Jack's Shirt, Deano's Bottoms
A Carlisle United Memoir

Tim Pocock

**Grosvenor House
Publishing Limited**

This book is published by
Grosvenor House Publishing Ltd
Link House
140 The Broadway, Tolworth, Surrey, KT6 7HT.
www.grosvenorhousepublishing.co.uk

A CIP record for this book
is available from the British Library

ISBN 978-1-80-381-077-5

Dedication

For Diane

Contents

Acknowledgments

Thanks to Rob Lees for the cover photo (that's me in Deano's top at Mansfield, Chapter 8, with Sam); to *The Cumberland News*, *News and Star*, CUFC programmes and BBC Radio Cumbria for quotes; also Sam, Bryan, Rob, The Bloke Behind Me and other Blues for their comments; Rebecca and Grosvenor Publishing for their help and advice; and of course the players and managers of Carlisle United, without whom my life would've been less stressful, financially more fruitful and a lot less fun.

1

The Warm-Up

This is the best story I've heard about being a Carlisle fan. It was in response to a question in the United fanzine I produced back in the nineties which asked, "What's been your worst moment as a Blue?"

A reader replied that it came early in the second half of a dreadful game on a bitterly chilly afternoon. He'd had enough and decided to leave early. In those days stewards weren't the presence they are today, and if there was one in the Warwick Road End, he couldn't be found to unlock the gates. That forced our man to climb out over them before sitting in the freezing cold of his friend's car with, for sustenance, "only a lump of cheese and a can of Special Brew."

But, he added, it was better than being inside the ground watching the game.

This book then, is dedicated to that fan. I don't however, want it to be another in the line of, "If you think you've had it hard, try being a fan of *(insert name here)* FC." That's because being a fan and following a team is not a

1

miserable experience. Here you might expect me to add "despite the football", in a wallowing-in-self-pity way. No. Supporting Carlisle brings me pleasure *because of* the football. Here's proof from my match report of a home game with Newport County:

"LOVE FOOTBALL! LOVE FOOTBALL!" A statement, a command! Arms raised above my head, me yelling into the Cumbrian air, Sam hugging me! LOVE FOOTBALL indeed. For oh, what a difference one kick of a football can make!

A second, maybe two, maybe less (don't know, don't care!) after the ball fizzed off the foot of Danny Grainger, nicking a defender's knee, rocketing (on Bonfire Saturday so of course 'rocketing'!) into the top corner, Everything Changed. So it was beer at home and the warm glow that tells you all is well with the world.

On the drive back Sam and I tried to analyse why one kick of a football can make us (and every other fan) feel this way. It was easy to quantify:

1. *The goal was a first-time volley from outside the box; spectacular goals aren't worth any more than a toe poke, but momentarily at least, they make you feel better.*
2. *It was the winning goal.*
3. *It came three minutes into the four of added time. If you're going to get a winner, get a late one.*
4. *It was unexpected. United were two up after 11 minutes but had that lead wiped out by two County goals, their equaliser coming in the 87th.*

After that, the only team who were going to score again were Newport. Theirs was the momentum.

5. *The context: five home defeats in a row and not one goal in those five.*

The world, well, my football world at the very least, seems a better place this morning because of that one boot of the ball.

You'll remember school assemblies, or rather you probably won't because so few are memorable. As a teacher I sat through three decades of them more than you. I can remember very few, but every now and then there would be a really good one, a nugget, I called it, amidst the silt I had to sift through. It was worth going to assembly in the hope that today's was going to reveal one such nugget in the bottom of the prospector's pan.

So too with going to a game. Chances are I won't see one that's awarded a five-star rating. Chances are I won't see United win, even less chance of an added time screamer. But that doesn't matter. I might.

Besides, any United win will do. The game doesn't have to be five-star. I'll save those, please, for ones which don't feature United, where I simply want to be entertained. If I do drive home with Carlisle victorious, the Feel Good Factor will last well into the following week. If I don't, I won't dwell on defeat too long because I'll soon be looking forward excitedly, *positively*, to the next game.

3

I'd say that the time I spend thinking happy thoughts about United exceeds by quite a margin the time I'm down in the dumps about them. Proof then, that Football is Good For You. This book will celebrate rather than berate the Blues.

Typing now as I am at the start of the coronavirus clampdown (two Saturdays with no game and it feels like two years) underlines again how much I love football because I miss it, I really do. I was sharing this hurt with someone, a non-football lover, who replied, "Yes, but what about Hannah *(my daughter)*? Aren't you missing her?" She was in Australia and, oops, yes, I was missing her too, but I'm used to her being away for months at a time. I'm not used to being without football, without United, not in March for Jimmy's sake, and not for the foreseeable future and beyond.

I've been meaning to write something about United for a while. Books by football supporters are, generically, much of a muchness. I can't pretend this will be different, but I won't have to rely on memory, as I've always written match reports, extracts from which will feature in the pages to follow. I'm not sure how this will end up but I'm looking forward to how it unfolds and, I hope, that I'll be happy with the result. A bit like a game then. So let's kick-off.

I'm not a life-long United fan. I saw my first Carlisle game when I was 18 and didn't watch them on a regular basis until I was 21. The first team I supported was West Ham United. They were the nearest club to where we were living. I doubt many fans ever had it so good as my first game, because that West Ham team had the World Cup winning trio, and at my first ever match (5th November 1966) there was a fourth, Fulham's right-back George Cohen. Future England manager Bobby Robson was in their line-up too.

West Ham won 6:1 with Geoff Hurst scoring four and Martin Peters two. I know that because I stuck a match report in a scrapbook which, thankfully, I've still got, along with the match ticket. My dad and I had seats in the Main Stand. Tickets were eight shillings (40 pence) each. 'West Ham's play had all the hallmarks of quality and gave the chilled fans something to glow over,' the cutting enthused.

I can't remember a thing about the game, alas, but I still have vivid memories of *going* to the game. I remember the crowd on the walk from Upton Park underground station to the ground; I remember climbing the stairs into the concourse at the back of the stand and how dark it was, how noisy, not scary though, simply different and exciting. I remember the view from our seats and at the end of the game, looking down from the stairs and seeing a mass of bodies leaving the ground to walk back to the station. I'd never seen so many people so close together before. I was hooked.

I'd like to think my son Sam had similar memories of his first match, but it was a trial run at Harrogate Town, just to see if he'd last the 90 minutes before I took him to watch United. He did, and his next game, his first as a Blue, was at Spotland, where a Rochdale steward searched his Fireman Sam lunch box.

I gave Sam everything he wanted to sweeten the experience, so much so that later that evening he called out to me from his bedroom, sat up in bed and threw up the remains of a Spotland burger and goodness knows what other junk I'd let him have. No matter. That was him hooked.

My dad preferred rugby, but that West Ham game was just after the 1966 World Cup, which he did watch. During the tournament I played football in the street outside. It wasn't a busy one and there weren't as many cars around as today, so we could often have a game on a decent sized pitch.

Just over a year later we moved to the Netherlands, where I pinned West Ham photos to my bedroom wall and was the only English boy in the village team. I must also have started reading the Sunday papers (flown out to the Forces) for scores, and listening to commentaries on the radio, because when my dad offered a Dutch guilder as a prize for which of his four children could guess where Doncaster, his next posting, was, I came closest. *Doncaster as in Rovers, white shirts and red shorts (thanks Subbuteo wallchart) and northern.* Ker-ching.

Belle Vue, then the home of Rovers, was nearer our new home than Upton Park and it didn't take long for me to switch allegiance to my local team. No sooner had that relationship been established, I was sent away to boarding school and, a couple of years later, we moved again, this time back south. But by then I was a Doncaster fan. West Ham were just another team.

I kept the faith in my teens, even persuading my dad to take me away from school the evening Doncaster played at White Hart Lane in the League Cup, but it was hard to sustain that long distance affair without a regular date, and what with starting work as a trainee journalist on a local paper, *The Kentish Gazette* in Canterbury, I had a strange few years as a fan. I followed the fortunes of Doncaster, Carlisle (dad's next move) and Gillingham, the nearest league team to Canterbury. Following, yes, but supporting? No.

That was partly because most Saturdays were spent reporting on Canterbury City, then of the Southern League. Canterbury wasn't a football city. The speedway team, whose track surrounded their pitch, attracted a bigger crowd.

The pinnacle of my three years in journalism was being asked to write a regular page for the match programme. That summit conquered, I left the profession to travel around the Greek islands. I was ridiculously ill-prepared which made my experience all the better before, prodigally and penniless, I arrived back at my parents in Carlisle, which is where this story really begins.

I first watched United on 26th December 1977 during my first trip home after nearly six months apprenticeship on the newspaper. What I remember, like that game at Upton Park, isn't anything about the match, but I do recall walking up the slight slope from the Paddock turnstiles to get my first view of the pitch.

The other thing I remember of the afternoon was a comment from the crowd. Carlisle's centre-forward and goal scorer was David Kemp, who had longer hair than most and was, more to the parochial point, a southerner. Perhaps that explains this comment from the Paddock after a mistake from the player: "Get back to playing your guitar, Kemp!"

I've never however, really bought into the terrace wit myth. Most of it is spontaneous, crude and abusive. That's how it is for me anyway. The wittiest cry I heard at Brunton Park was in a game when a referee made a decision that was as bad as the football. "Ref!" the Blue somewhere along the terrace groaned. "You're spoiling a shite game!"

I've seen a fair few of those but this book isn't going to dwell on them. In 43 seasons of supporting United (the three before were little more than me being mildly partisan), I have enjoyed five promotions and two Wembley Final wins. That doesn't seem a bad return, or maybe I'm just easily pleased.

It has however, been 11 seasons without either, the last eight in the fourth tier, quite a contrast to when United did have the limelight and were the best team in England, albeit only for a week. I wasn't alas, a Carlisle supporter back in August 1974 when United won their first three games to head Division One, the top tier of English football. I did though, listen to a radio commentary of one of their first home games, because I recall the commentator saying he could see sheep in the fields behind one end.

United's rural roots have been picked up on by opposing fans ever since and it's something to throw back at them: "One nil to the sheepshaggers!" we'd sing. In similar vein, taunting Burnley fans lost its edge when they'd return our chants with: "We *are* the bastards in claret and blue!" Given the way things are these days, that might shock younger, more sensitive readers, but yes, Carlisle and Burnley were once on an equal footing.

Mention of United's rivalry with Burnley brings me to a series of games that made me feel more a Carlisle United fan than any others but, paradoxically, they're not ones I look back on with particular pride. They were the three seasons' worth of games against Leeds United from 2007-10. The reason the memory of them does embarrass me is simple: I hated Leeds United.

Sometimes it's easy to define who you are by what you're not, so because I was a Carlisle fan it was obvious, almost natural, that I was no fan of Leeds, no fan at all. For reasons every football follower is well aware of, Leeds were an easy club to dislike, but living closer to Elland Road than most non-Leeds fans, as we did in Harrogate, made disliking them easier, more intense. And when Leeds, for the first and only time in their history, dropped into the third tier, that dislike turned to hatred.

Carlisle had won promotion to League One a season earlier and for three seasons the two teams shared a division. Games between them more than dominated the football year for me; they defined it.

My very worst moment as a Carlisle fan came against Leeds at the end of the Second Leg of the Play-Off Semi-Final in May 2008. Carlisle had blown their chances of outright promotion to the Championship with a calamitous run of results. To make matters worse, finishing fourth in the table meant they would face Leeds in the play-offs.

Leeds started the season with a 15-point deduction for going into administration but still made the play-offs. Their first defeat came at Brunton Park in November. I don't have to look to check the month of that fixture. It was *the* home game of the season. The date hasn't faded from my timeline. Memory of that game hasn't either.

So, before we get to that 'single worse moment', enjoy the following extracts from my report of the league game (Leeds' first defeat, I repeat with glee) on 3rd November 2007:

Football does not get any better than this. Tonight I'm a supporter of the most popular team in the country; for Carlisle United, my Carlisle United, ended Leeds' unbeaten run.

I'm delighted United won but relieved it's over and I can go back to normal match-day emotion. For my feelings before and during this game weren't healthy.

Never have I wanted Carlisle to beat another team so much simply for the sake of beating them.

And not just seeing Leeds beaten; not just seeing the nasty little chip-on-his-shoulder runt that is Dennis Wise beaten, but also to see their supporters beaten. They've been crawling out of the woodwork into their armchairs this season. School is full of them. I can understand children doing it, but when colleagues in the staffroom jump on the band-wagon sofa, it more than irks. It hurts.

"We all hate Leeds Scum! We all hate Leeds Scum!"

It's not adult, it's not Christian, it's not even personal. Leechy and Will were in the Waterworks End; they're good lads and Sam's mates, for heaven's sake! But they were We-Are-Leeds. So sorry, lads, you'll have to take the abuse.'

Leeds were much better than United in the first half and Jermaine Beckford scored in front of the Warwick. He didn't celebrate, having made his league debut at Carlisle on loan from Leeds a couple of seasons earlier. He just turned and walked away. I was impressed by his reaction. That though, was the only good thing I was prepared to say about Leeds.

United improved in the second half and on the hour the 3,400 Leeds fans were silenced. Simon Hackney equalised with a low shot from the edge of the box, then Joe Garner headed in at the near post from a corner. I can replay them both from the memory bank as I type.

There were still 20 minutes left, and another four added on, when...

Danny Graham chased a defender down and Carlisle won a corner. Hackney and Mark Bridge-Wilkinson needed to waste time. MBW had the ball at his feet, two defenders closed in. The sensible thing to do would have been to turn his back and shield the ball. Waste a few seconds.

Not MBW. He surprised them, slipped the ball between the two static defenders, took a touch into the box and drove it low across goal. "Why did you do that?" I started to wonder. "Oh. I see, if the ball goes out beyond the far post it'll take time to recover it for the goal-kick, and there's only 90 seconds or so left..."

Only that didn't happen. For MBW had put curl on the ball, and BLINKING HECK IT'S IN!

That did it. We were all over the place in the Warwick. What a moment! I hugged the bloke next to me, I was grabbed by the two Blues in front; it really was "D-I-S-C-O!"

At full-time we hadn't even left the Warwick before Sam received the first of many texts from mates (and mates of mates) congratulating us on doing the world of football a favour. We really were the nation's favourite Other Team.

The return game was in April. United lost 3:2, having led twice. After Leeds' first equaliser their centre-back,

Paul Huntington, a Carlisle lad, made a big show of turning to us in the corner and kissing the Leeds badge on his shirt. Before the game apparently, he'd had abuse on social media. He suffered far more after it. We told him what we thought of that, and he replied in kind, gesturing *'wankers'* from behind his back so the ref and officials wouldn't see.

In my match report I wrote that defeat had been 'the single most painful experience of my Carlisle United life.' It was and hurt like hell for a month. That's when we had to venture back to Elland Road for the First Leg of the Play-Off Semi-Final. I could see no reason to summon up any feel-good factor. It wasn't in my bones, water or in any other substance of man.

I had no hope, so I felt relaxed. I didn't even feel quite as much animosity towards Leeds. I'd gone through so much bile, angst, agony and, yes, pure hatred of Leeds United before and during the league games, that I'd burnt out (so I thought) that black bit of my soccer soul. I'd come through. I was out the other side into the light.

I resigned myself to United's fate. They were on a shocking run of form too. Yet with four games of the season left, things had looked very different. A goalless draw at home to leaders Swansea in front of 10,500 at Brunton Park had given United a six-point cushion in that second promotion spot. United then lost to Leeds, Southend and Millwall. Promotion as runners-up to Swansea was out of reach. Carlisle were in the play-offs.

Leeds in contrast, were on a roll. Plus, no doubt, they'd be spurred on by their sense of injustice, for the Football League had confirmed, just two days before the end of the season, that Leeds wouldn't get their 15 deducted points back. There was no sensible reason why Sam and I should have gone to Elland Road, nor why we already had tickets for the home leg three days later, except that is, loyalty. But hope? Not this time. We didn't fear the worse. We expected it.

There had been an alcohol ban for the league game but not that Monday night. We had a pint and Balti chicken pie in the bowels of the stadium beneath the away corner. We had just managed to get two tickets for the league game but for this, the play-off, there was no problem, especially with the game live on Sky. United had returned nearly half their 2,000 allocation.

We made a lot of noise regardless. So did Leeds, with nearly 40 times our number, but the longer the game went on, the quieter they became. Or maybe it was just because we stayed noisy, very noisy. *"Shall we sing a song for you?"* and *"You've only got one song!"* we jeered, for United played really well. The *Yorkshire Post* went so far as to say, 'Carlisle were, quite simply, superb.' And against the odds, United won.

The first goal came from the boot of Simon Hackney but took a deflection. When we'd finished bouncing, taunting Leeds and belting out *"D-D-DDD! SIMON HACKNEY!"* we wondered who the deflection had come off. "Please let it be Huntington!" I wished. It had actually hit United striker Danny Graham. Not that it mattered but a Huntington own goal would've been oh so sweet.

At the start of the second half Bridge-Wilkinson slid onto an Evan Horwood cross in front of their Kop and United led by two. The Leeds fans "went a bit quiet," an admission the next day from a Sixth Former who was in the Kop. All you could hear on Sky, a friend said, were the Carlisle fans.

Huntington, quite rightly, was signalled out: *"Wanker, wanker, what's the score?"* And during the half this ditty grew louder: *"15 Points? Who gives a fuck? You're Dirty Leeds and you fucked it up!"*

An extra four minutes appeared on the fourth official's board. Gary Madine dived into a tackle on half-way, the Leeds defender (it had to be Huntington) stepped round him with ease and hoofed the ball into the United box. Kieran Westwood, who'd had a blinder, started to come, stopped, and in that moment's hesitation, the bounce favoured Leeds. The ball broke loose and the one player I didn't want to get a sniff in that situation, Dougie Freedman, got a sniff. Goal.

For the first time I glanced down at my watch: 50.47 it read. Added time had been six not four minutes. The referee blew for time soon after. We celebrated but Sam wasn't happy, cursing the Leeds goal. I didn't mind as much. "Let's face it," I told him, "we'd have settled for a 1:2 defeat before kick-off, so a 2:1 victory is more than we could possibly have hoped for."

"It's a turning-point," Sam replied. "Madine should've stayed on his feet. It's only half-time in the tie."

And that's why I wasn't crowing at school next day, maintaining a dignified front (*"it's only half-time"*) whilst laughing inside. It was just a shame the win couldn't be celebrated in isolation, and only held sway for three days. Unless, of course... unless... The season had started at Walsall and 'Walsall to Wembley' had an alliterative ring to it. Three days later came the return leg at Brunton Park. Here's what I wrote. Brace yourselves.

What goes around, comes around.

The truism that football is a metaphor for life was never truer than tonight. For every good time there's a not-so-good moment, for every bad thing that happens, a good one will come along to restore the balance. It's not pessimism, no. I see a half-full glass. It's more to do with Dad's saying: "Every good time must come to an end, otherwise how would you know it was a good time?" Truisms, sayings, metaphors. All part of the narrative that is football, that is life.

"Tonight's Carlisle United Man of the Match sponsored by blah blah blah... is Peter Murphy!"

I turned to Sam. "Why announce it now? There's extra time to come." (Leeds had scored early to level the tie.)

The announcer added, "The fourth official has indicated there will be a minimum of one minute added time."

And in the next breath, Leeds scored. I looked at my watch. It read 45.09. Too late. The Fat Lady was stepping up to the microphone.

Nine years earlier when Jimmy Glass scored That Goal, at the very back of the stand that is the Memory Bank, someone whispered, "One day, there'll be a pay-back." There it was. The shot wasn't the strongest, but from where we were, at the back of the Warwick, the ball was going in from the moment it left Howson's foot. The ball rolled past Danny Livesey, rolled past Kieron's outstretched left hand, rolled inside the post and against the inside of the net.

I won't be able to look at the Warwick Road End goal again in the same way. It's tainted, stained.

What hurts most is Getting Beat By Leeds. "I'm not looking forward to tomorrow," I texted all and sundry on the way home. Sam was looking forward to it even less. Tomorrow was his last day of teaching practice in south Leeds "and they're proper Leeds fans too," he said. Every class had given him a chorus of 'Marching All Together!' on the day of the game. At least they knew the words. The Leeds plastics/part-timers/woodwork-crawlers in Harrogate probably wouldn't even know the title, but they'd be crowing too.

And they were. "Name your team!" I spat at one colleague who'd become Leeds for the day.

"Howson and Huntington!" he replied. Bastard. But I did ask for that. I almost told a vicar's wife to "Fuck

off!" after she gloated. She got the score wrong too. Leeds United. Yuck.

At the final whistle a few teenagers ran on the pitch, but most Blues were too much in shock to do anything more than stand in silence before shuffling out. The ground emptied quickly. Sam and I stayed only until we realised that a lap of honour wasn't going to happen then left in silence too.

The Public Address had prepared for this. The classic 'Story of the Blues' accompanied us out of the ground. For once we didn't run down the Warwick to catch the BBC Cumbria report. The music changed. Morrissey wailed, "Heaven knows I'm miserable now."

An angry Blue kicked the boot of a Leeds car. His mates tried dragging him away, but he broke free for another kick. Beneath the windscreen wipers of the cars down Warwick Road were flyers advertising Wembley coaches. I've kept that flyer. One day Blues will need Wembley coaches. What comes around, goes around.

Come round it did, quicker than expected. Leeds lost the Play-Off Final to Doncaster (thank you, Donny) and less than two years later Carlisle faced Leeds in another semi-final, this time in the Johnstone's Paint Trophy. The prize wasn't on a par with the Play-Offs, but the final was at Wembley.

The First Leg was again at Leeds. It was on a cold evening in January and the crowd was only 13,000. There had been over 36,000 for the Play-Off semi.

United won by the same score, 2:1, but this time the late goal was Carlisle's, as was the momentum.

Of the five games United played at Elland Road in those three years, United were unbeaten in the last four: three wins and a draw. Leeds however, had won three in a row at Brunton Park. The second leg attendance was 9,500 at Brunton Park, only 3,000 down on the Play-Off semi. Leeds hadn't sold their allocation; it didn't matter as much to them as it mattered to us.

Carlisle midfielder Adam Clayton scored after 32 minutes, which meant United led the tie by two goals and Leeds only had an hour to score twice and draw level, and that was assuming United didn't net another. But even when celebrating United's goal, I was thinking, "Well, that's another 30 seconds knocked off the clock, another 30 seconds when Leeds are less likely to score." It was that sort of night, that sort of game, one to be endured rather than enjoyed.

Two goals in 45 became one in 44 when Leeds equalised straight after half-time. Then Ludo Michalik (later to be Carlisle's finest ever Slovakian centre-back) missed his kick completely. Kevan Hurst, for a moment, seemed to have expected the clearance and stopped. The Warwick roared him back onto the loose ball, he dropped a shoulder on a defender, made space, and shot. I didn't see the ball hit the net but I knew it had from the noise coming from the right of me. United were two goals ahead in the tie with less than 18 minutes to go.

Those 18 became 17, 16, down to 11. Surely, surely United wouldn't blow this lead? But the fickle foot of footie fate was about to kick me well and truly where it hurts. Leeds scored twice; the tie was level at 3:3 and it was straight to penalties.

Adam Collin saved Leeds' first spot kick. "He has the biggest hands I've ever seen," said Clayton on the radio afterwards. The next five were scored; Ian Harte, Hurst and Madine for United. With two spot-kicks each remaining and United 3:2 in front, Richard Keogh strode up, put the ball down, strode purposefully back and charged at the ball. We knew what was going to happen next.

There was little subtlety about Keogh at the best of times, and we loved him for it, but his shot cleared the bar magnificently. Sam got a text from a friend in Harrogate: 'I've just seen the ball bouncing down the A1.' Keogh pulled his shirt over his head and was in tears by the time he got back to half-way.

Grella ('the little shit,' I added in my report) scored his penalty and was the only player on either side to make a big show of his success, badge kissing in front of the Warwick. Clayton showed more restraint, though no less accuracy, as did Gradel for Leeds. Five kicks each and the shoot-out was all square at 4:4. Into sudden death.

Horwood, who I feared might do a Keogh, swept his kick high into the net; Kilkenny of Leeds buried his; and Mattie Robson scored too. Only just though. The ball was too close to keeper Casper Ankergren. The replays later showed it had gone through his hands.

Next up was their left-back Shane Lowry, not a well-known name. As he stepped forward, a little voice in my head said, "He doesn't fancy it." His placement of ball on the spot and run-up seemed that bit more hurried. He hadn't stared the goal in the eye much either. His kick wasn't bad, to Collin's right, but that was the side he dived to and YES! Almost in an understated, matter-of-fact way, Collin saved. And that was it. Wembley.

Sam legged it onto the pitch ("I gave Harte and Hurst big man hugs!") but I was stunned into inertia. For a moment or so anyway, then Vera Lynn came over the tannoy and that sparked me back to celebratory mode. I kissed Rob's wife Sue, I kissed Rob, and broke into song. I gave Vera Lynn a run for her money as, for the first time since kick-off, I could now say the word: *"WEM-BER-LEY!"*

'And breath.' That text from Steph Thirlwell, wife of United's captain (I'll explain the link soon) said everything about the evening.

I should, of course, have been used to United's gut-churning, spirit-draining, strength-sapping wringer, especially in Wembley semi-finals. Sam and I had relived the previous four successful semis (and the two failures) on the drive up. Each one had put us well and truly through it. This however, mattered more than any of the other four, because it wasn't against Rochdale, Stockport, Shrewsbury or Macclesfield, clubs with little history with United. No. This was against Leeds. We had a cellar full of vitriolic vials with Leeds. It was personal.

In The Sportsman before the game I had wondered aloud, as is my wont before every Very Big Game, "Why do I do this? I don't want to be here. The next two hours will be agony. In my next life I want to come back as someone who likes DIY or gardening." I must, I mused, have done something very bad in a previous life – or very good.

"In two hours you'll know why you do this!" Sam replied.

In two hours he was right, of course. Come the journey home, we were in full song. Just before the Harrogate turn-off we were passed by a Leeds coach. "WE'RE GOING TO WEMBLEY! WE'RE GOING TO WEMBLEY! YOU'RE NOT!" we yelled. We were indeed. And half the sweetness, half the joy, half the *Yes-Yes-Yes-Get-In!* joy was that Leeds, this time, weren't.

And breath indeed.

United were hammered in the final by Southampton and Leeds were promoted at the end of the season. With that, Leeds disappeared from Carlisle's football life. They haven't played each other since and, unless the two are drawn together in a cup tie, which is unlikely to be a semi-final, our paths are unlikely to cross again. That's a relief.

I'm a kinder and more forgiving person again. I don't hate Leeds, I really don't. I don't like them either, but my feelings are those of a divorcee towards their former partner now that the tempestuous marriage is well in the past. I'm relieved it's over and mildly interested in how the ex is doing. But I'm pleased they are out of my life.

2

Ashurst, Beardsley, Chester

In the early eighties Burnley were United's Leeds, their big rivals. The decade began with the appointment of Bob Stokoe as Carlisle manager. One of the first things he did was order the removal of a sign that hung from a floodlight pylon welcoming the visitors.

"Welcomes are for after the match," he growled. "It's not a friendly place teams are coming to. It's a battlefield, a place where they will find it hard to get anything."

A friend told me about a charity golf tournament when he was in a foursome with Stokoe. His partner was friendly enough, but Stokoe didn't say anything until the end of the round, so focussed was he on winning.

Stokoe didn't suffer fools either. I once spotted United's rising star, a young Peter Beardsley, sat in a car outside the ground with kick-off fast approaching. "Must be injured," I mused. But he wasn't. Stokoe had told him to play in one position, Beardsley said he preferred another, so Stokoe told him to get out of the changing room and go sit in his car (or words, I guess, to that effect.) I reckon that might've been the making of the lad, who was praised throughout his career for being a selfless team player. Once bitten, twice shy.

Beardsley was, without doubt, the best Carlisle player I've ever seen. He was smaller than most, quicker too and boy, could he dribble! Two months after his debut at the start of the 1979-80 season, I watched him for the first time in a 3:1 win against Barnsley.

'He had three devastating runs in the first half which made me hold my breath,' I enthused. *'I have never, I think, been so excited by a footballer. On the third occasion his shot beat the keeper and had to be cleared off the line by a defender, but the applause was still ringing round the ground as the corner came over.'*

One goal in the 80-81 season against Plymouth not only had me waxing lyrical, but also spending some of my dole money on a *News and Star* photo of the last touch at the end of this solo run. *'A Carlisle corner and the ball's knocked out of the box; defenders rush out, hoping for an offside. The ball's returned to Beardsley. A brilliantly quick turn and he breaks clear, a goal is a certainty. But instead of shooting or executing one of his favoured chips, he dribbles round the keeper, round a defender and strolls almost to the goal line before tapping the ball over. Absolute magic.'*

The photo has the Plymouth keeper, yards behind him, easing himself up onto his elbow as Beardsley scores. The defender is on his back.

Stokoe named Beardsley in a team of the best players he'd managed. That early run-in with Stokoe kept him grounded too. In an interview with *The News and Star* when Beardsley was an England regular, Beardsley said, "When you've swept factory floors for a living, pulling a basket of football gear is no big deal." He was still doing that long after he finished playing.

A friend's son was an apprentice with York City and Ian went to watch him play against a Newcastle youth team. At the end of the game, when they were getting in the car to drive home, Ian watched the young Newcastle players stroll onto the team bus, followed by a familiar figure with the kit basket which he loaded on his own into the boot of the coach. It was their manager, Peter Beardsley.

At the start of his Carlisle career I sent Beardsley a Q and A sheet for an interview in *One Off*, a punk fanzine I produced. I asked who his favourite players were. One was Kenny Dalglish, the mercurial and prolific Liverpool forward; the other Bobby Parker, United's full-back, whose strengths were dependability and consistency. Flash he wasn't.

Beardsley's transfer to Vancouver came in March 1981 but part of the deal was that he stayed with United until they were safe from relegation. It took a while; he couldn't leave for another seven games. He also returned on loan for four months at the start of the 1981-82 season. When he left for good, Carlisle were top of Division Three.

Beardsley had started every match from early October to the end of the 1980-81 season, which was surprising given the way he played. Defenders would target him but Beardsley was a step ahead, usually. He also had more protection than when he was playing for Wallsend Boys.

"I remember hammering a side who were reckoned to be a tough bunch," he said in an interview in *The Cumberland News*. "They lived up to their reputation all right. When we'd changed after the match, they waited outside for us with axes and blocks of wood. The police had to be called to get us away. One player went onto the field with a knife down his stocking. You don't get that in the Football League."

Beardsley however, was once caught by a brutal tackle, which did force him to miss a game through injury for the only time in that season and a half. It still rankles as the perpetrator wasn't even booked. The guilty party was Gillingham's Steve Bruce, his former Wallsend Boys Club mate, who went in hard, high and late.

'One of the worst fouls I've seen north of South America,' I wrote. 'It left a bitter taste to this sweet nectar of success.' Carlisle won the game 2:0. Badly bruised, Beardsley had to be carried off the pitch by Stokoe and the physio. Beardsley recovered and the rest is football history. After Vancouver Whitecaps he played for Manchester United (just the once), Newcastle, Liverpool, Everton and Bolton in the Premier League, then lesser lights Manchester City and Hartlepool in the Football League.

His last appearance in a Carlisle game came at the age of 39, playing for Hartlepool two matches from the end of the 1998-99 season. He almost scored too, a powerful long-range strike that was tipped over, just, by Carlisle keeper Jimmy Glass.

Stokoe was a canny operator. Carlisle had conceded 70 goals in 80-81, so he signed two centre-backs, Tony Larkin from Shrewsbury and Jack Ashurst, who'd been Blackpool's record signing from Sunderland at £130,000 two years earlier. To help finance the promotion push, admission prices went up. It cost me £1.70, a rise of 20p, to stand in the Paddock. United didn't drop many points at Brunton Park; Stokoe succeeded in turning the place into an inhospitable battleground where United won 17 of 23 league games.

They were top by Christmas. A few weeks earlier I'd been to Darlington for an FA Cup tie. It was the first time I had travelled to a United away game. I don't regard a game at Gillingham in December 1978 as a proper away day, as I was living and working in Canterbury. I went on the train, met a Blue I knew at Newcastle and had a pint with him in a Darlo pub, which had a glass thrown at its window by a group of Carlisle youths, despite the pub being full of United supporters.

It was feisty stuff inside the ground too, with plenty of Blues in the crowd of 4,000. United came back from two down to draw. I shouted and sung myself hoarse. It was 'Rugby League support', I noted, with reference to the atmosphere at Brunton Park on Sundays in Carlisle RL's inaugural season (they were promoted too.)

'*I have a sore throat, had a four-and-a-half-hour journey home, I'm skint for the replay,*' I wrote, '*and I couldn't give a fuck! U-NI-TED!*' Safe to say I had caught the away-day bug; I've since watched United at well over 100 different grounds.

The year ended with a cold snap that wiped out the holiday programme. I remember it uncomfortably well; I was on the night shift at Carlisle station working for the GPO, when temperatures dropped to minus 13, the coldest night in the city for 20 years. United didn't play another in the league until the end of January.

And after the cold, the floods. United's Second Round FA Cup tie (they beat Darlington 3:1 in the replay) with Bishop Auckland was postponed five times before it took place in a monsoon. Despite the weather, the crowd was over 5,500, which was at least 1,000 more than at any league game. The FA Cup had magic back then.

After 70 minutes the match was abandoned. The tie eventually had to be played at Workington. The attendance was still 4,536, also better than anything in the first half of the league season at Brunton Park, despite United being top of the table.

Workington was my second away day. I went with friends from university and we celebrated on the pitch at the end to warm ourselves up after a 1:0 win, which had needed four weeks, one false start, seven postponements and a change of venue to complete.

At the start of April United beat Portsmouth to go second, a game watched by less than 4,000. The day before Argentina invaded the Falklands. That was a worry. *'It's put a dampener on my life right now,'* I wrote. My dad was based at the RAF depot 14MU, which was at full stretch to fit out the task force.

He did however, find time to take me to Deepdale. He wasn't impressed by the match day congestion, muttering he wouldn't be watching Carlisle away again in a hurry. United were *'as lucky as a hard-on in a harem,'* I wrote (I was at that age and didn't say that to dad) with strikers Bob Lee and Paul Bannon having all the punch *'of a mugger with a sausage.'* I enjoyed mixing my metaphors.

Thank goodness then, for evergreen veteran Pop Robson, who scored his 14th of the season, and the referee, who denied Preston what looked a certain penalty at the end. To make the away day even better (despite what my dad thought) Lincoln and Fulham, who were first and second, both lost. United went top again and stayed there until the penultimate game of the season.

Starting with the Preston victory, United went on a run of five wins and a draw. I also had a run of five in six: of United's last half-a-dozen away games, I made it to five. I had a real taste for them now. Gillingham was first. *'I felt like an Argentine in London,'* I wrote, before finding some strength in numbers with London based Blues.

The task force invaded the Falklands the day after. On May Day United beat Wimbledon 2:1, the fifth win of the five. United's defence, again, was solid, their luck better. United won thanks to an own goal and penalty. Win at Burnley the following Tuesday and, if Lincoln lost, United were promoted.

Burnley became my Leeds of the 80s but not yet, not on my first visit to Turf Moor. I got there okay but had no idea how I'd get back. There was no late train and the only bus I could catch out of Burnley terminated at Preston. I'd worry about that later, I reasoned, and wouldn't worry at all if Carlisle won and Lincoln lost.

Come kick-off there must've been 1500 Blues on our side of the wire mesh (to stop missiles) of the huge Longside terracing. There was a lot of nerves, a lot of noise. United started like the champions-elect we assumed they were, seven corners in the first 10 minutes. They couldn't keep it up. *'Would Carlisle scrape through again?'* I wondered. Answer: no. I couldn't bare to describe Burnley's goal, noting simply, *'I got the shakes, rage and tearful.'* Defeat hurt.

But in the great scheme of promotion things, it wasn't that bad. Oxford and Lincoln, second and third, lost too. What's more, I hitch-hiked back to university in two hours, despite being showered by beer cans from a carload of Carlisle fans. Mistaken identity, I'm sure.

With four games to go United were three points clear at the top. That 81-82 season was the first when a win was worth three points not two. I didn't go to Reading, the only one of United's last 11 games I missed, where United came from behind to draw 2-2. The table looked even better afterwards as United's rivals dropped points again.

Win at Wimbledon on Tuesday and United were promoted. A colleague from my days on the paper in Canterbury had moved to Wimbledon, so I had a bed for the night and someone to celebrate with when United won. I was sure they would. Wimbledon weren't good; they were about to be relegated. They were no Burnley.

That page in my diary has this header: *'Today was to have had a big, thick, juicy red border around it, only now a black band would be more appropriate.'* Next to that is the cutting for my star sign for the day from *The Mirror*: 'You may be offered promotion,' it said, 'but you should consider it carefully.' There must have been a fair few Cancerians in the United team.

Wimbledon was going to be my Wembley; a train trip to London to see United play at a ground beginning with 'W' where they would 'W' (win) promotion. I wasn't the only one fooled. I walked to the ground with two Swiss tourists who thought they were going to the famous twin towers.

The crowd of 2,002 was the lowest United appeared in front of all season. Dreams of the away following making it onto on the pitch were hit for six, well, three actually, as Carlisle were well beaten 1:3. Yet United were still, remarkably, in a strong position. Burnley, ominously, had won again and were up to second, but Fulham (third) had drawn and Oxford (fourth) lost.

They were playing each other in their last game which meant United only needed a point at home to Bristol Rovers to go up.

Carlisle had lost just twice at Brunton Park in the whole season: to Fulham in November and Huddersfield (FA Cup) in January. Bristol Rovers were in the bottom half of the table. "How many more gift horses do United need?" I wondered before kick-off.

Brunton Park had its biggest crowd of the season, 6,600. The sun shone, supporters were singing in both the Scratching Pen and Waterworks and gave the team a rapturous reception. They walked to the centre-spot and waved to the crowd before kick-off. United were milking the moment. Stokoe had also picked the right team: Gordon Staniforth was in, Bob Lee dropped. We weren't massive fans of Big Bob, so my dad's post-match comment was damning: "Stokoe left out one Bob Lee and played 10 others."

United lost the match 1:2 and along with it the best home record in the league, a very good chance of finishing the season champions and, worse still, the point needed to secure promotion. For 10 minutes they'd turned on the style but then *'like milk and Andrea...'* (I can only assume the latter was my latest unrequited love) *'...things turned sour.'*

United were undone by Bristol's speedy right-winger in his debut season as a professional. He later switched to centre-back, where he went on to play in the First Division and, once, for England. Yes, the player who set up both Bristol's goals was Keith Curle, United's manager three decades later.

That was the final Saturday of the season, but back in 1982 there was no ruling that all league fixtures had to finish on the same day. On the Tuesday Fulham were at home to Lincoln in fourth. If Lincoln lost, United would be promoted before their last game on Wednesday at Chester, one of the rearranged fixtures from the harsh winter.

Fulham and Lincoln drew. United therefore, dropped to fourth, out of the promotion places for the first time since the end of March. Burnley drew too. United would need a point to be promoted and a seven-goal victory to be champions on goal difference. A point would do me.

I journeyed to the game with Jimmy, a Hearts fan from university. As at Burnley, we'd have to hitch-hike back, not that it mattered on the way down. The only thing that did was that point. I'd not been to Chester before, a town of Tudor properties with electric gates. Chester's Sealand Round ground wasn't so plush. It was, I unkindly noted, 'crap.' The game was too but Chester were 13 points adrift of the team second bottom (Bristol City) and, thankfully, not very good at all.

After 37 minutes, from United's seventh corner, Paul Bannon headed the ball on and Pop Robson scrambled it in. Chester weren't going to score twice. Carlisle were going up.

Ten minutes from time the chant changed from *Going Up* to *We Are Up* and 10 minutes after that, United were promoted. I was up and over the wall on the final whistle. Out of the corner of my eye a policeman felled one invader, which was mean and futile, because there were over a thousand Blues in the ground ('more than half the gate of 2,535,' the *News and Star* reported) and most got on the pitch at the end. I hope the felled Blue got away to celebrate with us.

I could see Jack Ashurst's yellow shirt rising to shoulder height as he was chaired off. I shoved through the crowd and tied my scarf round his neck, tightly, to ensure no one nicked it before Jack reached the safety of the Directors' Box. A few minutes later scarf and skipper were there.

Reporter Ivor Broadis wrote that even Bob Stokoe ('he lives 10 years over every 90 minutes') was in a benevolent mood afterwards: 'He allowed me to smoke my pipe in the dressing-room, and that's the equivalent of allowing hobnail boots in a mosque.' Promotion meant it was Newcastle and not Newport next season, Sheffield Wednesday instead of Walsall. For a convert to the joy of travelling away, I couldn't wait.

Stokoe had done a remarkable job. United finished on 80 points. One more and they'd have been champions. United used just 20 players all season, and four of those had just a handful of games between them. Ten played 30 or more of the 46. Contrast that to a more recent season when manager Graham Kavanagh used 48. It's no plot spoiler to reveal that Kavanagh's Carlisle didn't win promotion.

Jim and I hitched a lift from the Chester carpark, where champagne was popped at the back of one car. The Blue who gave us the ride back to Lancaster was a Dalston lad called Nige, who fed us Opal Fruits too. Belated thanks, Nige. That page in my diary *does* has a thick red border.

It was Carlisle's fifth promotion since they were elected to the league in 1928 and my first, which means I've now shared over half their nine promotion seasons in my time as a Blue.

I wrote to Jack Ashurst a few days after the Chester game, thanking him for promotion, telling him he could keep the scarf and hoping that he'd read between the lines and send me his shirt. He didn't, but at least that gave me a fanzine title. I sent him the debut copy of *So Jack Ashurst, Where's My Shirt?* which appeared at the start of the 1992-93 season, Michael Knighton's first as owner. By then Ashurst's career was almost over, bar a couple of games at Rochdale.

As his career wound down, mine was taking off, as player-manager for the staff football team Athletico Aidan's. I'd started it mainly to give myself a regular game. As gaffer, I wouldn't drop myself from the line-up (any other manager would) and having formed the club, I could satisfy my statistical needs by keeping a complete history.

We are all, as I once heard at a school training day on autism, on the spectrum, males more than females. Some are further down it than others and I'm proud to say I'm probably slightly further on than you. I wouldn't be writing this memoir without those contemporary match reports.

Seven years and 77 games in (see what I mean), Athletico would celebrate its 100th different player. Graham Kavanagh's liking for an unsettled line-up had nothing on mine. The game was at a proper ground, Station View, home of Harrogate Railway (one of the PE teachers played for them) which in itself was exciting.

The 100th player was going to be a History teacher, one of the staffroom's characters if not its footballers. We only played friendlies and anyone who could walk in a straight line could play. Even those who wobbled got a game. The changing rooms were a couple of old railway carriages. As I was getting ready, an unfamiliar head poked round the door, an opponent I assumed. "Next one along," I told him. He didn't move. I did a double take. It was Jack Ashurst.

The lads I played with had been in touch with him and Jack accepted their invitation to be the 100th player instead of the History man who, like the rest of the team and staffroom, was in on the secret. I changed the line-up at once. I would partner Jack at centre-back. We kept a clean sheet and won 5:0. I made him look good.

After the game he said he'd send me the shirt but I couldn't accept it. I wasn't worthy.

I spent the summer of 1982 hitch-hiking around Europe and didn't get to the first games of the new season. My first was United's fifth in Division Two. Not a bad one either. New striker Malcolm Poskett, whose moustache and straggly hair gave him the look of a villain from a spaghetti western, scored all four against Palace. United coped pretty well at the higher level; they were never lower than 18th, even if they didn't get above eighth. Attendances at Brunton Park rose because bigger teams came. The average was up by a quarter to nearly 6,000.

A big chunk of my university grant went on following United. There were no student loans back then and because I'd worked for three years, I received a full one. I also had complimentary tickets at some games. Tony Larkin, a neighbour, left tickets when he could, the first at Elland Road where I sat with players' friends and family. That meant a nerve wracking, head down and scarf-most-definitely-out-of-sight walk through the motorway underpass afterwards. I survived unscathed, no thanks to a university mate shouting, "You were lucky!" when he spotted me. United had drawn 1:1.

The next comps were at Oldham, a less threatening but equally entertaining afternoon, despite United losing 3:4. Larkin headed the first, karma for leaving me those tickets. "It felt like it flew in!" he told me afterwards. "But we didn't start playing until the second half," he added in a World Exclusive interview for the diary.

I was enjoying the season. United beat Chelsea and Newcastle at Brunton Park but lost to Middlesbrough, when away fans sneaked into the home section of the Scratching Pen and a few minutes into the game the trouble started.

I used to stand in the Paddock in those early days with my dad. Later I would watch from the front of the

Warwick when Sam was little and needed to see the action; Sam also liked the noise. When we went as a family, we started in the Warwick before graduating to seats in the East Stand, until daughter Hannah realised that few little girls spent their Saturdays traipsing up a motorway to sit in the cold to watch football.

Diane stayed at home with her so Sam and I headed back to the Warwick. As he got older (and taller), we began to make our way through the gate in the corner to the Paddock. That's where I have a season ticket now, albeit to the left of the dug-out rather than the right, from where I first stood with my dad.

I've never watched a game from The Waterworks End, which is odd given that I've been going to Brunton Park for over 40 years; also because there are other grounds (Elland Road, The Valley, Bloomfield Road, for example) where I have seen games, not all featuring United, from all four sides.

In the middle of the 1983-83 season I became an uncle for the first time, enrolling James, aged 13 hours, in the Supporters Club at their Dickensian office in Old Post Office Court. At the same time I started courting Diane. I've got the first letter she sent me. 'I thought of you cursing and chanting and waving your precious Carlisle scarf,' she wrote. Nephew James has never watched United (my brother Guy, his dad, isn't much of a fan) but Diane would fairly soon have a scarf of her own.

I spent New Year's Eve 1982 in South Shields with Steve, another university friend and as big a Sunderland fan as

I was fast becoming a Blue. Carlisle were at Newcastle on New Year's Day, so it made sense to be just a few miles away, especially after New Year's Eve celebrations. There was no public transport but a Newcastle United Supporters Club coach would leave from Shields.

Steve's uncle gave us a lift into town to catch it, only his car broke down so we had to race to make the coach. We arrived before it left but we weren't allowed on after we showed our match tickets. It would only take home fans. Steve frantically phoned his mum, who picked us up and drove us to Newcastle, only for her car this time to stall at a roundabout. Thankfully it restarted and we were at the ground, just, for kick-off.

There were nearly 30,000 inside and I'd never felt so small or vulnerable. The Geordies in the Paddock were close enough for me to see the whites of their eyes. I didn't look at them long in case they recognised me on the walk to get our lift back to South Shields.

United were caught in the headlights at the start too, a goal down to Kevin Keegan's header after three minutes and other chances quickly followed. Carlisle found their composure and discovered that Newcastle were more a collection of talented individuals than a team. Alan Shoulder equalised. A minute into the second half Paul Bannon placed the ball past the keeper and United led. "I don't care if we go down," someone yelled, "so long as we beat the Geordies twice!"

"Andy Pandy boot boys!" jeered a group of United skinheads in front of us.

"If they're Andy Pandy, I'd hate to see Big Ted," came a reply.

They couldn't gloat for long. On the hour defender Dave Rushbury was sent off and soon after Keegan headed his second. With over 20 minutes remaining Newcastle pressed (13 second half corners to nil) and pressed again before, mercifully, the referee blew for time and we danced on the open terrace. The police kept us locked in for a good half hour afterwards, but that didn't prevent angry Geordies throwing stones over the wall. When we were eventually let out, the streets were eerily deserted.

The following season I went to the game on a football special. The train was bricked at Prudhoe and we were given a heavy police escort up the hill to the ground. Every pub emptied as we walked past, the Geordies stood on the pavement, staring at us. If it was meant to intimidate, it worked. *'I didn't feel like a foot soldier in a conquering army,'* I wrote, *'more a Christian off to the Colosseum to face the lions.'*

United were hammered 5:1. The police opened the gates straight away and every Geordie was a friend. "All the best for the rest of the season, lads," they said.

Ten days after the 1982 New Year's Day draw there was another tasty atmosphere for a FA Cup replay at Burnley, who were fast becoming big rivals. It was no fun travelling back to Lancaster after the 1:1 draw with a train load of oafish away supporters.

Burnley won the replay 3:1 with two late goals. Travelling fans weren't happy. A letter in *The Cumberland News* had the headline: *Treat United Fans Properly!* 'I find it disheartening the way the Carlisle fans were treated at Burnley,' Disenchanted Supporter complained. 'They cheered United on for the full 90 minutes and the Carlisle players did not even show the decency to come over and applaud the fans who spurred them on, even when they were losing. This has happened at every game this season. Is it any wonder Carlisle lose fans? They should take a lesson off the Geordie players.'

There was a better response at Sheffield Wednesday and the thanks given by players and management to supporters is now a regular feature of the away day experience. It's good to be appreciated.

The early eighties were a time when football wasn't the jewel in the country's sporting crown that it's marketed as today. It had too many rough edges. Prime Minister Margaret Thatcher wanted identity cards for supporters, all of whom were tarred with the hooligans' brush. On the bus to Hillsborough before a 1:1 draw, I got talking to an older Sheffield fan. We walked to the ground together, had a good chat, but when I said I was off to the away end, he asked, "You're not one of them yobbos?"

I wasn't. I've never hit anyone in anger in my life, but football does, without a doubt, bring out the dark side. Supporting a team is, as the anthropologist Desmond Morris wrote in a study of football supporters, tribal. His book's title was *The Soccer Tribe* and it made sense about how it felt to be a fan, though I should really use the unabbreviated word 'fanatic', for that was what I'd become, proudly too.

I'm embarrassed now to think back to a game at Burnley in the eighties when United scored and I was straight at that mesh barrier on the Longside. Had it not been there I reckon I would have started lashing out at the Burnley supporters. I had well and truly lost control. That's what football can do to you. More precisely, that's what supporting a team fanatically, especially away from home, can do.

I am not proud to remember that moment, that feeling, at Burnley. Yet I do take pride in being a Carlisle supporter, especially at an away game. Just being there is a badge of honour, a mark of respect from other fans, because you've proved your support by travelling so far to watch them. For me, with every home game a 184-mile round trip, that still matters and means something every time I set off for Brunton Park. I live near Ripon now but it was 218 miles for 33 years when we lived in Harrogate and for Sam in Pontefract it's 258.

I am impressed when travelling to a game to see a scarf in the back window of a car or someone in a team shirt on a train, because I know the occupants feel the same as I do about their team and I know the effort they're making. That includes Leeds or Burnley supporters. I have mellowed over the years.

There is an edge to this tribalism, which is exciting but isn't fun at its extremes. With no game on FA Cup 4th Round in 1983 (thanks Burnley) I went with Jim to watch Hearts at Queen of the South. Hearts fans, no doubt from different parts of the city, fought each other in the pub beforehand (then asked for donations to compensate the landlord) and again in the ground, seemingly to lure the police in so they could unite and fight them.

At Charlton in February during a drab 0:0 on another freezing afternoon, we few Blues in the 4,500 crowd were joined by a handful of local youths with tribal greetings of their own: "Do you want to feel my knife?" and "You're dead too." We moved seats and at the end of the game there was scuffling as we left.

At Charlton Station the friendly local who'd welcomed us so warmly caught the same train as the Carlisle fans. Outnumbered by something like 50 to one, he was strangely subdued. That's the thing about being a noisy fan. We're usually more bark than bite.

Middlesbrough was my last away game of the 82-83 season and I hadn't seen United win once on my travels. They only won twice away all season but United were pretty strong at Brunton Park. Only champions QPR scored more than United's 44 on their home patch. Alan Shoulder was top scorer with 21 and partner Poskett got 14 in the league. Oh, and Burnley were relegated.

The highlights of the next season, 1983-84 (and there were a few), included two home games in three days against Newcastle and Sheffield Wednesday, watched by a combined total of nearly 25,000. On Boxing Day I'd been on one of the eight Supporters Club coaches to Ayresome Park, where a Jack Ashurst goal from a corner and a stressful backs-to-the-wall second half brought United a 1:0 win. It was, I wrote, *'Pressure,*

pressure, pressure from Boro; the tension made my stomach hurt.'

Two days later came Newcastle. Their line-up included Peter Beardsley, Kevin Keegan and Chris Waddle. It was Beardsley's first game back at Brunton Park since his transfer to Vancouver Whitecaps. Keegan had missed the previous season's due to injury. *'It's going to be one hell of a game,'* I wrote in the morning.

Beardsley led Newcastle out and we sang his name. There were 5,000 noisy Geordies inside the ground, packing the Waterworks End, half the Paddock and a sizeable chunk of the Scratching Pen. Waddle scored early in front of them when his cross caught the wind and whipped over keeper Dave McKellar.

After 34 minutes Shoulder was fouled in the box by Newcastle goalie Martin Thomas. Penalty! "Please God!" I whispered, and Shoulder answered my call. His kick sent Thomas the wrong way. The football wasn't as good in the second half but there was no let-up in the pace. I was expecting and not really minding a draw.

Then three minutes from time Malcolm Poskett had the best chance of the half: *'A great ball over from the left and Mally headed straight at Thomas. He caught it and kicked the ball out, but it held up in the wind. Tommy Craig got to it first and Russell Coughlin, from over 30 yards, chanced his luck with a long-range shot. The wind took this one too. It went low, hit a post and bounced in.'*

Two-one United and they weren't finished. A minute later Craig coolly curled the ball in for a third. A Geordie ran out of the Waterworks to punch his own goalkeeper while 10,000 Blues were cheering and hugging. Even the Paddock was singing. My brother claimed my dad (never the most demonstrative supporter) had his hands above his head in applause.

A newspaper cutting in my diary described how the last few minutes were like pulling a giant cracker. My simile was seasonal too: *'It was like a thousand Christmas Days rolled into one moment!'* I wrote. *'I'm pissed without having drunk a drop! I shalln't, I can't, forget it.'*

I haven't. To cap it all, guess who I saw in The Crown at Stanwix that evening? Russell Coughlin! "Nice goal, mate," I said.

"Thanks," he replied.

"No, thank *you*!"

I proudly wrote up that exchange in the diary. I was a Friend of the Famous.

The wind was even stronger at Brunton Park three days later. "A Force 10!" I declared. Playing against it, United only got the ball over Wednesday's goal line once in the first half. The visitor's Gary Megson used the gale better with a chip from 25 yards to score, and I was planning my diary report headline (*BLOWN OUT!*) when Don O'Riordan flicked the ball in to equalise. We were singing and dancing again.

United's good form continued. From the end of October they lost just one of 21 league games, half a season's worth back in a 22-team division. Promotion to Division One (now the Premier League) was a strong possibility.

Before the visit of Charlton in March, United were on a roll, unbeaten in six, including a point at leaders Chelsea and with three successive home wins behind them. Nevertheless, I wrote before kick-off, 'United had to play better than in their last three games because Charlton, eighth, are a better team than Derby, Oldham and Swansea.'

Play better they did. United won 3:0, the third scored by Tommy Craig: *'Another corner, another clearance and another first-time volley, this time from Craig's left foot. It didn't dip an inch. If anyone had got in the way, the ball would've gone right through them.'*

Manchester City lost 5:1 and Newcastle had only won by two, so United were up to third on goal difference. *'There's a joke doing the rounds that if United aren't careful, they'll go up. On this form they're living very dangerously!'* That's how I finished my report. Carlisle had been favourites for relegation in August.

United however, couldn't hang onto the heady heights of third place, the highest league position Carlisle have reached in my time as a Blue. A week after the Charlton victory, I followed United to Blackburn, where a defence that hadn't conceded a single goal in six games shipped four.

'Blackburn nailed the myth that Carlisle's defence was harder to penetrate than a Scargill picket line,' *The People* newspaper gloated. Defeat was the start of a 10-match winless run. United finished seventh, which wouldn't even have got them a play-off spot today. Both Newcastle and Wednesday were promoted.

Midfielder Craig lodged with full-back Dave Rushbury a few doors down our street. Opposite him had lived Tony Larkin, centre-back the previous season. Larkin was moved on by manager Bob Stokoe. He lost his place in the team after he was given the run around by a young and incredibly quick Leicester striker, one Gary Lineker. Larkin's lack of pace ended his time at Carlisle, which given Lineker's exceptional quality seemed a bit harsh on Larkin. He was a good guy and the first player to leave me complimentary tickets at away games.

Larkin did some voluntary work with the visually impaired during his playing days then worked full-time with them. He coached the GB team in the 2012 Paralympics and on his retirement was awarded the OBE. There can't be many former Blues who have done the Olympian and Queen's Honour double.

Despite three players living just a few doors away, I rarely talked to them. Quite the opposite; I avoided them. I still feel there's an aura around a Carlisle player, which is daft because I know there isn't. They're just people after all, but they are living my dream, not just professional footballers, but Carlisle United professional footballers!

I'll illustrate what I mean with reference to Paul Thirlwell, who'll go down in United history as one of two captains to lift a trophy at Wembley, which he did in 2011, the last time United won anything.

Several years earlier I had a taught an A Level student called Steph, who was a delight, not only because she was bright and made me look good (she passed English Language with a Grade A), but she was also a fanatical Sunderland supporter. I was always a teacher who enjoyed being distracted with football talk and Steph had plenty of that.

Her choice of A Level subjects meant that, by an unfortunate freak of the timetable, she had three long A Level exam papers on the same Friday. The school gave her the option of sitting one on the Saturday morning, providing she went into lockdown overnight at the home of a teacher. Steph asked if she could stay with me, which is probably something that would never be allowed in this day and age, even though I was married with children. I was probably the least-bad teacher option because there'd be some football talk to break any awkward silences.

We didn't have mobile phones, which meant Steph couldn't ask her classmates the questions from the Friday afternoon paper. I did of course, exchange phone numbers with her parents so they could know Steph was safe and well. She breezed through the exams, passing with flying colours. She left school and trained to be a solicitor at Northumbria School of Law. On a night out she met Paul Thirlwell, then an up-and-coming Sunderland midfielder. They fell in love and married.

I was aware of this because every now and then I bumped into Steph or her parents in Harrogate. I was pleased she was doing so well, both in her career and choice of husband. I asked for a signed photo of Paul as Sam was at the age where he collected memorabilia like that, but when all was said and done, Paul Thirlwell was only a Sunderland player.

He was with them seven seasons and was obviously highly regarded. He was made captain for a while despite his age and relative inexperience. Thirlwell played in the Premier League and had, Steph told me, Dennis Bergkamp's shirt framed in their house. He'd asked for it after a game and had insisted it wasn't washed. The shirt still had grass stains on it.

His Sunderland career ended soon after he fractured his skull in a reserve game against Everton. The first Steph knew of the seriousness of the injury was when a club car arrived to rush her and Paul's parents to a Merseyside hospital. Paul recovered but soon after left Sunderland for Sheffield United then Derby. I followed his career because he was Steph's husband after all.

Then in September 2006, he signed on loan for United. Within minutes of hearing the news on Sky Sports I had found Steph's parents' phone number. "Hello, it's Tim Pocock, Steph's English teach-"

"We thought you'd call," her mum interrupted. Moments later I was on the phone to Steph. I'm not sure if she or her husband shared my excitement that he was on loan to a club many miles and one division below Derby, but I was. I now had a foot in the door of the inner temple!

Steph was, of course, too discreet and professional to pass on any spicy titbits (she was a practising solicitor for a big law firm in Leeds, which probably made her football's cleverest WAG), but we drove her to a couple of matches and Paul left us tickets at away games when they weren't in demand from his family.

One anecdote she did tell me, which will add to the USP of this book with a World Exclusive tag, was the time they went to Paris for a few days on a mid-season break. They visited the Sacre-Coeur Basilica in Montmartre where, purely by chance, they bumped into Paul's teammate, right-back David Raven. He was there with his girlfriend. Any prayers proffered between them didn't, alas, help United. They missed out on promotion to the Championship in both 2007 and 2008.

Paul signed permanently after his loan spell and went on to make some 250 games for United and was even player-manager very briefly in 2014.

I've met former England international and broadcaster Danny Mills on several occasions because I used to teach his son and we've exchanged friendly banter on Parkruns. At Parents Evenings Colin Cooper, the ex-Boro player and manager, would seek me out to talk football. Ditto, whilst I'm name-dropping, well-known actor Mark Charnock, who plays Marlon in *Emmerdale*.

He a proper Manchester United fan; he and his son have the season tickets to prove it.

I've chatted to Gareth Southgate and I've also played against Dean Windass, Stuart McCall and (this will impress older readers) Jim McCalliog, all very famous players in their day. They are bigger names than Jack Ashurst, Paul Thirlwell, Paul Raven, Dean Walling and Luke Joyce (more of the latter three later) but although Southgate, Mills, Cooper et al achieved more in their careers, none of them played for the Blues.

So I make no apology for the blue-tinted, myopic vision that sees me star struck whenever I meet a Carlisle United footballer.

3

Knighton, Deano, Micky Tash

The 1983-84 season had seen, for the fourth in a row, United improve their league position. By that criteria alone, I've never had it so good since. It was another 20 years before United went on a similar four season run, and that only ended with fourth place in what is now League One.

The 1984-85 season was an anti-climax. I only went to 11 games. That was partly because my parents moved to Gloucester. The only times I went up to Carlisle now were to watch United. Diane and I lived just outside Lancaster while I trained to be a teacher. She was from a big family of Rugby League fans in St Helens and we watched Saints as much as United. We were engaged before the start of the season and married at its end.

Four games into the next season, 1985-86, Bob Stokoe stepped down as manager. "I've had enough of the job and maybe people have had enough of me," he said. You could almost hear the sigh of relief. It had been a miserable summer for English football. The season ended with the Valley Parade fire and Heysel crush.

In September I started work as a teacher at a Harrogate secondary school. Diane and I didn't have a car or much money. Carlisle was a long (and expensive) train journey away. I started to watch the local team, Harrogate Town, then in the Northern Counties East League. It didn't feel the same as watching United, it never would. Nothing, for that matter, came close. But it was regular, albeit stress-free, football.

That wouldn't have been the case had I been at Brunton Park. Pop Robson took over as manager in the September but 49 days later, Stokoe returned, reluctantly. "There's no way I want the job again. I don't even want the title of caretaker boss," he enthused. This time, you could almost hear the groan.

He had good reason to be anything but cheerful. United were relegated. Defeat at Oldham sent them down. There was fighting in the away end and Stokoe went onto the terraces to try to calm things down. "We had a good following but a few hotheads spoiled things a bit," he said. It was a sad way for Stokoe to end 25 years in management. United haven't been back to the Championship (Division Two as was) since.

Sam was born on New Year's Day 1988, when United lost 3:4 at home to Burnley, and Hannah in September 1990. Coincidentally Carlisle also played Burnley on the day of her birth, a 1:1 draw. I did my best to coincide visits to Gloucester and St Helens with an away game (Newport or Bolton for example); otherwise it was those within an easy train journey of Harrogate, York being the closest.

I didn't miss much. Over seven seasons from 1986 to 1992, Carlisle only finished higher than 20th twice. They were in freefall, crashing straight through Division Three, then only saved in 1988 from a third successive relegation to what is now the National League by Newport County. They could claim a promotion of sorts in 1992 when they found themselves in League Three, but so did every other club; Division One became the Premier League and lower tiers were renamed.

In 1990 (one of the two seasons out of the bottom four) they were a game away from the Fourth Division Play-Offs, only to lose at Maidstone. The season before they made it to the FA Cup Third Round, drawing Liverpool at home. I'd written off for a ticket then written off any chance of getting one as the tie drew near, until the club phoned me a few days before the game to tell me my ticket application had been successful; a few were left. An exiled Blue who made it to just a couple of games a season was low down their priority list. Fair enough.

The crowd was the largest I'd been in at Brunton Park. The Liverpool's fans among the 18,500 were soon taunting, "Going down!"

Carlisle replied with, "Arsenal, Arsenal, top of the league!" and "Wimbledon!" given their shock FA Cup Final win the previous summer, and that old favourite, "What's it like to have no job?"

The Scousers response: "What's it like to *have* a job?"

They were at it again a little later, for having jumped on the Sheepshaggers band, well, tractor-wagon, the away fans queried a refereeing decision with, "Who's the shepherd in the black?"

Over the years Carlisle fans, away from home mainly, have made plenty of noise at games, but not too many chants or songs are original. The best I heard was when Ayatollah Khomeini was Public Enemy Number One and two lads started up behind us: "He's hiding in Kabul / He loves Carlisle-ul!" I can't think why it never caught on.

Liverpool won the tie 3:0. Peter Beardsley, by then an England international, stayed on the pitch to applaud the home support.

My return to more regular service with the Blue Army took a turn for the better with the publication of the football fanzine *Each Game As it Comes*, which I did with my Best Man Steve. He wrote about Sunderland, I wrote about Carlisle and we sold most copies at Harrogate Town, which we also covered as there was a captive football audience (though not a big one) at their Wetherby Road ground.

The fanzine lasted 12 issues. Its demise wasn't because I'd fallen out of love with doing it; the reason was down to me producing a spin-off, *So Jack Ashurst, Where's My Shirt?* I had the credentials to publish a fanzine about United because I'd started going to games more regularly, which was directly thanks to *Each Game as it Comes*.

One summer afternoon in 1991 there was a knock at the front door from a man clutching the latest copy of the fanzine. "Hallo, I'm Bryan," he said, "and I've got something to show you." Before I could stop him, Bryan was peeling off his top. All sorts of horrors flashed through my mind. Had the fanzine's address been published by mistake in *Sado-Masochism Monthly*? Was he a member of the Harrogate Railway Ultras who'd been angered by our fanzine's pro-Harrogate Town bias?

But before I had time to slam the door, Bryan's true identity was revealed. What he had to show me was a Carlisle United shirt. So yes, there was another Carlisle supporter in Harrogate. What's more, he went to games and had a car. I was now half The Harrogate Blues. In our first season, 1991-92, we didn't see them win once.

We came close in the last home game, the Big One against Burnley. It was half the title decider we'd hoped for when the fixtures were released; a Burnley win would make them champions while victory for Carlisle would lift them off the bottom of the table. The five previous attendances at Brunton Park hadn't passed 1,900. For the Burnley game it was a little higher.

We'd only driven beyond Skipton when we infiltrated the Burnley convoy and we had to queue to exit the M6. There must have been at least double the 4,000 away fans the police had estimated. Inside Brunton Park they spilled from the Scratching Pen into the Waterworks, then the Paddock, and all the time more were being hauled over the walls. We felt like the Brits in *Zulu*.

A hundred or so idiots (Burnley always had more than its fair share) charged the Carlisle fans in the Paddock and there was fighting on top of the dug-outs before police established a barrier between them and us.

Burnley scored first, which kept the invading hoard's attention on the game, but any fears of being caught up in the trouble were replaced by a baser instinct, namely for United to put one over on them. Enter Gwyn Thomas (a player whose pebble barely rippled the surface of the United pond) with the equaliser, and exit the Harrogate Blues, smiling. Full-time 1:1.

United's points tally at the end of the season was a paltry 34 and yes, United did finish bottom. They kept their Football League status only because Aldershot were declared bankrupt in March 1992 and had their record expunged. There would be no relegation from the league. If there were tears in Hampshire, there was a mighty sigh of relief in Cumbria.

An article in *The Independent* on Aldershot's demise speculated that other impoverished clubs were to fold, 'and some may take the lead of Carlisle United, who announced yesterday they will go part-time next season.'

"We've simply got to get our overheads down," warned chairman Andrew Jenkins. With money short, attendances low and the team singularly unsuccessful, United needed a knight in shining armour. They got him. Into Brunton Park charged Michael Knighton.

Knighton couldn't have timed it better. One moment we were told the club was likely to lose its status as a full-time professional outfit ("frankly, it breathed an air of death," was how he later described his arrival at Brunton Park); the next, Knighton was not only breathing life into "the dilapidated stadium," he was promising United would be in the new Premier League in 10 years.

I don't think any Blue really believed that would happen (I'm not sure even Knighton did), but that didn't matter, for here was someone with the same ridiculous optimism and faith in United as us. What's more he would put his money where his mouth was. Knighton was someone we had heard of, the Manchester United director who'd put on a kit and juggled a ball from centre circle to Stretford End goal. It was an iconic image.

Knighton was going to buy Manchester United. That didn't happen but he did secure a seat on the board. He clearly loved the limelight so when it stopped shining on him at Old Trafford, he grabbed the spotlight that a smaller, provincial stage promised. He was the new owner of Carlisle United and he wanted the world to know.

A friend went for a job at Brunton Park where he was interviewed by Knighton. The meeting lasted nearly two hours. My friend got the job but Knighton asked him just two questions. The rest of the time he talked about himself. Knighton didn't lack self-belief.

There was no doubt Knighton was a successful man so it was easy for Carlisle fans to believe he would make a success of United. Okay, maybe a place in the Premier League was stretching things a little, but we were prepared, as audiences do in the theatre (and Knighton loved the theatrical), to 'suspend our disbelief.'

Even without Knighton's arrival, I was excited about the new season. The opening game coincided with the first issue of *So Jack Ashurst*. I was also looking forward to taking Sam to his first match at some point. Having finished bottom of the league, things, at the very least, wouldn't get any worse. The front cover of that first issue showed Dean Walling stooping to head the ball. "I can't get any higher," the speech bubble from an opponent said.

"Don't worry, we'll still finish lower than you," were the words I put in Deano's mouth.

I sold over 100 copies before kick-off, which was as many as the total number sold each issue of *Each Game as it Comes*. Over 15 issues in four years, sales of *So Jack* averaged 400. I made £7.50 profit per issue. It was another labour of United love.

Knighton promised United would win that opening game against Walsall, who had been their first opponents in my first game at Brunton Park 15 seasons before. They didn't. Nor (plot spoiler alert) did United make it the Premier League by 2002. United lost 3:4. It was an eventful game, as was the entire Knighton era.

Rochdale away was a historic one because Sam, nearly five, came with me for the first time. He was too young to appreciate the game itself, I knew that, but he loved being with dad, the excitement of travelling on trains (made even better by having to run for a connection) and being spoilt.

"We had five packets of crisps!" he told everyone, including Mum (he hadn't learnt that what goes on tour, stays on tour) but what did for him was the Spotland burger, which reappeared all over his bedroom wall later. I loved having him with me at Rochdale, sitting him on the crush barriers, telling him what the Carlisle fans were singing (PG version), watching him run up and down the terracing, playing football with plastic beakers.

At times watching Sam was better than the match, but in fairness Rochdale wasn't a bad one at all: four goals, three sendings-off and United didn't lose, despite blowing a two-goal lead and the chance to play the last quarter against 10 men, because a minute after gaining that numerical advantage, Darren Edmondson was ordered off too. Fellow youngster Jeff Thorpe followed and United were themselves a man down for the last nine.

Edmondson's dismissal was in keeping with his gung-ho enthusiasm. He was a friendly lad as well. Sam's place in the Warwick became a spot behind the perimeter wall to the left of the goal, from where we could call players over at a convenient moment during the warm-up for autographs. The only one who ever refused was Clive Allen, a prolific scorer for QPR and Spurs. He had three forgettable appearances for United right at the end of his career, but obviously hadn't lost Premier League airs and graces.

Edmondson on the other hand, was always happy to sign. We've almost as many programmes with his autograph as Tony Caig's (being the keeper meant Caigy was closest.) Before a game with Barnet, whose dangerman was a fiery striker called Sean Devine, we asked Edmondson where he'd be playing.

"Don't know yet," he said. "All I've been told is, 'Get Devine!'" Sure enough, fairly early on, Darren got Devine and was yellow-carded. So too was Devine (retaliation) and for the rest of the match the striker was more concerned with catching Darren than scoring. Job done.

Knighton's first season didn't live up to expectations but wasn't as bad as the previous two. United shuffled around lower mid-table, finishing 18th. Bury in February was particularly bad. Indeed, I would challenge any Blue to come up with a worse 45 minutes than the half/hell we suffered in Gigg Lane's aptly named Cemetery End. From there we were perfectly placed to watch Carlisle concede six, yes SIX. And Edmondson got sent off again.

After the third Sam's bottom lip trembled. "I want to go home now. Every time Bury come up here they score," he sniffed. Right on cue, Bury scored the fourth. Sam burst into tears. I was rapidly going off United; they were making my boy cry.

But our first season as Harrogate Blues Two did finish on a high, a very big high indeed. The last game was at

Scarborough, where Diane and I took Sam and Hannah for donkey rides on the beach beforehand. Mum and daughter stayed there, Sam and I headed for the game. Scarborough let all fans in for free, which was good of them but meant a few idiots came looking for a fight. Sam didn't see that, thankfully.

The match was the season in a 90-minute microcosm: a promising start (a goal after seven minutes); significant achievement (two up early in the second half); frustration and anti-climax (final score 2:2.) Rory Delap and Tony Hopper made their debuts as second half subs. At the end Player of the Season Simon Davey and top scorer *OO! George Oghani!* threw their shirts into the crowd, which didn't please Knighton when he came on for his bow *("that's two I'll have to replace now")*, but it was all a bit of a non-event. I wanted something to remember over the summer's football-less months. We got it at York Station.

Having already boarded the Harrogate train, Diane said it would be a good idea to buy the children a drink before departure, so off I trudged with Sam and Hannah in tow. Passing the phone booths, I spotted a blue, red and white tracksuit.

"I think that's Dean Walling!" I told Sam, so back we went and spoke to him, for it *was* Deano.

He'd come to Carlisle as a striker, having been an apprentice at Leeds where he used to clean Jack Ashurst's boots, but he wasn't exactly prolific. He was given a go at centre-back and that was the making of him. Deano was at York Station waiting to board the Harrogate train too, alighting at Pannal, one step further down the line. His girlfriend would meet him. By coincidence, she had been a pupil at the school where I taught.

"Is it all right if Sam brings his programme for you to sign on the train?" I asked.

"Sure!" said Deano, but rather than having to search him out, Deano came and found us, chatting away the whole half hour to Harrogate. He told us he couldn't believe the *'Deano! Deano!'* chants he received during the game, especially as he wasn't playing and sat high in the stand.

"There's not many teams I'd rather play for," he said, adding that he hoped to be at Brunton Park next season. He was back in Carlisle on Monday to see Knighton and discuss (I suppose that meant listen to) terms. Deano signed Sam's programme and asked the lad about his school and football. To cap it all, as we neared Harrogate he took off his tracksuit top.

"Could you make use of this?" he said, handing it over. In doing so he made one lad very happy indeed. Sam was pleased for Dad too. Mum later admitted she wished he had stripped off his bottoms instead. At least Sam was out of earshot and didn't hear that. Leaving the station, we turned to Deano and, from the opposite platform, gave him two-fisted salutes. Deano replied in kind! And at that moment, though it hadn't been a great season, the Harrogate Blues felt champion.

Deano was a top bloke and, as those chants at Scarborough proved, hugely popular with United supporters. He played like any Carlisle fan would, were we given with the chance to represent United. Deano put in a shift and more, not just for United either. He was named in the PFA's fourth tier Team of the Season three times (twice with United, once with Lincoln). Few strikers could outjump him and he could tackle too. A challenge he made in a game at Sunderland was so impressive I described it as 'a Beresi' after the Italian World Cup winning defender.

It was easy to warm to him as a player, and easier still to warm to Deano as a person. He was a lovely man, really friendly with no airs and graces. When he spotted Sam once in a big away crowd at Darlington, he broke into a chant of "SAMM-Y! SAMM-Y" to the tune of our terrace cry "DEAN-O! DEAN-O!"

United had a new manager, rather, Director of Coaching, in Mick Wadsworth for the 1993-94 season. His wasn't a name we knew, unlike the two Player-Coaches beneath him: David McCreery, ex-Manchester United, in charge the previous season; and Mervyn Day, who'd played for West Ham and Leeds in the top tier.

Knighton's interview technique obviously worked. He'd made Deano an offer he didn't refuse and gave Wadsworth his first job in charge of a league club. The *So Jack Ashurst* end of season survey had invited readers to submit marks out of ten for Knighton. Responses averaged out at a lukewarm six, but by the end of his second season, his rating was up to eight.

Appointing Wadsworth was astute for all sorts of reasons. He'd done plenty of coaching for the FA at national level, which is how he knew Roddy Thomas, a teen prodigy. Thomas had out-performed Alan Shearer in the England schoolboy team but his career didn't develop the way he must have expected, partly I suspect, because he stopped growing. When he was released by Watford, Wadsworth persuaded the young Londoner to make his new home in Carlisle.

Thomas was joined in the October by another forward, David Reeves from Notts County, United's most expensive signing at £121,000. We saw Reeves score at Wigan in November. I had Sam (now five) and Hannah (three) with me. In the morning Diane said she wasn't feeling well so I'd have to stay at home to look after them. There was an alternative: take them both on the train to Wigan.

We had lunch at McDonalds where they were given a toy dinosaur with their Happy Meal. They were good omens, I hoped. Like dinosaurs, defeat at Wigan (three in four seasons in the FA Cup) would be a thing of the past. Hannah was happy enough running up and down the terracing, not that it pleased a steward. "Stop her doing that in case she falls over," I was told. The long cross-country trek, and that cheery welcome, did make me wonder why I'd bothered. The answer came just after four o'clock when Reeves scored.

In that wonderful moment, everything clicked into place. Yet perversely, there then followed the worst 27 minutes of the day. Until Reevesy's goal, the game had been a pretty dull affair and "Why am I here?' kept springing to mind far more than a United forward in the Wigan box.

The Ancient Greeks might've been the first to ponder, "Why are we here?'" Had they invented football as a pursuit instead of philosophy, such a poser would've been dismissed as too trivial, for with United's goal came 27 minutes of anguish. I wondered, nay, physically felt the pain of a bigger existential question: "Will United hang on?"

A second goal from Reeves' strike partner Andy Flounders provided the answer. Thereafter I never once questioned the point of our cross-country day-out.

For the season's derby with Preston the crowd was close to five figures. Carlisle had a buzz about it. Fanzine sales topped 250 before kick-off, thanks to Skipton Tim doubling the sales force. Sam failed to get Deano's autograph down by the Warwick wall because he was so popular ("I only wanted to say hello") and nearly missed out on Day's, only for Merv to glance back, spot him, sign his programme and pat him on the head. That made Sam's afternoon.

Preston were managed by John Beck, whose teams were well-known if not well-liked for their boorish and brutal football. Their centre-forward was Tony Ellis, a perennial scorer against United. Sam joined in the abuse: "Tony Ellis is a homosexual!" he was singing, or so I feared. How would I explain that to his mum or teachers?

I needn't have worried. I listened closely to what Sam was chanting: "Tony Elliott is a true professional!" Phew. Tony Elliott was United's reserve keeper.

This was in the days when homophobia wasn't frowned upon the way it is now. Five-year-olds swearing still is, which is why I was a tad worried when Sam said afterwards, "The referee was a wonker." I told him that wasn't a nice word, even though Sam had a point. The referee had disallowed two Carlisle goals and a strong case for a penalty. With 10 minutes remaining, Tony Ellis scored the only goal.

At Darlington Diane complained about the cold and Hannah the noise of the away support: "It hurts my ears!" she cried. There were that many Blues we lost travelling companion Skipton Tim in the away end and Bryan had to ask a steward to deliver our Sunderland cup tie tickets, because he could see but not reach us. United won 3:1 and once warmed up in the car afterwards, Hannah combined *Away in a Manger* with *Glory, Glory, Carlisle United!*

The size of United's support was even more impressive given the team's erratic results. They started New Year in 16th with an average home attendance of 5,900. Over the season attendances at Brunton Park showed a bigger increase (over 50 per cent) than at any other league ground.

At away games the Blue Army manoeuvred in numbers. United were drawn at Roker Park in the FA Cup. Sam and I took the train with Sunderland Steve and a couple of other Mackems. We changed at Newcastle and hopped on the football special from Carlisle, where departure had been delayed half-an-hour. With so many fans on the platform, extra carriages had to be attached.

In ours were some of the lads who produced another Carlisle fanzine, *Watching from the Warwick*. Mentioning Sam in so many match reports ('*Harrogate Blues on Manoeuvres*') and getting him to illustrate the players had given him celebrity status. A Blue at Bury shook his hand: "So you're Sam!" And that was how we met Rob, like Bryan a great bloke, good mate and someone we'd never have met had it not been for United.

On the Sunderland train the lads serenaded Sam with, "Sammy, Sammy! Give us a wave!" which brought a lump to dad's throat. Sam on the other hand was frightened.

There was a big police presence at Seaham station but as we were with three Sunderland fans, we were allowed to slip through. Sam and I wore Carlisle scarves and en route to the ground faced a large group of home supporters leaving a pub and heading for the station. They didn't look the friendliest of welcoming committees but simply moved out of the way as we walked through them. We had a pre-match pint in a (safe) pub with our Sunderland travelling companions before we headed for the ground to see the Carlisle coach arrive. Deano seemed very relaxed.

"Happy New Year! How's school?" he asked.

"School?" I replied. "What does school matter on a day like today?"

We were inside the ground early to find Sam a crush barrier to sit on. There would be close to 5,000 Carlisle fans on the terracing. When United emerged, the ticker-tape welcome rivalled, in our eyes, anything at the World Cup. Buoyed by our support, the team were on top from the off. Sunderland's goal came against the run of play, which the home support acknowledged: "One shot! We've only had one shot!"

Carlisle continued to be the better team in the second half, but when the ball fell to a United player in or around the Sunderland box, it wasn't to likely scorers David Reeves, Rod Thomas or Simon Davey. United, attacking the goal in front of us, were heading for honourable defeat.

With 10 minutes to go, Thomas's cross was deflected to the edge of the box. Full-back Tony Gallimore shot, low and left-footed. The keeper had it covered, parrying his strike, and from our angle he was going to drop on the loose ball, despite it rolling away from him and nearer, yes, nearer to Darren Edmondson. This sequence of play couldn't have lasted more than a couple of seconds, yet as traumatic or tremendous moments do, it seemed to last much longer.

Suddenly it was all over. Darren had got to the ball first and it was in the back of the net. He ran behind the back of the goal and stood directly in front of us, his right hand raised high like the Statue of Liberty, palm outreached and waving once, twice, three times to the massed terrace of manic humanity in front of him.

It was an image I'll take to the grave. I can only feel sorry for non-football folk who've never experienced such joy, such jubilation, the moment made all the more intense knowing that 5,000 others around you were feeling exactly the same. My celebrations were suddenly cut short: "Help Daddy! I'm falling off!" I lifted Sam from the barrier and jigged with him in delight.

Darren's goal was the overwhelming winner of the season's best moment in the fanzine's End of Season Survey: 'I don't think I've ever felt such elation watching United, an unbelievable feeling... Unbridled ecstasy... That bout of temporary insanity from 5,000 fans...' readers wrote. Another Blue added, with commendable understated, 'Probably the best moment of all time.'

Afterwards Sunderland Steve admitted, through gritted teeth, that the Blue Army had been "pretty impressive" and an old lady on the train back to Newcastle said, "Well done Carlisle! You must be really proud of your team and support. There was no singing in the Fulwell End." *Proud*. Yes, that's how I felt. The previous three seasons hadn't given us much to feel proud about. Sunderland was different.

Carlisle lost the replay in extra-time, an anti-climax. I persuaded friends from school to drive me up to watch a cup upset. Safety concerns had slashed the capacity to less than 13,000, yet the ground was no different to how it was five years earlier when 18,500 were allowed in for the Liverpool tie.

Carlisle couldn't repeat performances like the one at Roker Park week in, week out. I heard a former player explain the difference between a top tier professional and one in the fourth. In terms of fitness and ability, there wasn't a great deal between them, he said, but a Premier League player is far more consistent. His lower division counterpart plays to his max two or three times every 10 games. When he does, and when his teammates manage to raise their game on the same day, then a team like Carlisle can match Sunderland.

Consistently good performances throughout the team (we're talking, in numerical terms, 7/10 ratings at least) mean a side would win more matches than it loses, which breeds confidence and that in turn, means better performances and more wins. It's a victorious circle. Two decades later, when United were on a good run, Bryan was chatting to one of United's management. "Why are they playing so well?" he asked.

"Confidence," was the one-word answer. Those top tier players then, have more confidence in their ability (how often are they described, perhaps unfairly, as arrogant?) and have more resilience to shrug off criticism or get over a bad performance. Carlisle's confidence at Roker Park had grown by the minute; every player raised his game.

But when lower tier players don't play well and lose confidence, things don't go so well. "The worst performance I've ever seen!" fumed Bryan just three weeks later when Carlisle lost at home to bottom of the table Northampton, who hadn't won in 20 games. The match after that they were almost as bad in defeat at Bury, despite the welcome they received onto the pitch from 250 Blue balloons, paid for and distributed by *So Jack*.

United were mid-table in the league going into March and, oh glory be, into a Wembley semi-final in the Autowindscreen Shield. They were underdogs; opponents Huddersfield were a division higher. The First Leg was at Leeds Road with 2,500 Blues plus cockerel in a crowd of over 10,500. The cockerel had been liberated from a pub garden somewhere between Carlisle and Huddersfield. It was released just as a Huddersfield player was about to take a corner. It wasn't the only cock on the pitch that night.

Home supporters invaded when their team scored, which they did four times. Simon Davey had equalised from the spot but individual errors undid the first half performance. Sam was in tears after the fourth goal and the Yorkies' regular pitch invasions didn't help our mood. On the final whistle and with the same clowns coming onto the pitch to goad us, one Blue snapped, jumped out of the away end and was immediately leapt on by police. This was too much for me. I picked Sam up and marched down to the fence.

"Why didn't you arrest any Huddersfield fan?" I demanded of the nearest PC. "They were doing it all game."

"That was nothing to do with me," he replied, avoiding eye contact.

I knew I had him then. "It had everything to do with you!" I retorted. "What sort of example is that for my son?"

A crowd of Blues gathered round. Whilst I was protesting at the foot of the terrace, Sunderland Steve overheard a Blue telling his mate, "See him with his boy? They go to loads of games. Proper fans..." That recognition from a peer was appreciated but Being There for the Second Leg was more call of duty than act of faith. There was no expectation that I'd be dancing on the pitch, oops, terracing should United turn the 1:4 deficit around.

Nevertheless over 5,000 Blues turned up. Huddersfield brought 3,000 themselves (they were three up after all) and a fair share of idiots, one of whom we saw picking a fight with a police dog on the Warwick Road before kick-off. He lost. The football, for the first 40 minutes of the match, lacked bite. Shortly before half-time however, Carlisle pulled a goal back when a defender flicked Gallimore's free-kick past his own keeper. I didn't get carried away. "That's one," I said. At least two more were needed.

United's next attack brought a corner from the left. The ball was cleared to the right where full-back Joe Joyce, under pressure from on-coming defenders, thumped it 25-yards into the top corner. A stunner, an absolute stunner! Joyce, who'd only scored six goals before in a career of 450 league games, was flattened by his teammates. The improbable now seemed possible.

United fancied it, you could tell. Paul Conway, an American midfielder ("the working man's Glenn Hoddle," according to Skipton Tim) was playing so well we wondered whether a World Cup call-up wasn't out of the question. United didn't score a third but they were applauded off by fans who ignored the Huddersfield idiots on the pitch. There was still the matter of breaking the news to Sam, who'd fallen asleep listening to the Radio Leeds commentary, but he took it on the chin. "Besides," I told him, "we'll get to Wembley in the Play-Offs."

United's run after Huddersfield was, as it had been throughout the league season, more of a jog. They were 11th with four games remaining. The first was at home to Wigan when, for the only time in the League, the attendance was under 4,000. Fanzine sales however, were good again: 200 copies of Issue Eight (*Promotion Special!*) shifted before kick-off.

'Whatever else happens this season, it's been fun,' I wrote in the editorial. 'But barring victories in the last four games, celebrations haven't lasted long enough.'

Four games and four victories later, United were in the Play-Offs for the first time. Like the rest of us, Paul Conway hadn't expected Carlisle to make the Play-Offs. His wedding had been set the weekend of the First Leg, a big society one in Central Park, New York, no less. He did delay his honeymoon though; Knighton was flying him back for the Second Leg.

Years later in a *News and Star* interview, Conway recalled his days at Brunton Park: "I remember when we went down to the McVitie's factory, the plant manager was telling us that production was always up on a Monday if the club had won. Wow! In America, our sports are a bit different, we're more an entertainment-first culture, whereas in England, the football is in the people, in the soul."

I had my doubts about the semi-final the moment Bryan told me Simon Garner was playing for Wycombe. Garner always scored against United in his Blackburn days. He did it again for Wycombe with their second four minutes from time. "We can still do it," I told Sam as Wycombe celebrated Garner's goal and a 2:0 First Leg lead.

"No we won't," replied Sam. Unlike at Huddersfield, there were no tears in his eyes. Aged six and old before his time.

There was a minor pitch invasion during the game. Matters weren't helped by stewards bringing down one invader and a couple kicking him when he was on the ground. That brought more supporters on to the pitch to confront the stewards, followed by police. In addition to the trouble on the pitch, rain fell throughout the afternoon. All in all, a wonderful day out. Garner scored again in the Second Leg and United lost 1:4 on aggregate.

4

Double then Drop

In spite of the Wycombe defeats, 1993-94 had been quite a season, the best since the promotion campaign to the second tier 12 years earlier. United had made it to not one but two Wembley semi-finals after all.

'Let's start the first issue of this (new) season with absolute optimism,' I wrote in the new issue of *So Jack Ashurst*. 'United will be champions in May. I make this prediction because I can't think of one good reason why not to.'

A very good reason to be confident was that the squad was stronger. Wadsworth had a penchant for centre-backs and anyone who'd played for Barnsley, his hometown club. Derek Mountfield came in the first category, David Currie the second. Mountfield had won the League with Everton; Currie was well-known too, more as a maverick. 'A team with him and Roddy in is capable of taking any Division Three opposition apart should the mood take them,' I boldly declared.

The season started with a home game against Wigan. A flat battery, A66 road works and being stuck behind a hay wagon meant we didn't arrive until seven minutes to three. Before kick-off we had to collect Sam's deckchair away shirt (red, green and white stripes), plus our father and son season tickets. We were now even more committed to the Blues.

As we gleefully brandished our season tickets at the Warwick turnstiles, Sam nudged me and said, "Daddy, listen!" They were playing his favourite song, D:Ream's *Things Can Only Get Better*. It became the season's soundtrack. United were two up when Deano scored an own goal. While prostrate on the turf, head in hands, the Warwick broke into chants of *"Deano! Deano!"* It made for a nervy last 20 minutes, but nothing compared to the stress of the drive.

I suggested we returned from our week's summer holiday at a Berwick caravan park a day early on the Friday evening, "to avoid holiday traffic," I explained to Diane, which was the case, of course. As was United playing at Scunthorpe on the Saturday. Swapping sunny seaside for Scunny turned out to be a very good decision indeed, albeit not for the first 80 minutes of the game.

United were dreadful and two goals down, partly because Wadsworth started with a five-man defence. He abandoned the system at half-time but things only improved when sub Jeff Thorpe came on. The young winger was the first Blue to cause Scunthorpe anything close to concern, but a United goal still seemed remote with 10 minutes left.

At that point Davey was fouled in the box. From where we sat, close to the action as United were attacking the away end, Davey's tumble was a tad dramatic. In any case, the defender would've been better off leaving his man well alone; United hadn't managed an on-target effort all match.

Davey's penalty was the first shot the Scunny keeper would have to save, and save it he did, but Tony Gallimore was following up and knocked in the rebound. Wadsworth gambled, sending Deano up from centre-back. It paid off. Deano's challenge saw the ball break to winger Thorpe just outside the box. He didn't shoot straightaway; he didn't even take a touch and have a go with his favoured left. No, instead he cut back onto his right-foot and curled a beauty into the top corner. A ninetieth minute equaliser.

Another attack. Rod Thomas's shot takes a wicked deflection and the keeper inches the ball around the foot of the post. Corner! Davey from the left, Thorpe rises, the ball arches towards the same top corner as the equaliser and I'm up on the wall, Sam's desperately looking for me, there are people on the pitch (it's very soon all over) and if there'd had been a Brazilian commentator exploding GOOOOOOAL! he would have run out of breath long before we'd finished celebrating.

I'm looking at the referee, he's looking at his watch, his hand goes to his mouth and there's a roar ringing in my ears. I'm not sure what, if anything, we're chanting now but at last there is some audio order. Everyone's on the wall, out of their seats, on the pitch: CHAM-P-O-NEE! CHAMP-P-O-NEE!

Oh yea oh yea indeed! Driving out of the car park we heard the other Division Three scores. With four wins and a draw from their five games, 10 goals scored and five conceded, United shared exactly the same record as Torquay, but when the tables were read out, United were top on alphabetical order.

United lost at home to Northampton in September and drew at Lincoln in October. After those games, they dropped to second, but they beat Hereford mid-November and went top again. That's where they remained right through Christmas, New Year, Easter and all the way to May Day. *Cham-p-o-nees!* by a mile, eight points to be precise, the title assured with games to spare.

But that doesn't tell half the story of a remarkable season for United and the Harrogate Blues.

Carlisle's cup form was decent too. United beat Rotherham in the First Round of the League Cup and drew Premier League QPR over two legs again in the second. The only goal at Brunton Park was headed by Les Ferdinand, the one opponent that season to get the better of Deano in the air.

There were nearly 10,000 at Brunton Park against QPR, nearly all Blues, and there was another big crowd for the FA Cup First Round tie at Guiseley, which was played on a Sunday at Valley Parade, Bradford. Valley Parade was the closest League ground from Harrogate. We'd taken some non-Blues with us who were mightily impressed with the following, most of whom travelled in a cavalcade of coaches.

Bryan reported how they had been made to wait outside Bradford for a police escort. Fans alighted to stretch their legs, have a pee and oh! there was a match on in the park opposite. So it was that a Sunday league game suddenly had a four-figure crowd, which disappeared almost as quickly once word was given for the cavalcade to depart. United beat Guiseley 4:1. Over half the crowd in a gate of 6,500 were Blues, most of us in the covered Kop.

A month after the Guiseley game and days after a home draw with Doncaster in front of 7,000, which kept Carlisle at the top of the table, I was diagnosed with testicular cancer. If that juxtaposition comes as a surprise to you, the news that "it's a tumour" was quite a shock to me. I won't go into detail, relax, but 25 years ago there wasn't the awareness of prostate or testicular cancer or, for that matter, other men's health issues.

I was asked if I'd talk about it on a BBC 2 series aimed at raising awareness about male illnesses. I was pleased to; I felt no embarrassment about having just the one. The only thing I was ashamed about was not knowing that you could even get cancer down there. We blokes just didn't talk about those things.

It was though, a worrying time. When the consultant told me, "I'm pretty sure it's a tumour but don't worry, there's a 98 or 99% success rate," I just thought: *"So there's a one or two per cent chance I could die."*

After the biopsy I had a course of radiotherapy. For one session I wore a Carlisle shirt, not purposely, just because I had, and still have, that many United tops. The radiographer recognised it; she had family in Carlisle. Football gets everywhere.

Less than two weeks after my operation I was back on the terraces at Scarborough. United won again, went six points clear at the top with the best record of any team in the top four divisions. The home fans inquired, "Where were you when you were shit?" A sure sign, if ever there was one, that United were on the up and up.

There was a confidence which spilled over into arrogance in my match reports: *'This will surely be the last time United have to play a league game at Scarborough... United's Farewell to the Fourth Tour rolled into Hartlepool's palatial stadium and rolled all over Hartlepool United...'*

Hartlepool was well-nigh deserted for the high noon kick-off on Boxing Day. Down one side, there was just a long wooden fence. The Blue Army was given what is now the home end, which was then an open terrace. The police bill was £7000, which would've been most of Hartlepool's takings from the travelling support. We got talking to a policeman outside who'd been drafted in from Guisborough. "Can't understand it," he said. "We were told Carlisle don't travel well but there's no trouble at all."

Hartlepool had decent stewards too. I asked if I could sell the fanzine in the away end. "Sell what you like son," one replied, and his chum patrolling the perimeter didn't stop grinning all game. He was probably a Darlington fan, taking delight in United's 5:1 win.

I could still feel sorry for Hartlepool, whose players had to travel all the way to Torquay straight after the game for the next round of league games. Carlisle were home to Bury, first v second in the table. The game merited a full report in the fanzine, which usually just covered the aways in such detail, partly because of the crowd, 12,400, with all four sides of Brunton Park full and fans locked out; and partly because it was one heck of a performance from United.

They didn't just have the better players but the harder workers. Richard Prokas, a Penrith lad, was quite magnificent. He rarely let United down. He was more piano-carrier than piano-player, but with each challenge he knocked a little more stuffing out of Bury's resistance.

I compared the visitors' attempts to make any ground to that of a seven-stone weakling on *Gladiators,* a favourite TV shows of Sam's (ok, I admit it, and mine): *"First Prokas hits them, OOMP! Then Deano, K-POW! Degsy (Mountfield), THWACK! And now, on their knees, they face Dazza (Edmondson), BOING! And Gally (Gallimore), YOW! Finally Caigy would grapple and grab the ball off them, G-ZOINK!"*

United won 3:0 and most of the 11,000 plus Blues stayed behind to applaud United off. It was the least we could do after such a superb performance. With half the season over, United had amassed 52 of a possible

63 points. They went into the New Year 11 points (ELEVEN POINTS!) clear of Bury in second, but they had proved the gap was much, much wider.

Before the Bury game I called Mick Wadsworth over to sign Sam's programme. Neither Sam nor I could remember mentioning Sam by name, but Mick asked, "It's Sam, isn't it?" Being the class act he was, Wadsworth was obviously planning ahead to United's next game, pondering over the team he'd pick and who he'd have leading them down the tunnel. The opponents would be Chesterfield and leading United out would be Sam as mascot, a day after his seventh birthday.

Unfortunately bad weather meant the match was postponed. Still, Sam's time would come at the re-arranged game. In the meantime, it was FA Cup Third Round Groundhog Day: Sunderland away. Carlisle's sequence of three FA Cup ties at Wigan in four years had been broken when they were drawn at Sunderland the season before, only for the same pair in the same order to be pulled out of the bag 12 months later. Once again, United drew 1:1 at Roker and lost the replay.

The Roker game wasn't as much fun as 1994's, not because United didn't play well or because the support wasn't as good, but because of the heavy-handed stewarding in front of us which restricted our view, first and foremost, and was unnecessarily confrontational.

Just like the previous year, Sunderland scored first and Carlisle equalised with 10 minutes to go, this time thanks to skipper Davey scoring with a rising shot from the edge of the box. By way of celebration, and in contrast to our mania, he sauntered towards us with a calm swagger. "Relax lads," he suggested. "We were always going to score."

The Tuesday night replay attendance was 12,200 when, for the first time in 20 league and cup games, United lost. There was another five-figure crowd of nearly 10,700 at Brunton Park the following Saturday to watch a 0:0 with Preston. United could only draw at Rochdale a week later. There were mitigating circumstances: the mid-week cup tie, a flu bug and not least Rochdale's will to win. *'From now on every mid-table, no-hope outfit is going to raise their game to beat the champions-elect,'* I wrote.

'Deano scored again with a strike right out of a sharp-shooter's manual. I was up on the fence giving a big YES! to Reevesy, who was giving it back too, when I remembered Sam and his cousin Christopher somewhere on the steps behind me. I found Sam coming back down from the fence himself, rubbing his knee and screaming, "That's seven goals for Deano, Daddy!" He was okay.'

Despite just one win (at Barnet) in five league games, United were still picking up points as the other four were drawn, including Doncaster. They were a club in trouble; even a half-time penalty competition had to be cancelled as only one lad turned up for it. Rovers weren't alone. A few weeks later Darlington's PA announcer apologised for no half-time scores as "no one's brought a radio."

United's unbeaten league run had to end somewhere. It was just a pity it was at Preston. 'Just like old times,' my report started. 'United lose, teams below win and we all feel pretty pissed off.' But, I added, not really. United's lead at the top had been slashed to a measly 10 points and at the final whistle we reacted with *GOING UP!* rising to a crescendo with *CHAMPIONS!*

We weren't wrong. United kick-started their season with another unbeaten run that hauled in 20 points from 24. The loss of Davey, transferred, didn't stop United's charge, and snow didn't halt the Harrogate Blues either. We had to stop at my brother's in Kendal after watching United beat Northampton as the A66 was blocked. Next morning the snow had melted and we drove home without a hitch. Rather like United motoring to the title.

Davey was sold to Preston, which blotted his copybook. He made his debut alongside a Manchester United loanee: David Beckham. Davey was named in the PFA Team of the Season, which wasn't a surprise giving his role in United's midfield. His replacement was Steve Hayward, a Derby midfielder whose debut came in the Autowindscreen Semi-Final Second Leg at Rochdale.

In the First Leg United had done to Dale what Huddersfield had inflicted on United the previous season, opening up a 4:1 lead. We travelled to Spotland to celebrate. Gerald, a godfather of the travelling support, came dressed in a Superman costume. Watching United at Wembley was, he beamed, a life's ambition, before he flew back up, up and away over the open terrace.

Twenty minutes in and Carlisle were two goals down. I came close to despair: 'If they can blow this, they can blow promotion too. That awful feeling struck me like a Cantona kung-fu kick to the gut.' (The Frenchman's assault on a Palace fan was the other big football story of the day.) That's how panicky I felt, but taking a deep breath, I reasoned that if United could only get the ball in Rochdale's box more often, they'd score, simply because Rochdale were Rochdale and wouldn't be in their lowly league position if they were any good.

Even that however, looked doubtful, seeing how United didn't seem to have a midfield. It looked a bad decision to debut Hayward in such a massive game. Thank goodness then, for central defenders at corners. Deano won a header, a scramble followed and suddenly arms were raised and players were wheeling away in celebration. No one around us knew who'd scored (it was actually Mountfield, Deano's partner at the back) and no one cared. We were dreaming Wembley again.

I didn't tempt fate. Yes, I sang my heart out for the lads but I didn't even mouth the word '*Wembley*', not until the last five minutes, by when Superman was flying again. The morning after I tried explaining the wonders of that Tuesday night in Rochdale to someone who wasn't a football fan. "But it's only a game!" the person interrupted.

"Only a game?" I gasped. "No! It is everything and anything but!"

As we partied out of Spotland the heavens, apparently, opened. But did anyone notice? I almost felt sorry for

Sam, who was on his way to Wembley after less than three years into his life membership of the Blue Army. Yet he too had known the pain that supporting United can bring; he'd wept at Bury when those six goals went in, and at Huddersfield in the previous year's semi-final. That pain however, is a pre-requisite for the pleasure and passion of nights like Rochdale 95.

Little wonder that Spotland has a special place in our hearts. I was misty-eyed there again a few seasons later. Sam had a choice of either going with a friend to watch Bradford City play Manchester United (David Beckham et al) or to come to Rochdale with Dad. It was probably the first time I'd been on the end of a withering look from my son.

"United of course," he said. He didn't add "stupid question," but he that's what he meant. I told folk what Sam had said in the Spotland clubhouse before kick-off (that's another reason why I like Rochdale; I've never been refused admission to have a beer in the bar, whether I've been in United colours or not.) Gerald/Superman was impressed.

"Let me shake your hand, Sam," he said. "That's loyal support." I turned away. There was a tear in dad's eye.

Sam remains every bit as fanatical as me about United, but put him in the centre of Carlisle and I'm almost certain he wouldn't know where he was. There's no need for us to go there before the game. We tend to have a drink in the Rugby Club or buy at coffee and pie at Claire's and stroll around the ground. Afterwards we shoot straight off; it's a fair way to Ripon and even further to Pontefract.

Sam ran through Carlisle in the Half Marathon but never having lived there, and with no relations in or around the city, he has little connection with it, but at the same time, he has a life-time invested in the club. I like to think I have brought him up properly. Evidence to back that up came when we took him to the Harrogate pantomime a year or two into his supporting life. The interval came and Sam asked, "Will they announce the attendance during the second half?"

United's trip to Wembley was so good on so many levels. 'Thank goodness for the Autowindscreen Shield,' I wrote in the last fanzine of the season. 'Without a Wembley final, this season might well be remembered as one of the dullest, because United are far too good for the rest of the division. The odd team might pinch the occasional point, but there's no side with the resilience, or brilliance, of United.'

Brian had collected our four final tickets a few days before the home game with Scunthorpe (no need to ask who won). He'd left them at home otherwise I'd have had a surreal moment of holding them in one hand and in the other, a cheque for nearly £18,000.

We'd taken out health cover when each of the children was born. I remembered one had a critical illness clause. I'd had a brief look when I was first diagnosed and didn't think testicular cancer qualified me to claim. A few weeks later Diane was queuing in the bank when she met the person who'd sold us the policy. Diane didn't want to tell her at first about my cancer in case it affected our policy (we were pretty innocent/ignorant back then) but she came clean.

"I think you can claim for that," the saleswoman said. A quick phone call, followed by receipt of a letter requiring little more than my doctor's details, and a week later a cheque for nearly £18,000 landed on the mat the morning of the Scunthorpe game. Wembley tickets and a five-figure pay-out on the same day. If Carlsberg did Saturdays...

The title bandwagon and Wembley roadshow rolled in to (and over) Mansfield on the first Saturday in April. We pulled up at a bus stop and offered a young Mansfield fan a lift so he could guide us to the ground. "I hear you're bringing 300 hooligans," he said.

He must have been seriously confused by our part of the convoy, compromising as it did of mum, dad and two little children. Sam and Hannah could be terrors, yes, but hooligans?

Others had heard the same as our guide. "Carlisle, Carlisle, where are your boys?" came the chant from the Main Stand next to us in the away end. There was clearly disappointment that our "boys" weren't interested in anything but the game. One Blue who had a seat in the stand said he'd been given a police escort to the loo at half-time. It wasn't a pleasant atmosphere.

Rumours were rife in both camps. We were hearing how a Forest firm had joined up with the Mansfield "boys" for some pre-Euros practice. The game however, passed off trouble free. United were oblivious to all that. They won again and would meet Mansfield's nearest and dearest, Chesterfield, at Brunton Park on the Tuesday. Chesterfield were second in the table and, get this, FOURTEEN points behind United.

For the Harrogate Blues, Chesterfield at home would be extra special whatever the result, because Sam was mascot. It had cost us nothing. We simply wrote in, asked and the club put Sam on the list, picking the original date because it was the matchday closest to his birthday. Season tickets for children, when accompanied by a grown-up, were just a fiver. For the Chesterfield game, we were given free tickets too. We had a tour of the inner workings of the Main Stand; a trip up to Foxy's, the new swish restaurant; and access all areas of the changing room.

As we meekly entered (don't worry, Diane remained outside), Darren Edmondson and Paul Murray looked up guiltily; they'd just been scrapping. Tony Hopper, quiet, serious and no doubt seriously nervous, preparing as he was for his home debut, stayed in the corner; Deano and Reevesy were the old pros, relaxed and laid back; Rod Thomas was on the treatment table.

The YTS lad Lee Dixon, our guide, then showed us down the tunnel. "This is it! THIS IS IT!" I wanted to yell. I was excited to the point of being petrified. I was aware of people looking down on us from above - there was no protective walkway back then. Thank goodness for the home dug-out to hide in.

Darren Edmondson and centre-back Jamie Robinson, in for Mountfield, were two of the first Blues out to warm-up. Lee called after them; they paused and took Sam. He spent most of the time with Edmondson, Hopper, Thorpe and Reeves. There was little in the way of warm-up routines. Robinson ("he was really nice!") brought Sam off. Earlier in the day I'd got in touch with the fan who videoed the games to order a copy. There can't have been a great demand for them, because the first 10 minutes of the tape focussed on Sam out on the pitch passing with the players.

Sam waited at the top end of the tunnel while Wadsworth gave his team talk. I kept craning my neck to look up the tunnel in readiness. I heard the teams before I saw them. There was a lot of shouting; Sam said later it was only United making the noise. The referee came round the corner, Reevesy broke into a trot and nudged Sam, who started to run too. There was a roar, a flutter of ticker tape and they were past me in a flash; Hannah was telling me to get her a balloon which had blown down from the terracing. But that image of Sam, my son, running out in front of United, my team, was worth its weight in Wembley-ticket gold.

My most nerve-wracking moment came next, having to walk across the pitch to photo Sam with the officials, Reevesy and the Chesterfield captain. According to Sam, Reevesy had called tails and won the toss, turning to Sam to ask which way they should play. "We'll stay this end," said Sam. Reevesy took his advice.

The ref let Sam keep the coin. "He gave me a pound!" Sam said excitedly after he'd run off the pitch. I kept my head down. It was another quick dash up the tunnel for Sam to get changed, then up into A Stand (where I'd never been before, or since for that matter) to watch the game from our free seats, Sam clutching his pound and Hannah her balloon.

Sam's mate the ref would've endeared himself to us all the more had he blown up immediately on 90 minutes. Nice guy Jamie Robinson had put United ahead only for Chesterfield to level in added time. Five regulars were missing from United's starting XI, not that their absence stopped United playing some lovely stuff. The lead at the top remained 14 points.

Carlisle beat Gillingham on the Saturday, which meant they could win promotion *and* be champions if they won at Bury. Two thousand Blues were in the Cemetery End ready to celebrate, but this was Bury, remember, where United didn't win. In any case, Knighton said beforehand that he wasn't too bothered about clinching the title there; he would rather the crowning glory came in front of a full house at Brunton Park on Easter Monday. Key players were rested and it was, irritatingly, no surprise that United lost 0:2.

"Don't worry boys," a policeman joked on the way out. "You won't be here next season. Pity me. I have to watch this lot every week." It would have been good to put one over Bury before United disappeared over the horizon. Never mind, we'd party on Monday and travel to Wembley as champions the following Sunday. What a week it would be!

United only needed a point to go up; three and they'd be champions. Hartlepool were the visitors, not that it mattered who United played. They'd win. "You mustn't come on the pitch at the end," a steward said, "but we've been told not to stop you if you do."

Except they didn't win. They didn't even draw. Having lost just twice in 37 league games over eight months, United lost for the second time in three days. Keith Houchen (he of the iconic diving header in Coventry's FA Cup win) scored the goal. United were poor, as Wadsworth admitted. "I've no magic wand to tell me why," he muttered into his moustache. At least he had Wembley to take his mind off things.

The record of the day fills a scrapbook: my report, newspaper reports, my photos, the newspapers', ticket stubs. I wasn't going to throw the Wembley car park one away either; it had cost me £7 after all. We'd made a whole week of it, staying with family and spending the Saturday afternoon at London Zoo.

On the Sunday, having parked and paid for London's most expensive piece of real estate, we enjoyed the atmosphere outside the stadium. It was buzzing, of course. Birmingham, who'd not reached Wembley in generations, brought 50,000 fans; United 28,000, nearly four times the season's average home attendance.

Only the FA Cup Final had a bigger attendance at Wembley that year. Not even the League Cup Final, Liverpool v Bolton, or England v Brazil attracted as many. There wasn't a hint of trouble. The club's two firms, apparently, had arranged their own Cup Final clash at Southend the day before. At Wembley I would happily have joined in the Brummies' *Shit on the Villa!* chants had it not been for the children. Diane had still not forgiven me for singing *Three-one to the Sheepshaggers!* at Hartlepool.

The police were friendly too. One officer told us to take our camera in despite the warning on the back of the ticket, "because all that will happen will be a steward asking you not to take any pictures, and they'll only do that if they see you in the first place."

Wembley looked decidedly shabby from the outside. Some of the paint on the Twin Towers had peeled and there was nothing special about the innards of the stadium either. It was only once we'd climbed the last set of stairs to the second tier and had shown our tickets to the steward that the splendour of the place hit us like a Deano header.

For all the over-pricing, the naff attempts to make the place all-seater by sticking plastic trays on terracing, for all the pillars and posts which blocked a clear view of the pitch, Wembley was still Wembley. It was big and it was beautiful and blinking heck! United were there!

I won't spend long on the match. United lost to a Golden Goal in extra-time. Tony Gallimore, legend has it, rushed to retrieve the ball from the net to re-start the game, yelling encouragement to his prostrate teammates. "Come on, lads! There's still time!" he urged. On being told there wasn't, he replied, "What's Golden Goal?"

Birmingham were the better team; our Man of the Match was keeper Tony Caig, which bears that out. They would shortly go up as champions of Division Two. I didn't level any criticism at United in my report: 'They tried their hardest and over the season have given me my best nine months as a supporter.'

Besides, United might've lost the match, but we'd made more noise. And as every travelling fan knows, that's (almost) as important as your team winning. "There's only Carlisle singing," I said to Bryan at half-time. He replied that it seemed that way because we were in the middle of the Cumbrian support. Maybe, but throughout both halves and those 13 agonising minutes of added time, the only voices I heard were United's.

More than once Hannah put her hands over her ears. "It's so noisy," she complained. When I asked if she was enjoying the game, she replied cheerfully, "No, not really." Deep in Deckchair Army ranks the cries were *UNITED!* and *WE LOVE YOU CARLISLE, WE DO!* A mate back in Leeds, listening to Radio Five, said that whenever commentators mentioned the 50,000 Brummies, all he heard was *UNITED! UNITED!*

"We out-sang them, didn't we?" I asked, seeking confirmation from Paul Newton of *The Cumberland Sausage* fanzine.

"We did, and that's why I'm happy," he agreed as we walked through throngs of Brummies. They might've won the Shield, but they'd lost the shout. These were the last paragraphs of my match report:

As Tait (who scored the Golden Goal) tore towards his fans, as manager Barry Fry bounced across the pitch, and as United's players collapsed to the turf, Something Special stirred in the rows and ranks around us. Men, women, children rose from their seats and burst into applause. The Blue Army was on its feet. We simply stood and clapped. It was the most moving moment of an emotional afternoon.

Next to me Sam was up on his feet too, his face buried in his sleeve. He was in tears but didn't want to show it. "He was trying so hard to be a good sport," Diane said. "I was desperate for Carlisle to win for Sam. That goal was like a spear through the heart."

To Bury 93 and Huddersfield 94, add Wembley 95 as a ground where young Sam shed tears over United. Not a bad place to complete your hat-trick. Birmingham might've won the match but the day was ours. We shall return.

And return we did.

Of more pressing concern was United securing promotion. Carlisle had a third attempt at Colchester the Saturday after Wembley. We didn't go. It had been an expensive month. We'd done the previous seven home and away. I was happy for United to do it without us, and thanks to Reevesy, chesting the ball over the line, they did. United won 1:0 and were promoted as champions with two games to spare.

United's last was at home to Lincoln, the fifth five-figure crowd of the season. At nearly 12,500, it was the biggest in Division Three all campaign. We were in the ground an hour-and-a-half before kick-off. Sam and Hannah sat in the shade, mercifully, on the Warwick wall. In the Paddock early arrivals wilted. One St John's volunteer was playing a blinder, distributing water in plastic cups.

The club had promised entertainment before the game, but despite the considerable improvements on the pitch and behind the scenes, United's attempts at pre-match fun were reassuringly naff. There were the obligatory dancing girls who didn't dance at all when their tape didn't work, followed by a couple of lads with mobile microphones (oh the innovation!)

"We'll have a penalty competition! You! You! And you!" they screamed, pointing to the Paddock. A couple of children ran to them, followed by a couple more and soon we had two latter-day Pied Pipers heading to the Waterworks with half the county's children in tow. Even the words of the Voice of Brunton Park Neil '*Now then lads and lasses*' Cunningham fell on deaf ears.

But at least we had Michael Knighton juggling a ball and scoring at the Warwick, then Reevesy was handed the trophy before kick-off. It was a moment I'd been wanting for 13 years. Hard-bitten fanzine hacks avoided eye-contact with their neighbours as he lifted the trophy. United lost the game 1:3, a scoreline Wadsworth said was "totally, utterly irrelevant."

A lap of honour was aborted so we joined the invasion then hung about on the pitch. The celebrations were over but we didn't want to go. We didn't want this wonderful season to end. United would start the 95-96 season in Division Two. Three seasons into Knighton's time in charge and the club was well and truly on the up. "This is not a return ticket. It's a one-way trip," Knighton said, and we believed him, we really did.

For the Harrogate Blues, the following season, 1995-96, was our most prolific. Sam saw 46 games, I managed 45 (I missed the last game of the season because Athletico, the staff team, were on tour), Diane 44 and even Hannah clocked up 34. Don't worry. The discrepancy between Hannah and the rest of us was due to her staying with grandparents. She wasn't home alone. At least, I don't think she was.

The reason we could get to so many games was thanks to the health insurance pay-out, which meant we could afford a new car, petrol and tickets. Also, Tuesday night games, home and away, were reachable because I only had to mutter, "I'm feeling a bit tired this afternoon," and I'd be excused staff meetings before I could finish the lie, oops, sentence.

I did the same on the one Saturday of the year, the school's Open Day, I was obliged to work. That always annoyed me because one of the reasons I became a teacher was to have Saturdays free for football.

United drew Preston in the FA Cup First Round and as ties went, this was one of the better ones and a likely candidate for extended highlights on *Match of the Day*. I told the Powers That Be that I wasn't feeling well again and headed up to Brunton Park. Whenever an attack came the Warwick's way, I'd make sure my hat was pulled down and my scarf was up over my chin, just in case I'd be spotted. The things we do for United.

Carlisle lost the tie but two away days later thumped Hull 5:2, despite gifting them a two-goal lead inside 16 minutes. My focus at the end was on the captain's armband that Reevesy had discarded after the players' salute. I asked a steward to fetch it. Sadly the armband was only a strip of sticking plaster as opposed to reusable material (I'd made myself Athletico's captain as well as player-manager) but I still have it.

That wasn't the only item of memorabilia I picked up. One of the extras in the epic that is the Carlisle United story is Danny Donachie, who had his 15 minutes of fame, almost to the minute, as a second half sub against Stockport in the March. United lost and the rest, for Danny, was history. He was only on trial, from what I remember, and probably got the chance because his dad was Willie Donachie, a Scottish international of the seventies.

We took special interest in those 15 minutes because Danny's aunt was Sam's primary school teacher. Sam must've mentioned he was a Carlisle fan (at least a couple of time a day if was like his dad) and at the end of term, she presented us with Danny's green United shell suit which doubled as a track suit. It didn't have the style or kudos of Deano's tracksuit top and I can't imagine that parting with it caused Danny much angst, but we were delighted with it.

Danny's career as a professional footballer didn't last beyond the end of the season. He trained as a physiotherapist and became Director of Medical Services at Everton. He might only have made the one appearance for United, but he'll pop up again later in these pages.

United struggled somewhat to adjust to life in League Two. In mid-January they were just a point outside the relegation zone but with 20 league games to go, we expected United to stay clear of trouble. Then came the bombshell. Wadsworth left.

Where was I when I heard the news? Answer: in the Gents at Twerton Park, Bristol Rovers' temporary home in Bath. Fellow fanzine editor Arnie, a temporary TV celebrity (he was being filmed on his travels for *Look North*) whispered in conspiratorial tones, "I've got some red-hot news but you mustn't tell anyone. Wadsworth's gone to Norwich! The BBC told me. I knew before the players!"

Minutes later, having told everyone I knew, I approached someone who worked for the club. "Is it true?" I asked.

"Who told you that?" came the reply, not in a *What rubbish!* tone, more *How do you know?* I didn't press my source and he wouldn't say more (Knighton would've been impressed with his reticence) except to add, "It's been a funny week. Wadsworth's just not been there."

Wadsworth's sudden departure was the first sign that not everything in the Brunton Park garden was rosy. The official line, Knighton wrote in the next game's programme, was Wadsworth had gone to Norwich as assistant manager simply because he was ambitious.

Knighton said he had lost a brother, that his exit had nothing to do with a lack of funds for new signings, a contract extension or salary issues. Maybe that was the case, maybe it wasn't. From our perspective it was a crying shame, because under Wadsworth the team had progressed. His rating at the end of the Championship and Wembley season was a massive 9.4 in the fanzine's poll. Knighton's was 9.0, the third season in a row the owner's stock had risen.

Mervyn Day was now Director of Coaching, i.e. manager, the title confirmed by Knighton. Wadsworth had never been listed as that in his job description in the programme, which might've been a bone of contention. We suspected there was more to it than that.

Wadsworth never said, merely suggested that "most people who've written to me know the answer." In that case it could be safely assumed that it *did* come down to a lack of funds for new players, for that was the most popular answer to the fanzine's End of Season Survey question. One reader even claimed Wadsworth told him so: "He said he tried everything he knew to get the chairman to put his hand in his pocket."

But we don't go to games to watch the manager, so if United stayed up and results improved, we'd be happy. We were pleased enough with a point at Bristol/Bath. There wasn't however, much of a difference in form between Wadsworth's last six months in charge and Day's first six weeks.

United didn't do much better in the Autowindscreen Shield. In the First Leg of the Semi Final they were a goal down at Rotherham with seven minutes to go when Nigel Jemson made contact with Deano's leg. Jemson put his dying swan routine into over-dive, virtually crawling into the box before collapsing. The newspaper photo in my file has him reaching out like an Olympic swimmer for the pool wall.

Two thousand Blues in front of him weren't fooled, but the referee, so far behind play he might've been officiating the previous game, blew for a penalty without so much as a glance at his linesman. "It was outside the box! Why didn't he ask the linesman?" If Sam, aged eight, could see the injustice *and* the ignorance of the referee not checking with his assistant who was in a better position, why couldn't the official?

Rotherham scored from the spot and United lost the home leg 0:2 as well, so there was no Wembley and nothing to divert attention from an increasingly dismal end of season. Of nine league games in March, United only won the eighth; small consolation it was against Rotherham in the league.

Form improved in the last two months, but four wins (and four defeats) couldn't prevent the drop. The Wrexham home game in April was an afternoon of celebration off the pitch with the opening of the East Stand, built in under 12 months. Blue bums on new seats were the only plus points. Carlisle lost 1:2, ending the day five points adrift of safety. That didn't stop us travelling to Brighton, admittedly without much hope that things could (only) get better. We had a picnic on the pebbles by the sea and watched United lose again.

Defeat meant that United were more or less down. The players knew it too. At the final whistle they came closer to us than they'd come all season. Our support had been long and loud. Deano led the line. He was in tears.

Brighton's supporters also came over to the away end to thank us for joining in their anti-Board chants, before storming the empty directors' box and frisbeeing cushions across the pitch. Their owner was selling the ground which forced the club out of town. At their last home game against United's relegation rivals York, a pitch invasion meant the game was abandoned and re-arranged for a morning kick-off the Thursday after the season had finished.

On that last Saturday Carlisle beat Bristol City and York lost. United, remarkably, were out of the relegation zone on goal difference. York however, only needed a point at Brighton, already relegated, to go back above United.

It was a strange feeling that Thursday morning. I was at school and had a free period, so I could listen to the

BBC Radio York commentary. Rather, I couldn't. I had to take myself off for a long walk around the site. Brighton scored and led at half-time. The hope was too much to bear. By the time I returned to my classroom York had scored three. United were back in the bottom tier.

5

Another Double, Another Drop

It was still a mystery as to how United found themselves back in Division Three. We hadn't expected promotion to League One (now the Championship) straight away, but the squad that started in Division Two was a strong one. It was almost the same as that which blitzed through Division Three.

Almost but not quite because Derek Mountfield's absence was, it is now clear a quarter century later, a big loss. Why wouldn't it have been? At Everton he'd won the FA Cup, the League and European Cup Winners Cup (second only to what's now the Champions League.) He had the class and kudos to make those around him play better.

United needed someone like him at the back again. A centre-back was second (behind a striker) on the wish list of fanzine readers in the End of Season poll, just ahead of "more teaspoons for the concourse bars."

Weddings would delay our start to the league season, so we brought forward our first fix to a pre-season friendly against Kilmarnock. United fielded a triallist at the back, a mystery man-mountain. We asked Caigy, called over for his obligatory autograph, who the hulk was. "He's French," Caigy replied. "He played in their First Division. We only met him today."

The *News and Star* had more success identifying him. *'Ooh! Aah! Who You Are!'* the headline declared on Monday. The mystery Frenchman was Stephane Pounewatchy. His name took some articulation (Poon-a-vatch-ee) but he was just what United needed. He oozed confidence and composure; he was one of those athletes who never seemed to break sweat. Stephane's job was to defend so defend he did, and very well indeed by Division Three standards.

The squad had another useful if expensive addition. Having dilly-dallied over the signing of Barnsley's Owen Archdeacon at the end of the previous campaign, complaining that it would cost too much, Knighton didn't miss out and mess up a second time. Archdeacon ("Gallimore with a brain," according to a mate) went on to finish top scorer, some achievement for a wingback. What a difference a goal or two from him might've made to United's Division Two survival chances a few months earlier. Gallimore had been sold to Grimsby for over £100,000.

'I couldn't care if United aren't champions,' I wrote in the fanzine's editorial. 'We had that thrill two years ago. Second or third would suit me fine. If that sounds arrogant or bitter, tough. This is a wasted season. I know it and many Blues know it too.' I was right in that respect; the average attendance would be 2,000 less than the title-winning season.

The first league fixture we saw was a 1:0 Tuesday night victory over Leyton Orient. The heavens had opened before kick-off and the gates were still locked at seven; the downpour put the game in doubt. When we were let in, we saw Knighton helping the ground staff mop up, 'which is what United should do over the next nine months,' I wrote.

And that's just what they did. From the start of September to early December they were never out of the top five; from December to May always in the top three, often as leaders. Being a keeper, Merv focussed on defence. In addition to Stephane and Deano, Will Varty, who'd come up through the ranks, was a third central defender. United's wing backs were Archdeacon on the left, Edmondson on the right; then, after Edmo's transfer to Huddersfield, the ever-improving Rory Delap.

Edmondson, Varty and Delap weren't the only youngsters who'd broken through into the first team squad. Lee Peacock and Richard Prokas were others. Youth team coach David Wilkes was doing quite a job. Edmondson's move netted the club £225,000. The rest had pecuniary potential too; Day later revealed the intention was to transfer one prodigy per season. The club's long-term plan suggested that taking one step back into Division Three would be followed by two forward.

Day explained the club's transfer strategy at a meeting of the Yorkshire Branch of the Supporters Club. We met for the first time in February at an Otley pub and the following season we even booked a coach for an away day at Grimsby. Not for the first time, it really felt that Carlisle were on the up.

At Hartlepool in September we enjoyed a finale almost exactly two years to the day to rival that of Scunthorpe (Thorpe's goals in added time.) United were a goal down with five minutes to go attacking the away end when Steve Hayward equalised direct from a free-kick. Then, in the last minute, United had a corner.

Archdeacon's played it short to Rod Thomas, who returned the ball immediately; Archie whipped in a cross and through the thick blue line of Blues on the wall at the front, I caught Reevesy diving in at the far post. There was a scramble, United arms went up, and for a fraction of a second I thought the ref had disallowed the goal. The ball had been clawed back out from behind the line by the keeper, but the linesman had seen it go over.

United's players raced away and there was pandemonium in the away end. I hugged the Blue next to me and crashed through the gap in the seat. I haven't a clue what happened to the squash bottle at my feet and the bananas inside Sam's bag were squashed beyond recognition.

United went top at the start of October; their only league defeat in their first 12 games was at Fulham. They were 11 minutes away from a second at home to Mansfield, especially as Rod Thomas had been red-carded, when Merv sent on his sub, another Carlisle youngster, Matt Jansen. It was quite a debut: *Almost immediately he dribbled goalward and shot just wide, and a little later, one magic Matt moment made the journey worthwhile; with the quickest of turns he flicked the ball inside, completely wrong-footing two defenders closing in on him.*

Jansen, an asthmatic, had to grab an inhaler from the bench, but returned to the action to play a part in United's equaliser. From his pass, Warren Aspinall was fouled in the box and scored from the spot. The point kept United top. There would be a fair few 'magic Matt moments' over the next two seasons, but such was the strength and success of the team that Merv could afford to use Jansen sparingly, bringing him on when the game needed something special.

Like United's youth policy, the season was developing successfully. Carlisle scored six against Shepshed in the FA Cup, then followed that with a 10-game unbeaten league run. Everything was going so well until the aliens spoiled it.

Knighton had an interest in UFOs. He attended a lecture in Carlisle with an extra-terrestrial expert, during which Knighton spoke up about a close encounter he'd experienced. His anecdote made front page headlines in the *News and Star* and in the national media. Knighton wasn't happy about that, not happy at all.

What upset him, he explained in a double page spread in the Cambridge programme (won 3:0), was that he'd been talking off the record. So upset was he, that he announced that he would be leaving Carlisle at the end of the season, blaming the *News and Star.* The last thing anyone wanted was for Knighton to quit the club and a return to the bad old days before he came. *'DON'T GO MICHAEL!'* the frontpage headline begged.

"You're one of the best chairmen in football. We're proud of you," the editor squirmed. "You are a man of vision. You have not just seen UFOs. You envisaged us playing at Wembley while others scoffed. The dream came true. You saw a brand new stand gleaming with pride on the east side of Brunton Park. It wasn't just a dream. It came true."

At least Knighton's departure wasn't imminent and the threat of it had little effect on United's form. Starting with the Cambridge victory, United won 10 and drew two of their next 12 league games. In the FA Cup a defeat of First Division Tranmere featured another highlight: John Aldridge's red card.

Aldridge had won the League with Liverpool and, as sometimes happens when decorated players come to Carlisle, had an attitude that suggested Brunton Park was beneath him. Tranmere were behind to an early Archdeacon goal and Aldridge, who'd been whinging all evening, then gave the linesman an earful close to us in the Warwick. The ref brandished the red and Aldridge had a mighty long walk to the tunnel. Did we enjoy that!

The largest Brunton Park crowd since the Liverpool tie, over 16,000, watched United lose to Premier League

Sheffield Wednesday in the 4th Round but United were heading towards Wembley in a competition they were making their own. For the fourth time in four years, they were in the semi-finals of the Autowindscreen Shield.

Opponents Stockport County were no mugs; they'd been promoted to Division One (now the Championship) behind Bury. That said, the County player who thought swinging a punch at Stephane was a sensible thing to do was obviously three goals short of a hat-trick. He was sent off and moments later Archdeacon, who'd already put United ahead, scored from the spot and Carlisle took a two-goal lead to Edgeley Park.

We followed them and weren't alone. Stockport's decision not to make the game all-ticket was made to look silly by the size of the Carlisle support; kick-off was delayed to let in 3,000 Blues. The open terrace behind the goal held 2,500 but that was soon full to bursting point. Carlisle fans spilled onto the pitch and made a dash for the seats. The stewards made a token gesture to stop them; one fan was ejected which was as pointless as it was petty. United midfielder Warren Aspinall, warming-up near the corner, made that clear as the lad was led away.

I first looked at my watch after eight minutes. "Only eight minutes!" I gasped in alarm, but on the plus side, there were eight less minutes for County to score. Remembering Rochdale two years earlier, I wasn't going to say or sing the W-word, but it slipped out once and seconds later, Caigy was beaten. If there was one man you'd want to save you from a runaway train, let alone a goal-bound strike in a Wembley (oops, that word's slipped out) semi-final, it was Deano. He had already acrobatically scooped one shot off the line and somehow Deano got his head to this shot too, and although I didn't dare say so at the time, the tie had its turning point.

Eight minutes into the second half Stockport had a player sent off after a foul on Prokas (the two had earlier been booked) but I was still not counting any chickens or the cost of four final tickets. At the end of the first half the referee played almost four minutes added time but, according to my watch, blew prematurely to end the game, seconds after a pitch invasion from the more boisterous Blues in the seats.

With stewards shepherding them off, the ref bunched the players close to the tunnel, and as soon as Caigy's goal-kick was in the air, they exited at speed. United had returned to Wembley.

"Come on! Let's get on the pitch!" Sam insisted. With hundreds already there, it was okay for us to follow. We joined the madding crowd around United skipper Hayward, who'd missed the dash to the changing rooms. Sam said he'd got close enough to touch his knee as he was lifted, beaming, onto shoulders.

I had a camera with me and took a photo at that moment. It was blurred, the light wasn't good and the snap wouldn't have won any prizes, but we had a copy done and sent it to Hayward. Almost by return of post, Sam received a poster signed by the whole squad. Top man.

It was a noisy and joyous celebration. Someone on a microphone urged us to retreat; we were drowning him out with cries of *"WEM-BER-LEY!"* (we could shout the word now) before the rest of the crowd hushed us. Merv was speaking.

"The players won't come back out until you clear the pitch," he said. "And that means everyone." We weren't going to mess with Merv. Over the perimeter wall we climbed, out came the players and nobody strayed back on. "We love you all!" were Merv's parting words.

United's league form wobbled but they were promoted before Wembley after a televised Friday night game at Mansfield. It was a low quality 0:0 but we didn't care. The title had long since gone; Carlisle finished three points behind Wigan and Fulham, who'd both done the double over them, but United were 12 points clear of Northampton in fourth.

There was now the small matter of that Wembley final. We weren't making a London weekend of Wembley. This time we it was just an away day, a special one yes, but we weren't going for the excitement of seeing United *play* at Wembley; we'd done that two years before. This time we were going to watch them win.

Our plot of real estate in the Wembley car park was now worth £8 (up £1 on two years previous). We arrived three hours before kick-off and were far from the first. We travelled the last few miles in a Carlisle cavalcade. Diane, now a trainee primary teacher, stayed in the car to prepare the next day's lessons. I'd borrowed a video camera so Sam, Hannah and I filmed our own Big Match preview, asking all and sundry to predict the score. The only person to guess correctly was a steward and he didn't know who was playing until we told him.

The last person we asked was our friend Grant from Leeds. The next shot would be his reaction when we returned once the game was over. It would be a split-second on video but in between would have passed four hours and a thousand stings from football's slings and arrows of outrageous, or tremendous, fortune.

Inside Wembley I met Bryan. He'd made a weekend of it, too much, he admitted; he couldn't eat breakfast. He'd been at Twickenham on Saturday to watch Cumbria win the county championship final. "What a stadium!" he said. "Makes this seem a dump."

The players, booted and suited, walked round in front of us while on the pitch a celebrity game took place, to no one's great interest. From the foot of the gangway we called out to United's squad who, to a man, posed for photos with Sam and Hannah in the foreground, our side of the dog track.

We were at the tunnel end and, when they emerged for the game; we gave the players the loudest of welcomes beneath a canopy of red, green and yellow balloons. I wasn't keen on United's away kit being the colours of a Stobart wagon, but the free balloons made for a great pre-match party, rounded off by the thunderous roar of a thousand explosions as we burst them. The Rio carnival had nothing on us. Amidst the din I glanced across to the Colchester end. They were waving flags but that was it. No balloons. What chance then, had they of winning at Wembley?

Carlisle started as favourites. Colchester were well below them in the table and United had easily beaten them at home and drawn away in the league. It was a cagey first half. United looked in control but didn't create much; nor did Colchester, thanks to United's trio of central defenders: 'Stephane was smoother than a Parisian fashion label; Will (Varty) far wilier than a lad his age should be; whilst Deano was not only the best defender, but most likely source of a United goal.'

Colchester's best spell was straight after half-time, but it was broken by a broken corner flag. Rory Delap ran into it and snapped the pole. Wembley might be "the Theatre of Dreams, The Home of Legends!" as the stadium announcer bellowed more than once, but it wasn't the easiest place to locate a spare corner flag. It took five minutes to find one.

After 70 minutes history was made: Delap thumped a free-kick with power and precision, forcing an opposition keeper to make a first serious save after nearly three hours across the two finals. Colchester's goalie Emberson did well to stop the shot and even better to hold onto the ball.

It wasn't until the 22nd minute of extra time that Colchester had their one and only shot on target, which

Caigy saved. It probably wasn't a game to amuse a neutral, but it wasn't a game for them. This was a Wembley final for two sets of supporters who couldn't give a hoot about entertainment. All we and the Colchester fans cared about was winning. The game ended goalless so a penalty shoot-out was going to decide just that.

United won the toss and penalties were taken in front of us at the Tunnel End, the Paul Tait End as I thought of it, given this was where the Birmingham player won the Shield two years earlier. Being at right-angles to the goal made the 12-yards between kicker and keeper seem that bit further when United's penalty takers were stepping up.

Colchester's skipper took the first to a cacophony of whistles and boos. I didn't jeer; I was too nervous. He scored, puncturing our abuse, and raised an arm to us. Paul Conway was United's first penalty-taker. We had no way of knowing its direction, me even less as I was looking through the lens of the camera. He scored. I wouldn't snap the others. My hands couldn't stop shaking.

Adcock took Colchester's second without even picking up and replacing the ball on the spot. "He's rushing it!" I thought. "He'll mi-!" But he didn't. Caigy dived the right way and looked cross with himself that he didn't get closer to the ball.

Owen Archdeacon was next, United's regular penalty-taker during the season. His late penalty in the

Semi-Final First Leg had carried United a big stride closer to Wembley, but he'd missed since against Hereford and he failed again now. Emberson saved and their fans, whom we'd hardly heard before, roared.

Teammate Green whacked the third in off the bar; another inch or two higher and it would have bounced back out. United were 1:3 down. They would have to score and Colchester miss or have Caigy save if they weren't to lose. Some responsibility therefore, would be on the third penalty taker. Presumably that would be Aspinall or Hayward, who'd taken them before, or ice-cool Stephane, maybe even one of the young lads, Delap, Peacock or Jansen, with the cocky confidence of youth. But Deano? No, surely not!

Whilst there was no one in that team I'd rather have gone over the top with because he'd have stopped, blocked or dived in front of every bullet, even we, Deano's Biggest Fans, had to admit that there was no one more prone to sending the ball half-way up the East Stand than Deano. Give him a grenade and you'd be anxiously watching your back.

But cometh the crucial penalty, cometh Deano. He scored. His kick, we saw later, was the best of the shoot-out. And to think I'd had my doubts. Colchester however, still had to miss (or Caigy save). Duguid, the young sub, was next. He shot, Caigy dived right and got a hand to the ball; it hit the post – and rolled back off it.

"YES YES YES YES YES YES YES!" I knew I was repeating myself but I couldn't stop shouting until the

twelfth or twentieth *"YES!"* by which time Warren Aspinall was ready for United's fourth, which he scored of course, for the force, the momentum, was now United's. Colchester's chance, I dared to think, had come and gone.

Deano and Caigy had dragged United back from the cliff edge. Now Colchester's shaven-headed centre-back Cawley teetered on the brink and 27,000 Cumbrians held their breath. Cawley drove the ball to Caigy's left and oh *YES!* Caigy saved again. United were one penalty kick away from winning at Wembley.

Steve Hayward was going to take it. I didn't look. For the first (and last) time ever in a game, I deliberately turned away. I looked sideways at Diane, Sam and Hannah. I wanted, I suppose, to keep the ones I loved the most in view, to focus on what really mattered should Hayward not score. Or maybe I looked at them for luck; I don't rightly know.

I kept my eyes on Sam. "It must've been the longest run up he'd ever taken for a penalty," Sam said afterwards, but it didn't take long between him turning and –

Sam's eyes told me before his smile. His hands shot up and before I heard the roar I was slumped in my seat, weeping uncontrollably. All that stress, all that tension, all that Wanting To So Badly, all that fear that if United didn't win… But they had. They *had* won. My team had won at Wembley.

When I stopped sobbing long enough to stand and get up onto my seat, I realised the players were celebrating at the corner in front of us. Bryan, six seats down the row, suddenly appeared next to me and hugging him, I started crying again! Then the old boy in front of Sam fell backwards off his seat, with Sam having to spring into the aisle to avoid him. Hurt or not, the old boy was grinning.

From our seats we couldn't see Hayward lift the Shield. There were too many flags been us and him, though I saw it glint as players passed the trophy along the line to be hoisted again. The celebrations continued below us. The photographers' priorities were clear. They wanted Steve with Shield, Steve and Caigy with Shield, Merv with Shield.

Caigy, United's Man of the Match for the second Wembley final, jigged this way and that, beaming and saying "Automatic!" (I could read his lips) to explain how he'd guessed which way he'd decided to dive to make those two penalty saves.

Michael Knighton came down from the Royal Box (HRH Glenn Hoddle had presented the Shield) spinning a scarf above his head and all around us we sang our cover version of the Sheffield Wednesday anthem which we'd made our own. The four of us stayed behind long after the players had disappeared. We were probably the last ones out as Hannah needed the loo, and while Mum was in the Ladies with her, I went back for one last look, for I might never return to Wembley again.

I wasn't bothered I might've missed United's last kick at Wembley because I'd seen the look in Sam's eyes when the penalty went in. And that's another of those priceless images, thanks to United, with which my life's been blessed.

We didn't go to any of the last three games. We didn't need to. United were already promoted but wouldn't catch Wigan or Fulham and those Wembley memories would keep us smiling over the summer. United had bounced back at the first attempt and it would be a case of once-bitten, twice-shy when it came to staying up next season.

Carlisle were back on course, back on the road to Better Things. Knighton had calmed down, didn't leave and was obviously enjoying the ride. Oh the sweet bliss of ignorance indeed! Within weeks of the new season kicking-off, the wheels were spinning off the United wagon.

Four points from 18 wasn't a great start to the 97-98 season, but injuries and suspensions were mitigating circumstances. There was no need to panic. It was early days after all. But Knighton didn't think the same. He sacked Merv.

Even now it is hard to fathom quite why he did that. Very often sacking managers comes down to money and Knighton might've been concerned that the club was going to lose too much if their form didn't improve. That said, having splashed out £200,000 on two players (midfielder Andy Couzens and forward Ian Stevens), it didn't seem the club were badly off. And there was a two-legged League Cup tie with Spurs coming up, which would generate extra income.

It didn't appear either, not to us anyway, that there had been a problem between Merv and Knighton. Wadsworth hinted the reason he left was because Knighton wouldn't strengthen the squad, but Knighton had done that pre-season. Day said he had been wanting to sign Couzens for six months and Knighton had delivered.

Merv also seemed an affable bloke. I met him when he came to talk to the Yorkshire Supporters Club. He came across as a pleasant, intelligent, reasonable man. Wadsworth had sounded rather dour, although that impression wasn't born out by limited personal experience of encounters with him for autographs. Neither Wadsworth nor Day struck me as pushovers. Successful managers need an edge and they had it. Maybe that was the problem.

Knighton had an ego and loved the limelight. I reckon the reason he sacked Merv was simply because he wanted a go as manager. *It's my club, my money, my turn!* You could almost hear him stamping his foot on the boardroom carpet. Knighton blamed Day's dismissal on results. In the first home programme after the sacking, Knighton wrote that Merv had to go because of results over an 18-game period at the end of the previous season and start of the new one. United's promotion was overlooked, as were five cup wins.

I was sorry to see Merv go and wrote to him saying so. I reckon mine was the first letter he received from a supporter after his sacking. Day lived in Leeds and I taught the daughter of his neighbour. I gave her a letter thanking him for what he'd done. Merv sent a reply via the student. She said there was a tear in his eyes when he read my letter. Sam's football coach knew Merv and said he was "on the floor" about the dismissal.

I wasn't the only supporter to write. "Letters such as yours have helped soften the blow considerably," Day wrote in his reply. "I admit to being shocked and dismayed at the chairman's decision to dispose of my services and even now find it hard to believe, especially in light of what we achieved last season."

Day wasn't the only departure. Deano was sold to Lincoln for £75,000 on the morning United lost to Spurs in the Second Leg of the League Cup. Hayward had been sold to Fulham for £175,000. Thomas and Conway, also regulars over the last three eventful seasons, had gone too. Their careers had peaked at Brunton Park. Conway was soon back in America and Thomas had little success at Chester or Brighton.

The Spurs game wasn't a sell-out but the crowd was still over 13,500. Spurs played a full-strength team and won 2:0 without much resistance from United, bar Jansen. Knighton didn't appoint a manager. Instead David Wilkes, in charge of the youth team at the start of the season, and John Halpin, the club's Community Officer, were listed in the programme as first team coaches. But it was clear to all who was pulling the strings,

Knighton's decision turned supporters against him but, fickle as we are, we would've accepted it, even forgiven him, had results improved. They didn't.

United might still have struggled even if Knighton had appointed an experienced manager. Couzens was finding it tough to fill the midfield gap left by Hayward (and Conway); Stevens wouldn't start scoring regularly until December; and United missed Deano. But no manager meant Knighton was well and truly the person to blame. Like *Macbeth*, Knighton's ego had got the better of him. That was the real shame of the Shakespearian tragedy that was unfolding. If only he had stuck to what he was best at.

The fourth of four defeats in a row in November and December was at Oldham, where I went one better than persuading family and Sam's football friends to watch United. I booked a coach and took the Year 11 football squad from school. They played games against a former colleague's teams in Oldham before watching United at Boundary Park.

With it being a Tuesday night in Oldham (surely the coldest ground in the country) and taking into account United's poor form, there weren't more than a few hundred in the away end. Of the three coaches in the car park, one was the team coach, another the Supporters Club and the third ours. It was a miserable night. United lost 1:3 but the lads from school loved it. I'd never been thanked so much for taking pupils on a trip.

United's next away game was at Grimsby. We went by coach again, this time with the Yorkshire Blues. It was the only time we travelled collectively; the Yorkshire Branch of the Supporters Club didn't survive much beyond the season. It became too depressing, an Alcoholics Anonymous self-help group: "I'm Tim and I'm a Carlisle United supporter..."

United were beaten 0:1 and things hadn't improved by March. We were in a black mood driving home up the A1 from Chesterfield after a 1:2 defeat when a big black BMW started to overtake us, then slowed to stay alongside. I assumed the driver wanted to turn off and would slip in behind us. I glanced over, as you do; the tinted window came down and – "It's Deano!" I shouted.

He waved and pulled in front of us. The BMW's number plate was D3AN.W. I assumed he was heading to Spofforth, the village his wife came from. The M62 Junction neared and Deano veered off. "He must be going to Leeds then," I said, and how nice of him to slow down and wave.

We drove on, yet a moment later D3AN.W came alongside us again. Deano signalled that we should follow him and he pulled into the next lay-by. Parked up, Deano came over and shook our hands, hugging Hannah and Diane ("he smelled lovely!") He'd spotted our Carlisle scarf in the back of the car. He didn't know United's score; he wasn't tuned into *Sports Report*. His BMW, the whole lay-by indeed, throbbed to music.

"I'm on my way to Leeds for a night out with Edmo *(Darren Edmondson)*," he said. He'd been playing for

Lincoln at Doncaster. "We were two up after ten minutes and I thought I'd have an easy afternoon." Deano puffed an imaginary cigar, but Doncaster fought back to level before Lincoln won with two late goals. Deano said he was off to the Caribbean a few days later for his international debut for St Kits. He'd been made captain. Deano was happy at Lincoln, renting a house near the Cathedral.

He also said he'd received our letter wishing him well after his transfer. "Oh! I must remember to send you my shirt," he added casually. *Your shirt!* "Yes, my old Carlisle shirt. I've kept it for you." Having missed out on Jack Ashurst's, I told him I'd be sending him a SAE asap. A few days later not just his shirt but also a *CUFC Champions 1995* Union Jack flag came through the post.

After more handshakes, hugs and kisses, Deano was off. "Deano knows me!" said Hannah proudly as we watched him drive off into the distance.

I just wished United could have renewed their acquaintance with Deano. United dropped into the relegation zone after Chesterfield, one of nine defeats in the last 10 games of the season. The drop was confirmed when York won at Brunton Park.

Knighton wasn't at the game. He was on the Isle of Man, listening to a crackly Radio Cumbria commentary in a Land Rover outside the farmhouse he was converting. Changes to the country's tax laws regarding residency had forced him to leave Brunton Park for two months, he explained, which didn't strike much of a chord with most United supporters.

United's 1998-99 campaign back in the fourth tier started with a 1:0 win over Brighton in front of over 5,000 but only one other Brunton Park game topped 4,000 until the last game of the season. Supporters were turning their back on Knighton's United. More stayed away after three defeats sent United to the foot of the table. So six years after Knighton arrived promising the Premier League, United were back where he'd found them: bottom of the Football League.

Frustration with United was personal; Knighton was to blame. Two decades on and that anger's left me. Like I say, I've mellowed. I've stopped hating Leeds United, haven't I? And it wasn't all Knighton's fault; it wasn't Knighton missing sitters and making other costly mistakes which made the drives home seem even longer.

But Knighton was, until just before Christmas, the manager, sorry, Director of Football. The buck stopped with him, buck being the appropriate metaphor, because money was as much a cause of fans' anger as the team. The way we saw it was the club had made millions selling Jansen, Delap, Reeves, Hayward, Walling and, at the end of the previous season, strikers Nick Wright and Alan Smart. Another youngster, Paul Boertien, would be off to Derby for £250,000 in March.

Yes, Knighton had signed players for six figure sums, but far more money had come into the club via transfers than had gone out. This was, of course, a simple fact of football and business life. Carlisle's best assets were always going to be sold. Let's not forget too, in Knighton's defence (and here I really am Devil's Advocate) that United were in a far worse position, financially anyway, when he bought the club in 1992 than they were in December 1998.

Now however, fans were staying away because of Knighton. It wasn't just his club but his team. The signings he had made at the start of the season ('a radical restructuring programme,' the programme termed it) didn't strengthen the squad. Quite the opposite. Left-back Damon Searle was the only one who would've held his own in the promotion-winning teams.

Eventually in December, 15 months after he'd sacked Mervyn Day and with Carlisle fourth from bottom of Division Three, Knighton appointed a manager, Nigel Pearson. It was the first management position for the former Sheffield Wednesday and Middlesbrough centre-back. 'It's not quite a new dawn,' I wrote, 'but at least Pearson's burly form can momentarily eclipse the black hole of Michael Knighton.'

For three weeks in January we also had the Autowindscreen Shield to distract us. United were drawn at Scunthorpe, one of the easier grounds to reach from Harrogate. The skies were clear as we left Harrogate but nearing Glanford Park the heavens opened. We arrived to find the game had been postponed, pitch waterlogged. We were given the sandwiches which had been intended for officials and headed home.

A week later we were back at Glanford Park and almost on our backs immediately we stepped out of the car. "Be careful, it's like an ice-rink down there," the attendant had warned us. He was right. United forward Scott Dobie cut his hand on frozen grass and the game was abandoned at half-time.

I wasn't going to let the tie finish without us, so off we set to Glanford Park on a third successive Tuesday. Thankfully, it was a case of third time lucky, and not just because the game was played to a finish, but also because it was a very good one with United much better than usual, a treat in itself. The game ended 1:1 and went straight to penalties, United's first shoot-out since Wembley.

United triumphed in sudden death. The hero was Tony Caig, who scored then saved. The players ran down our end to celebrate. Young defender Peter Clark came too close; I grabbed his hand and dragged him into the seething mass (or semi-seething, seeing there were just 58 Blues.) We left elated.

There wasn't much to cheer in the league. Before the transfer deadline in March, Caig was sold to Blackpool and Couzens joined him on a free transfer. Caig was "astounded", especially as the fee was just £5,000. In his place United borrowed a 19-year-old from Derby, Richard Knight.

With four games to go we travelled to play-off hopefuls Rotherham. Against the odds and definitely against the run of play, United scored with their one and only attempt of the afternoon on the stroke of half-time. There were at least 15 minutes to savour the lead. Not even Carlisle conceded during the interval.

The second half was like the Stockport semi all over again, wristwatch-watching every other minute... 5, 10, 15, 20, 25 passed; convert to second half time and it was 71, 72, 73 minutes. Carlisle were never going to score a second but that wouldn't matter if they kept Rotherham out. Then, after a moment of relative light relief when the ball was over halfway, Searle slipped, Rotherham broke, Leo Fortune-West headed in. Six minutes later he had a hat-trick.

I penned United's epitaph: *'In the scrapyard behind the rear of Millmoor's away end, rejected locomotives, which once blazed trails across the land, rotted, never to rock the rails again. On the other side Carlisle's Football League Days neared their end too. Rust in peace.'*

That defeat at Rotherham left United three points off the bottom with three games to go, but Scarborough had two matches in hand. At the start of these Memoirs I promised I wouldn't wallow in dark, depressing places, so what happened next follows later, Chapter 95 to be precise.

6

Collins, Cardiff, Conference

Starting with that 1998-99 campaign, United had six seasons at the bottom end of Division Three, finishing either second or third bottom bar one glory-glory season in the middle, when they reached the heady heights of seventeenth.

At Cheltenham in November 1999, we waited outside the Players' Entrance so Sam could collect autographs. First out was midfielder Steve Soley, not blessed with great talent but a player we liked because he always got stuck in, cared and gave his all.

"We're really sorry, we're really frustrated," he apologised after the 1:3 defeat, adding, "the keeper must go," and in the next breath, suggesting the management should too. "At Portsmouth *(his previous club)* we worked on systems every day. Cheltenham's midfield flicked the ball on and everyone pushed up. It wasn't pretty but it was effective. At least they had a system. We don't know what ours is."

Next out came coach Neale Cooper (Pearson had left at the end of the 98/99 season), moaning about the players:

"This just wasn't good enough. I told the players they were getting twice as much as Cheltenham's."

Captain Paul Brightwell pulled Knighton aside (we didn't ask for his autograph.) "Can I have a word, Mr Chairman?" he said. I doubt if they were discussing the contents of Cooper's Christmas Box.

Scott Dobie was putting his kit in the luggage compartment. He was one of the few players who could hold his head up. He'd scored despite been stuck out wide. "But why weren't you playing centre-forward?" I asked.

"I don't know," he replied. "I've only ever played there four or five times. They want me up and down *and* in the box. I've just had a few words so I don't know if I'll be picked next week."

The 1999-2000 season didn't improve. After a 0:4 home defeat to Hull in April, we found a scrap of paper beneath a windscreen wiper. It was from Bryan, whom we planned to meet at the end. He wasn't there. "Couldn't stand anymore," he'd written. It read like a suicide note. United only stayed up because a Peterborough player, Richie Hanlon, scored at Chester to send them down to the Conference instead of United, who were losing in their last game at Brighton.

The following season (2000-01) at Blackpool on a bizarre wet and windy October night, United were three goals and a man down when, despite not having an on-target shot or header all game, they scored twice:

the first an own goal, the second straight from a punt from goalie Peter Keen. The gale swept the ball deep into the Blackpool half where it bounced high over their keeper and into the net.

Our next game was Southend at home when, for the first time in 14, we saw United win. As Carlisle came into view at the end of our drive up the M6, black clouds loomed large above Brunton Park. The sun however, smiled either side and a rainbow arched over the city. Indeed, not one but two. We'd clutched at every straw going the past three seasons, so why not at rainbows?

"They're a lucky omen!" I declared.

They were too. Stevens and Dobie both scored in the first half. It was a happy half-time and it was about to get even happier. As usual I'd bought a Golden Goal ticket. Once when Danny Donachie (he of the 15-minutes and tracksuit fame) made the draw, I'd been two numbers from the winner. This afternoon Paul Murray, a former starlet who was then at QPR, hobbled out on crutches. I glanced at our ticket before the draw: 1-9-0-5.

Sam and his mate Phil chatted away, oblivious to the draw. I didn't give it much attention either; I didn't catch the winning amount. It wouldn't be as high as it once was, given the attendance of barely 2,000.

"ONE, NINE" – and I already knew what was coming next (the rainbow moment) – "O, FIVE."

I waited until the number was repeated, showed it to Sam and Phil as Man With Microphone read it a third time, before heading down the steps, showing the ticket to a steward who let me pass onto the pitch, and there I was, jogging across to shake hands and collect my winnings.

I gave the East Stand a quick wave. Someone gave a cheer; the Paddock usually cleaned up on the Golden Gamble. I directed another to the Warwick (why not?) before a handshake and hug with Paul Murray. Then it was up the tunnel to collect a cheque for £145. Suddenly it seemed a huge amount.

I asked Murray why he was on crutches. "I've broken my foot again," he said.

"Still," I replied, "every cloud has a silver lining. If you hadn't, you wouldn't have drawn my ticket and I wouldn't have won £145!"

He didn't smile. At least the Man With Microphone managed one when I offered to give the cheque back to buy the club. I was well chuffed and walked round the pitch trying not to look like a smug bastard. United won the game 3:1. Being a Carlisle supporter that Saturday was very good indeed.

It wasn't bad on FA Cup 3rd Round Saturday 2001 with a 15,300 sell-out for a tie with Arsenal. United went into the game six points adrift at the foot of the league, Arsenal second in the Premiership. Given that gulf, a 0:1 defeat was a creditable scoreline. One of our loudest chants was for manager Ian Atkins, appointed at the start of the season, who was doing his very best to keep United up in the last, dark days of the Knighton empire.

Buoyed by their performance in the cup and thanks to Atkins' efforts, Carlisle's league form improved. In April they went to Rochdale on the back of a run of seven points from nine, during which they'd not conceded a goal. Rochdale in contrast, hadn't won for 12. The game didn't follow the form guide: United lost six-nil.

We'd been entertained en route to Spotland by my teenage nephew Christopher, who told us of a disastrous double blind-date he and a mate had made over the internet. It was so bad that his friend made an excuse to go to the kitchen, only to leg it out of the backdoor. "I was left with both girls and couldn't think of anything to say to them, so I stuck on a video, a musical, which I'd seen before and hated. It was the worst day of my life."

After the game I told Christopher, "You've just witnessed the worst of mine!" It was an exaggeration but judged simply by the scoreline, it equalled the worst of my time as a Carlisle supporter. Even the six-nil defeat at Bury had something in mitigation, United having played over half the game with 10 men. But that's not why I'm giving the Rochdale game space, for I wrote afterwards, 'I doubt if any team slaughtered six-nil has ever been so well supported.' Here's why:

On the final whistle United's players, almost to a man, turned immediately towards us and applauded. There was no sheepish shuffling off this particular mortal coil. They stood, arms above heads, saluting those who, let's face it, had seen United die before them.

Yes, there was anger after Rochdale's second goal. A couple of Blues were ejected and a pie was thrown on the pitch (a waste as Spotland does damn fine pies.) But after the third and fourth goals, frustration manifested itself in fanaticism. "IAN ATKINS' BLUE AND WHITE ARMY!" must've lasted a good 15 minutes during the second half.

"That support was God-like!" Christopher enthused, with just a hint of teenage hyperbole. "That chant sounded like a Red Indian war cry. I thought all the Carlisle fans had painted faces!" In the midst of it Rochdale scored their fifth and sixth goals but you wouldn't have noticed had you been listening not watching. The noise level didn't drop. Indeed, it only increased.

"ONE IAN ATKINS! THERE'S ONLY ONE IAN ATKINS!" we roared. "ONE GOAL! WE ONLY WANT ONE GOAL!" we urged. Had it come, we'd have celebrated it with the delirium of a Wembley winner.

Driving away, hoarse, I was lost for words to describe our support. "United were so bad," I eventually managed, "but the support was so good."

Christopher pondered a moment. "In that case, why don't you hire a hall and create an atmosphere like that without the football? It would be a lot cheaper and you'd save yourself the stress of watching the game."

United lived to fight another season in Division Three with a game to spare and a cushion of two teams below them for the first time in four seasons. A goal from Carl Heggs at Lincoln did the trick. We celebrated on the pitch and even made it up into their Main Stand where former Blues Deano and Prokas were watching.

Knighton's days at Brunton Park were now well and truly numbered. In December 1999 a court had banned him from being a director or being involved in the management of any company for five and a half years. The disqualification related to Knighton's running of the school he'd bought. Knighton had resigned from Carlisle's board but still owned 93 per cent of the club.

The News and Star joined supporters' calls for him to sell. It was safe to say their relationship was back on the rocks. The newspaper distributed red *GIVE US OUR CLUB BACK KNIGHTON* cards for supporters to brandish. Knighton did introduce one potential buyer but he turned out to be (and I kid you not) a barman from a Peebles curry house.

Knighton stayed but Atkins left to be the assistant at Cardiff City. Understandably, he'd had enough. United's new manager was Dubliner Roddy Collins, brother of boxing world champion Steve and built not so much like a brick out-house, but a three story lavatorial block.

Carlisle had a strong Irish influence in the 2001/02 season. Baby-faced Richie Foran scored 16 goals; he picked up almost as many yellow cards. Peter Murphy also made his United debut. His Carlisle career would last 12 seasons and he would play over 400 games, scoring some famous goals too. The Irish link wasn't always appreciated. At Shrewsbury I saw a United fan rip a tricolour down from the fencing.

A year after Heggs' crucial goal at Lincoln, Foran's equaliser at Halifax seconds from the end of added time confirmed that United would stay up with six (SIX!) games left. We celebrated on the pitch again. The police wouldn't let the players come out so we made do with John Courtenay, rumoured to be the new owner, who'd stood amongst the thousand travelling fans, serenading him with: *"John Courtenay! He's from the Emerald Isle! He's rich, he's buying Carlisle!"*

Seven teams finished below United, two more than in the previous four seasons combined. The drama however, wasn't over. Collins told Radio Cumbria that he would quit Carlisle if the club wasn't sold to Courtenay. The club (i.e. Knighton) didn't appreciate Collins' comments. Two games after Halifax, Collins was sacked.

Knighton's 10 years as owner eventually ended in the summer of 2002 with United just five league places better off than where he'd found them, and a long way from the Premier League. The decade had seen United promoted (and relegated) twice and brought two trips to Wembley. The ground had a splendid new East Stand too. But Supporters had lost all faith in Knighton. With the new season approaching, it was reported that United's season ticket sales numbered a grand total of three.

The sale of the club was on the cards, but we'd heard similar rumours before. We were desperate for that to happen so in one respect, stress remained. On holiday in France, we read nothing in the local papers about a potential deal or, surprisingly, anything at all about United. On the ferry back to Dover the Sunday after United's first game of the 2002/03 season, I bought an English newspaper and quickly turned to the football results. United had lost 1:3 to Hartlepool but the score wasn't what I was most keen to check. It was the attendance.

The crowd was over 10,600. "He's gone!" I told Sam. "Knighton's gone!" Fans had returned, yes, in their thousands. Knighton had sold the club. Courtenay reinstated Collins and declared their aim was for Carlisle to be in Division One (the Championship as it is now) in three years, four at the most.

The morning the sun rose on Courtenay's New Dawn there had been queues at the ticket office. By the end of the season, the average home attendance of 4,800 was fifty per cent higher than it had been in any of the previous four seasons.

A week after Hartlepool came United's first Saturday away day post Knighton at Lincoln. It was quite a game. Foran and a Lincoln defender were sent off after six minutes;   United finished with eight players after two more dismissals; John Courtney was arrested for threatening behaviour after celebrating Lincoln missing a penalty; and, strangest of all perhaps, was the travelling Blues chanting, *"THE BLUES ARE **GOING*** (as opposed to staying) *UP!"* United were 1:0 winners.

At York in November there was a bucket-collection in aid of home club funds. City were the latest club to announce they were in financial trouble. Having seen Carlisle come close to the edge, the least I could do was toss in a pound, despite their away end being one of the worst in the league and their irritating habit of putting one over United at Bootham Crescent.

I'd never seen so many Carlisle fans at York, where there usually was a decent following anyway. The pub on the corner near the away end was packed before kick-off. Leechy (Sam's latest friend to share The Carlisle Experience) was wide-eyed and terrified when *"UN-I-TED!"* took off. The pub ran out of Tetley's and glasses.

With the Blue Army out in force and the rain streaming down, stewards had to open up an extra section of seating. That meant the more boisterous fans were close to each other and things did kick-off. I saw smashed seats thrown towards York's mob. The announcer told them to stop. "That's the last thing we need at the moment!" he pleaded in vain. The stewards didn't seem to be having much luck either. What did the trick were the half-time Dancing Girls, four lasses in thigh high white boots, short skirts, and a willingness to wiggle. The fighting stopped at once.

Carlisle lost 1:2 and were second bottom at the end of January when they were boosted by a handsome 3:0 home win over Orient. I'd asked the club if, before the game, they could arrange for Roddy Collins to present Sam with a shield marking 200 appearances for his boys club, Harrogate Hornets.

United agreed, which they've always done to personal requests like this. I can't imagine Liverpool or Manchester United being so obliging. Given the size of Collins I was quite relieved when he gave Sam a Masonic-style handshake. "I've a broken finger," he explained. Rather his than one of Sam's.

The club's PR wasn't always that good. We set off to Carlisle for the LDV semi-final with Shrewsbury in February, despite fears of frost. Bryan had been down to buy his ticket, strolled into the ground and posted on the message board that he'd bet his house on the game being postponed. The club however, said nothing when I phoned them. We only heard the game was off thanks to Radio Cumbria just before we reached Temple Sowerby. The club must've known the game was in severe doubt, yet still allowed Shrewsbury fans (and exiled Blues) to travel.

We had a full carload too as it was the first trip for the Harrogate-Knaresborough Blues. United had signed experienced defender Paul Raven, who'd played over 300 games for West Bromwich. I'd been tipped off the night before the signing was announced; his brother-in-law, also a Paul and a teacher friend from Knaresborough, phoned to tell me.

We took him and Raven's dad Ron with us but the closest we got to meeting Paul the player was a couple of phone calls as we travelled, the second to tell him the game was off. United hadn't kept their players any better informed either.

We were soon back at Brunton Park for the rearranged game. Bryan was confident, pointing out that on the two previous occasions United had reached the Final, they'd played the first leg at home. I wasn't so sure. History might have been with United but against them was the rotund form of Nigel Jemson. It was his dive that had cost United a final place when he was at Rotherham and he did much the same again, trying to get Raven, already booked, sent off, collapsing like a tranquillised hippo. What's more, Jemson wouldn't give Leechy a Jaffa cake when we saw him munching a packet afterwards.

The main action was condensed into five first-half minutes. On seventeen midfielder Stuart Green was fouled in the box. Penalty! Foran was first to grab the loose ball. This was significant because striker Craig Farrell (who'd taken the recent spot-kicks) and Foran had an agreement that whoever was first to the ball took the kick, which smacked of school playgrounds.

"It's okay when it works," said Collins afterwards, "but I think we'll have to look at something more professional."

Foran's kick was too close to keeper Dunbavin who made the save. (Remember the name; the goalie will feature again in these pages.) Four minutes after that miss, United did score. Farrell galloped down the right, outstripping all Shrewsbury cover, then pulled the ball back across goal for Adam Rundle to have a touch before lifting it over the goalie. United had a 1:0 lead to take to Gay Meadow a week later.

Shrewsbury on a Tuesday night was a long way to travel for so much stress. But we had to be there for the Second Leg. Paul the brother-in-law came with us. We stopped just outside Shrewsbury for fish and chips at a place called Wem, which got me thinking Wembley, even though the Final would be at Cardiff. A van parked in front of us. It was a LDV one. Another good omen.

My experience at the Stockport semi-final had taught me not to keep looking at my watch. The quality of football at Shrewsbury made that easier. It was awful. United kicked-off, passed back to right-back Mark Birch who sliced the ball into touch. That was the benchmark for the first 45 minutes. United couldn't string more than two passes together; Shrewsbury weren't any better.

I wasn't assuming anything, not even when Jaffa Jemson was substituted, but Shrewsbury didn't score so United were through. There was no pitch invasion. The heaviest police presence I'd seen at a United game saw to that. They even sent over a helicopter as we came out.

So United were off to the Final at the Millennium Stadium. As the song said, we were, *"Down to Cardiff, to see United!"* with a chance of returning with the trophy again. *"Take me home, Warwick Road."*

We broke our journey at my parents in Gloucester before heading into Wales via country roads to avoid the Severn Bridge and Bristol City's fans. Traffic flow as we neared Cardiff was well-organised but the colours were wrong: the signs directing the Blues were red. They were bilingual, which must've been a great help to all United's Welsh speaking supporters.

Carlisle had the Cardiff City carpark from where we were bussed into the city centre. If the Millennium Stadium looked like a spacecraft just landed by the Taff, Ninian Park was a scrap of space debris. I couldn't recall a shabbier facade than that of their Main Stand. It cost £5 to park but bus rides were included. My brother-in-law had taken his boys to Twickenham the day before to cheer on Gloucester in the Rugby Union cup final; he'd paid £15 just to park.

The Millennium was the best stadium I'd seen United play in. The view was pillar and back-of-the-head free, and what a view it was too. Beneath the seats the concourses were wide, the prices reasonable and the staff friendly. They smiled. At Wembley everyone looked like their surroundings: grey, miserable, run down.

United supporters made up a quarter of the 51,000 crowd. The following was well down on Wembley 95 and 97, but over 12,000 Cumbrians made it to Cardiff for a one-thirty kick-off on a Sunday despite the lack of success (and that's putting it mildly) over the five previous years.

Bristol's chairman obviously didn't think so. He said his club deserved two-thirds of the gate receipts. I was so angered by his greed that I phoned *Talksport* the Thursday before and told them so. Birmingham took twice as many as United to Wembley and didn't ask for a proportionate share and, as I pointed out to the nation, how many Bristol fans would travel to Newcastle for a 1330 Sunday kick-off?

Bristol's fans impressed me as little as their chairman. True, there were three times as many, but you wouldn't have known that was the case from the noise (lack of) they made. City were in a Division Two promotion battle, United in a Division Three relegation scrap.

United however, raised their game. It was one of the better performances of the season. The defence set the standard. Raven suffered a bloody nose after one challenge; the big screen hanging from the rafters showed him with cotton wool up his nostrils to stem the blood. The scores were level at the break. I thought United had edged the half. "Let's face it," I said to Bryan, "Bristol can't be that good if Lee Peacock's their centre-forward."

Peacock had played for United in the 1997 Shield Final. I should've kept my mouth shut. With 13 minutes to go, Bristol sub Liam Rosenior, whose pace turned the game in their favour, had a shot parried by Mattie Glennon and Peacock tapped in the rebound. Rosenior added a second and that was it, game over.

Appearing in the final didn't kick start the season. We took a carload of Sam's friends, all part-time Blues now, to Wrexham on Easter Monday. United lost 1:6 and we taunted Liverpool fans stuck in M62 jams on the way home, belting out: "We're going to Tamworth, you're not!"

With three games to go and without their best outfield player (loanee Stuart Green was back at Newcastle after a fall-out with Collins), the end for United looked nigh. Remarkably however, Carlisle stayed up and, even more of a surprise, they did so with a game to spare.

In the space of four days they won 3:2 at both Torquay and at Shrewsbury. We didn't make it to either. Shrewsbury was on a Tuesday night again; funds were a factor, so too was a 'club v country' dilemma as Sam and his Carlisle-supporting mates had a football match of their own for Harrogate Hornets at Otley.

We listened to the commentary (the game was live on the BBC) driving back. Brian Wake, who only managed nine goals in the season, scored a hat-trick. It kept United up and relegated Shrewsbury. Although this would have been no solace to them whatsoever, we now at last had a club that really, really disliked United.

Not only did Carlisle send them down, United had also stopped them getting to the Cardiff Final. It has long been a bugbear that Carlisle is so far from anywhere that we have no derby rivals or no team that hates us. We might dislike some clubs more than others and even, as you've read already, hate them for a time too, but fans of other club don't hate Carlisle. Newcastle, the nearest, have Sunderland; Darlington have Hartlepool; Preston have Blackpool. Barrow are the same; they'd rather beat Morecambe than United.

Come the summer of 2003 however, United were hated by Shrewsbury. I know this because as luck had it, a friend was courting a Shropshire lass. I met her just the once and she rounded on me with venom when I told her whom I supported. Far from being an unpleasant experience, it made for a refreshing change.

The hatred didn't lasted long. Shrewsbury bounced straight back. United meanwhile... Well, prepare yourself. The next few pages will be a bumpy ride.

United's first away game of the 2003-04 season was at Yeovil, not the easiest place to get to on an August Saturday. We stopped overnight again at Gloucester and avoided the motorway on game day, so we arrived in decent time, whereas the Supporters Club coach had to be escorted off the motorway and was still late for kick-off. Those Blues missed the most memorable moment of the afternoon.

It came in the warm-up. We'll skirt over the game itself; Yeovil won 3:0 as easily as the score suggests. United keeper Mattie Glennon was preparing in front of us. His routine included half-volleyed drop-kicks. Goalkeepers, as their role suggests, are better with their hands than feet, so it was tempting fate that Mattie practised by aiming towards his coach on the touchline.

With Yeovil's neat and tidy ground having shallow stands close to the pitch, this was asking for trouble. Sure enough, it didn't take many efforts before Mattie sliced one. It missed his man and hit a Yeovil fan flush in the face. That would've been painful enough. Rob was once caught by a stray rocket during a warm-up at Charlton from Kevin Gall who, coincidentally, scored two of Yeovil's goals. "I still had the pattern of the ball on my grid at half-time," he remembered painfully. "It was one of Sue's happiest memories watching Carlisle."

But what made it worse for the Yeovil fan was that she was a very elderly lady, no doubt a lifelong supporter, who must've dreamt of this day, her club's first ever home game in the Football League, and then had it ruined. Mattie and various medics rushed over to the poor lady. I assume she recovered; we didn't hear otherwise, which was a blessing and the only good thing to take away from Huish Park.

There was one another thing to note about the game. My match report included, I suspect, the first use of the adjective *'suited'* as a swear word, as in: "COLLINS! YOU **** *SUITED* ****!" which came from an irate Blue.

United lost their next two games and Collins lost his job. He was replaced by Paul Simpson, whom Collins had signed as a player during the summer. Simpson was a Carlisle lad but he'd slipped through United's net, going on to have a successful career with Manchester City, Oxford, Derby and Wolves.

Simpson's managerial style was more measured than Collins'. He dropped himself for his first game in charge and recalled centre-back Lee Andrews, banished to Rochdale the previous season. His team talk was less bellicose. "I told the players that this was the time of their lives," he said, "so go out and enjoy." Simpson's side stopped the rot; they drew 0:0 with Cambridge and Andrews was Man of the Match.

A week later United were at Darlington, where the result was settled even quicker than at Yeovil. A Darlo striker, unmarked, headed two goals in 12 minutes. It would take a pretty dire display to reduce 1700 away fans to miserable mutterings, but United had achieved that by half-time. There was a muted chorus of, "We'll score again, don't know where, don't know when..." as a fifth game without a goal neared the end, but the rest was silence.

We drove Paul Raven to his car at Scotch Corner afterwards. Raven was struggling for fitness and had been on the bench. I asked him whose job it was to have marked the scorer. "Chris Billy," he replied. Billy hadn't got near the ball or an opponent all afternoon, so that was no surprise. We gave him 1/10 in our post-match ratings.

Billy got better, much, much better, but that wouldn't come for a while. Indeed, Billy and Simpson both came close to legendary status at Brunton Park, which seemed highly unlikely after the Darlo defeat. The problem for Simpson was that the squad he inherited had been assembled by Collins and was even shorter on confidence than quality. The forward signed in the summer, Steve Livingstone, only played six league games; he didn't score but got himself sent off twice.

United's fortunes didn't change. Darlington was the first of 12 league defeats in a row. Cheltenham away was Number 10. It was a sign of the times that the Harrogate Blues didn't set off until the Saturday morning. Instead of a stop-over at his grandparents, Sam, now 15, was partying Friday night. He slept all journey.

Paul Simpson opened the scoring and United found themselves ahead in a league game for the first time in two months. Then Cheltenham scored twice and United lost again. It was lucky 13 when, at last, the run ended with victory over Torquay the Saturday before Christmas. Right-back Paul Arnison scored from 30-yards to seal success after a first half goal from debutant Andy Preece. The striker had been Bury's player-manager but the Lancashire club, mid-table in Division Three, had to let him go because they were, not for the last time, in financial difficulties.

As that old United favourite from D:Ream had promised, things were going to get better, not in a dramatic blaze of PREMIERSHIP-IN-TEN-YEARS glory that Knighton had proclaimed, more a light-at-the-end-of-the-tunnel fresh start. Preece joined two other wily pros at United: left-back Tom Cowan, who'd been released by Dundee as they too were running seriously short of money; and centre-back Kevin Gray from Tranmere. All three were strong characters; all three became the embodiment of a new team spirit.

What I best remember Tom Cowan for was sprinting off the pitch in a game when substituted late on. United were desperately trying to score so not for him a gentle jog and turn to the crowd; the sooner he was off the pitch, the sooner a striker could come on. Gray's crowning glory was, legend had it, pinning a teammate to the wall by the throat at half-time because, in Gray's opinion, the victim had pulled out of a challenge. That was the last time anyone did that when Gray was in the side. "He won't accept anything less than good and he leads by example," United striker Karl Hawley once said of Gray. "Not many people will cross him."

The trio, you might gather, didn't take kindly to defeat. They were resilient characters and weren't perturbed by an act of injustice at Bury on Boxing Day when the referee ruled a Raven tackle to have been a foul. Injury meant Raven couldn't kick with his left, according to brother-in-law Paul, but that wasn't going to stop him playing either. He and Gray were a formidable partnership.

Bury scored from the spot but Gray headed an equaliser before half-time. There was nothing fancy about Carlisle; their preferred option was to get the ball to Preece as quickly and often as possible, and with United attacking the Blue Army second half, there was no way United weren't going to win. Thanks to Preece (he was still Bury's manager in the match programme), they did just that. He made two goals by beating his man and whipping in low crosses which were slid in first by Brendan McGill then Kevin Henderson.

Preece went off to a standing ovation from all sides of the ground. United's third goal came with 21 minutes still on the clock, and what a joy it was to be two up, seeing United in complete control and singing my head off for the lads with 900 other Blues. *Jingle bells* never sounded so sweet. "This time of year is, after all, about Belief," I ended my report, "and there's now a bright star of hope above Brunton Park."

I wasn't the only one thinking that. Eight thousand Carlisle fans agreed, forcing a delay to the kick-off against Darlington. Preece set up McGill again to give United an early lead before Darlo equalised. Both teams went at it hammer and tong. Paul Raven alas, was tonged early and came off after 20 minutes. It was his last game for United.

United picked up 10 points from their four Christmas and New Year games. The transformation was remarkable. In 21 league games since the start of the season, United had won only once and scraped just five points. But starting with the Torquay victory, they lost just three of 15, winning seven.

Next up was Rochdale away. The journey across the Pennines was horrible. The whole country was battered by strong winds. Two games were abandoned because of it, and an Everton fan was killed by flying debris outside Leicester's ground. I had serious doubts that the game would be go ahead. We'd endured a similar experience a couple of seasons before, diverting to watch Bolton instead when we heard Spotland was waterlogged.

We arrived early but we weren't alone. An hour before kick-off and there were longer queues waiting for the turnstiles to open than at the excellent chippie the other side of the road. It was the biggest following I'd seen at Rochdale, and that included the night United got to Wembley. Blues packed the whole of the stand running down the side of the pitch, making up over half of Rochdale's best gate of the season. There were 2,400 of us and boy, did we make a noise!

Sam, Rob and I made sure we were at the centre and one row from the back of the stand. Behind us was one Blue who was so frustrated during the first half that he whacked the plastic seat in front. A chunk of it hit Sam. It was that sort of afternoon. Half-an-hour into the game, Cumbrian Grant Holt went over in the box as Glennon challenged. The ref rushed to the area, pointing to the spot, and we knew United's keeper was off.

Was it a penalty? It looked like Holt had, at the very least, played for it. He'd knocked the ball too far ahead of him, saw Glennon charging out, and went for the easy option. He pushed the ball wide of the keeper and fell over. Rochdale scored from the spot, United were down to 10 men and the game was, to all intents and purposes, over. Holt added a second and we left Spotland certain that United, despite their second half of the season heroics, were down.

Heading for Scunthorpe the following Tuesday, I didn't feel frustrated but sad. It would be the last time for some time (a long time?) I'd do that drive. I felt sad that I wouldn't sit in the away end and remember Jeff

Thorpe's double or Caigy's penalty shoot-out heroics. The match report, I expected, would be an epitaph for United's 75 seasons in the Football League.

But hold on! What's this? A five-goal thriller to make it a hat-trick of happiness at Scunny? Chris Billy scoring his first-ever goal for the Blues, a stunner to win the game? And the Fat Lady missing her cue, waddling back to the wings? Glory! Glory! Carlisle United! The Blues go marching on!

Billy unleashed a waspish drive from the angle of the box. The ball fizzed into the top corner of the goal in front of us (the Jeff Thorpe corner) and we went bonkers. The cry was "STAYING UP!" echoes of which would still be reverberating around Glanford Park's rafters at the start of the following season, with or without United.

That win sparked a return of 10 points from 15. Teams above hadn't anything like that form. With four games to go, United were, remarkably, just two points from safety. That was the good news. The not-so-good was that three of those would be against sides in the top six.

Lincoln were on an eight-game unbeaten run and, on the day, were the best team I'd seen over the season. United didn't played badly, it was just that Lincoln were better. Their second goal, in added time, came after Glennon charged upfield for a free-kick, but even if he'd scored, it would've been too late to get a winner. The ball was cleared to right-back Mark Bailey, well inside his own half and just below us in the East Stand.

He gave the ball a hefty thump and it beat Glennon to the Waterworks net.

On another day we'd have been chuckling about that goal on the way home, but with relegation rivals winning, there was nothing to smile about. The gap was five points (in effect six because of United's inferior goal difference) with three to play.

To Mansfield then, with defeat likely to send United down to the Conference. For the second game in succession, United were up against one of the best of the division; Mansfield were as good as Lincoln. The game was a belter.

Forty-seven minutes and 36 seconds. United have 24 more seconds to survive and preserve, for a week at least, their League status. Sam's said Rochdale are leading; The Bloke Behind Me that Scunthorpe are ahead; United are relegated if Mansfield score.

They've a penalty. It wasn't even disputed. Cowan clumsily flattened his man in a last-minute moment of panic. Liam Lawrence is taking it. He's on a hat-trick. Tom Cowan's a great player and my favourite Blue, but Lawrence gave him the run-around. With most opponents Tom can afford to stand off them, knowing he'll win the tackle if they run at him. Not Lawrence.

What's more, he's already beaten Mattie twice from the spot: once down the middle, then (the kick had to be retaken) low to Mattie's left. Sam and Leechy have gone down the front. Here comes Lawrence...

We'd parked easily enough down the lane. A Mansfield fan stopped to talk, running through a ridiculous scenario of results which would see his team promoted outright. They were secure in the play-off positions, whatever happened today. Carlisle needed the win more. Defeat would see United relegated if Rochdale and Scunthorpe got better results.

It was another all-ticket affair. Next week's home game is too, as is Doncaster, of course. Just short of 1,000 Blues were with us. It was a warm day and the atmosphere was red hot. We were behind the goal. Mansfield's singers were in the Main Stand to our left. There was an edge to the atmosphere. The players emerged from a pull-out tented tunnel between us. At kick-off my ears rang with the noise of our welcome.

Mansfield were good. They won early corners but United threatened on the break and scored from a set piece of their own. McGill swung the ball in from the left and Kevin Gray, at the far post, powered in the header. Mansfield could/should have scored with their next three attacks, didn't, and I had the feeling it was going to be our day, which got stronger after 20 minutes.

Preece won a free-kick in their half, near enough from goal for a strike. He struck it well, but the ball cleared the bar. Referee Mathieson however, ruled a Mansfield player had encroached. He booked the offender and moved the ball 10 yards nearer the edge of the box (as was the rule then.) Preece had a second chance and boy! did he take it. Roberto Carlos had nothing on him. He hit the ball with such power that the keeper barely twitched before it was in the back of the net. Two-nil and "THE BLUES ARE STAYING UP!"

If that was reason enough to pump up the volume, what happened next upped the noise levels another notch or three. Lawrence's trickery forced Gray to foul him just below us. It was a penalty, no doubt about it. Gray looked to the heavens in anguish. Lawrence put the ball on the spot, walked back and beyond the D. In front of him on the edge of the box stood Foran and Andrews, denying Lawrence that extra yard or two in his run-up.

He refused to budge, insisting the referee order the defenders to move which, of course, he couldn't do. Eventually Lawrence was persuaded to start his run-up inside the area. He must've been one confident (or cocky) sod. Usually defenders try to put penalty-takers off. Here was Lawrence unsettling, it seemed, himself.

His kick, when it came, was typical of the man: a cheeky chip down the middle as Mattie dived to his left. Lawrence raced into the net, picked up the ball, turned to taunt the Blues behind the goal only to see the referee pointing to the spot. He had to retake the kick, encroachment, presumably. Mattie, and United, had a second chance.

As Mansfield protested, Tom Cowan dug his heel on the spot to rough it up. Mathieson extracted himself from the Mansfield posse, raced over to Tom and booked him. Lawrence took the kick again, this time to Mattie's left, and scored. He ran to collect the ball again, only Foran stood in his way and knocked him over. Lawrence went down, claiming he'd been elbowed; Richie was having none of it, and one mêlée later, Foran was booked, Murphy too. It could've been worse. A lesser linesman might've been conned and told the ref to send Richie off.

We were cheesed off the referee hadn't cautioned Lawrence, but we had our moment when Lawrence dived over Gray and the ref, this time, booked him. Oh how we celebrated! Lawrence however, was chuckling three minutes later, beating Glennon at close range to equalise.

To rub salt in our wounds, Wayne Corden, a Mansfield attacker, gave the Blue Army two fingers. Cue an angry surge, Corden scuttling away, the hoardings taking a hammering, the police rushing forward. Most of the Carlisle fans down at the front seemed keener on reporting Corden's offence than settling the score personally, but Corden couldn't have enjoyed his half-time trot to the tunnel. I'd never seen a referee throw himself in front of a player to keep a madding crowd at bay.

The second half was, for a while at least, quieter. United defended that bit deeper to deny Lawrence room and he wasn't quite the threat he had been in the first period. That's not to say the atmosphere and tension were any less. Mansfield's fans fancied their team's chances as much as I did United's.

Cometh the hour, cometh Foran. He took the ball through two tackles on the left, cut into the box, laid the ball square to sub Kevin Langmead, who bided his time, turning down the first opportunity to shoot, taking an extra touch and striking the ball low and hard to the keeper's right. We were directly in line and the moment the ball left his foot, we knew it was in.

Langmead's celebration took him straight into the crowd. He was booked for it; Mathieson had probably, and sensibly, told both teams to cool it at the break.

Mansfield were muted. We weren't. "LIKE A TEAM THAT'S STAYING IN THE FOOTBALL LEAGUE, WE SHALL NOT BE MOVED!" Langmead had the smell of goals in his nostrils (it was his first ever after all), but a little less single-mindedness on more than one break would've set up his senior partner Preece.

Not that his profligacy mattered much, not with United winning, not with the minutes disappearing, not with one, two minutes of the three added on gone, not with 30... 34, 35 seconds gone – not with another ball into the box cleared, and Cowan covering...

And there it was, the referee almost apologetically pointing to the spot. He could do nothing else. Cowan had clattered into his man. In the cold light of the seconds which followed, Tom would've known there'd been no need to do that. But with seconds left and your team hanging onto survival, considered opinion doesn't always come easy.

Sam said later Lawrence had scored 12 from 12 spot-kicks this season. Lawrence must've been thinking,

"I've gone down the middle, I've put it to his left, now I'll go for his right."

Mattie must have thinking the same: "I'll go to my right."

There was nothing wrong with Lawrence's kick. It was hit hard enough; the ball was heading for the corner. There was nothing wrong with Mattie's dive either. He took off to his right, meeting the ball in mid-flight and pushing it clear of goal and post.

The away end took off. I hugged the Bloke Beside Me (he had £1 on a 3:2 win at 66-1!) then stood rigid with sheer, sheer joy. And at the far end United were celebrating too and Mansfield were trooping off. It was all over. Mattie's save and Brian Shelley's hoof to clear were the last moments of the match. United were, for a week at least, "STAYING UP!"

We were in no mood to leave. The players thanked the crowd, but even after they disappeared down the tunnel, we stayed. We cheered the subs who came out to cool down, we cheered Courtenay who came over from the Main Stand, we cheered Mattie Glennon, who stuck his head round the tunnel to clap us.

The win probably won't make much difference. With Rochdale and Scunthorpe winning, United will need to take six points from six and hope one of the pair or Macclesfield lose both their games. But we weren't going to let that stop the party.

Paul Simpson's done one heck of a job to bring us this far, to make us feel this happy, to get off (get this!) the bottom for the first time since late August. York lost and were relegated. Simpson's got this motley crew playing as well as they possibly can and brought us Glory! Glory! Away Days like this. Staying up? Who knows? But if we do go down, we'll bounce right back. ...

The crowd for the last home game was 9,500, United's best of the season. Precious few were from Cheltenham, though there was one in a chicken suit and others in fancy dress. After eight minutes United took the lead. Foran crossed from the right, Preece stuck out a foot, the ball rolled across the box and Brendan Brazil, sorry, McGill tapped in at the far post.

It was the goal United needed to settle their nerves, but the game went flat thereafter. Attention was elsewhere. Leechy was texting scores through, folk around us were relaying them too. It looked good for United. Scunthorpe went behind at Cambridge, equalized, went behind again and Cambridge added a third.

Six minutes remained. From a corner Cheltenham sub Odejayi won a header, the ball hit the underside of the bar, bounced down, up and in. United couldn't raise their game again.

The final whistle wasn't greeted with boos, and there was no sense of bitterness either. The Cheltenham chicken applauded us as he left the ground. I felt sad, a tad embarrassed about being a non-league supporter next season, but on the way home a Plymouth fan passed us (they'd celebrated the Division Two championship at Hartlepool.) He took his hands off the wheel and clapped. And I felt proud. Proud of the efforts Simmo and the players had made to stay up, proud of the complimentary attention the club had received, and proud, indeed, to be a Cumbrian.

United's last game in the league was not a depressing wake, quite the reverse. It was some party and made all the better for the Harrogate Blues because, until Paul Raven's brother-in-law Paul phoned on Saturday morning, we weren't even going. He had a spare ticket, but only the one. With Sam committed to playing cricket, I declined the offer. I'd told Diane that Cheltenham was my last game of the season and it wouldn't have felt right being at Belle Vue without Sam.

We continued to talk on Paul's landline, then his mobile rang. It was Paul Raven's mum. He had found us extra tickets. Sam feigned injury, I apologised to Diane and we were off.

The streets were busy with Donny fans in celebratory mood. It's strange, considering how I loved that club in the seventies, that I was totally ambivalent about their success. When you've One True Love, when you give *I'm Carlisle Till I Die* full welly on the terraces, every other club is, well, just another club.

It had been five seasons since we'd been to Belle Vue. Donny had been in the Conference for four years, came up via the play-offs and walked through Division Three. Belle Vue looked worse than ever, the stand propped up, it seemed, by portacabins. The club would soon be moving to a new ground, "where we'll be playing in two seasons time," I predicted.

Some 1,800 Blues had a third of their Main Stand and Paddock. I knew we'd make a noise, but the difference between the Blues' vocal support and Rovers' was as wide as the gap between top and second bottom of the table.

Don't invite a Doncaster fan to a celebration, my match report began. *As the song said, you'd find them in the kitchen at parties, well out of the way of all the laughter and excitement next door. There were over 7,000 of them at Belle Vue. They filled the run-down ground but you would've thought it was us, not them, who were celebrating the championship.*

"Will you ever sing a song?" we chorused.

"You even had to start singing 'Champion-ee' for them," Sue said. It's true. We did.

Their team might've won the Championship on the pitch, but off it, the Blue Army is Champions League. To the tune of Staying Up (let's hope we never sing that again) we roared, "We'll be back! We'll be back!" And though, in the scheme of things this'll take getting used to, we roared, "Like a team that's going to win the Conference League, We Shall Not Be Moved!" Of more immediate concern was the question raised by the Blue Beside Me, who started this chant: "Where the fuck is Forest Green?"

"Are you watching Brunton Park?" we asked, followed by, "East Stand! East Stand! Give us a song!" Back at BP, Bryan said all he could hear on the big screen was

United. As for Rovers (their supporters at least), it was a case of: "Champions? You're having a laugh!"

We had something to celebrate too when, for the second away game running, Glennon saved a penalty. Soon after however, Doncaster scored the only goal of the game, not that the three-points mattered to either team in terms of league position.

United's most successful period in seven seasons had almost kept them up. Their record over the last 25 Division Three games was 11 wins, 7 draws, 7 defeats – an average of 1.6 points per game, which worked out as 74 for the season. That would've got United into the play-offs.

At the end a celebrating Doncaster fan threw his flag to a Carlisle fan, who threw his back. When we eventually left the ground, we saw the Doncaster fan walking to the pub with it round his shoulders. We wouldn't have given our flag away. It was going to accompany us around the Conference before returning to the League.

"We're going down, but we don't care, because we'll be back, this time next year!"

7

Simmo, Story, Stoke

A friend of mine, a Mansfield Town fan, said he preferred his team being in a lower division where they'd win more games rather than in one where they'd struggle for most of the season. I disputed that. I said I'd love Carlisle to have a season in the Premier League (though the Championship would do), even if that meant they'd lose the majority of matches. On reflection however, I'm inclined to agree with my Mansfield mate.

Here's what I wrote a couple of months into the Conference season: *If United don't go up as Champions, and if they fail in the Play-Offs, then I have a confession: I won't be that upset. The Conference really is okay. I haven't noticed any difference in the standard of football but the reason I like United being in the Conference is simple: they're winning, and with some style too.*

Victory brings the Feel Good Factor, as outlined right at the start of these memoirs. Defeat doesn't. It might, as it did during Simpson's first season, leave fans feeling proud and satisfied with the team's efforts, but that's not the same as the feeling when you see them win.

The 2004-05 season was United's first outside the Football League in 75 years. Carlisle were one of the few full-time clubs in the Conference. Things are different now. It's much harder for a relegated team to bounce straight back. Carlisle's first fixtures were against Canvey Island, Northwich Victoria, Forest Green Rovers (far from the fully professional outfit they went on to be) and Farnborough.

It wasn't just the calibre of the opposition which made us confident that this would be a successful season. United were relegated as a team in form. The line-up was almost the same too. Of greater long-term importance, United had a new owner: Fred Story, a very successful Cumbrian housebuilder. He was local and loaded.

It's hard to think of better criteria for an owner, or one who lived up to expectations so well. Story had been a boyhood fan of the club, a season ticket holder, and although his sporting days were on the rugby rather than football pitch (Fred was a bit of a unit), he maintained a deep affection for the club.

He didn't interfere with team selections, lent the club a million pounds and didn't ask for it back. When he did sell, Story left the club much better off, both in terms of finance and league position. Little wonder we lauded him so warmly: "WE ALL LIVE IN A FRED STORY HOUSE!" Given the success of his building business, a fair few did.

As for the players, Richie Foran moved to Motherwell and Paul Raven retired, which was a shame as we enjoyed the company of brother-in-law Paul and dad Ron; plus we'd have to start paying for admission to all away games again.

Neither however, had been regulars in the relegation season. Foran had lost form and Raven struggled with injury. To replace Foran up front, United signed Karl Hawley from Walsall. The other main additions to the squad were the splendidly named Carlos Roca and, even better, Magno Vieira. Roca sounded exotically foreign, but he was a Manchester lad released by Oldham Athletic. Vieira was one hundred per cent Brazilian. No wonder we were excited.

So too was the Conference about United being there. Carlisle were arguably the biggest club to have played in the fifth tier; they were, indisputably, the only one to have spent time, albeit briefly, in the top tier of the English game or who had topped it, of course.

That also meant that United would be the team every other really wanted to beat. Carlisle would have the largest number of supporters, home and away. It would be very different being the big fish in the small pond.

It would be difficult too. Canvey Island proved that in the first game of the season. Over 7,000 Blues turned up expecting the season to get off to a flyer. It didn't. The game was a 0:0 anti-climax. The first away game was at Witton Albion; opponents Northwich were ground-sharing because they hadn't one of their own.

"It's not very professional this," remarked nephew Christopher, "a man eating a pork pie taking a quid off you for parking."

"Coming somewhere like this must really bring it home to you," a Sky Sports reporter said in the car park.

"In five years it'll be the San Siro!" I replied, putting on a brave face. The burnt-out wreck in the car park, the three bus shelters for stands, the one tiny trough for a thousand bladders in the gents would, I reasoned, be tolerated for a season and reminisced about on flights to Champions League stadia.

Northwich saw us as a cash cow. We paid £9 to stand behind the goal. Four days earlier on holiday in France we'd paid less to sit and watch Auxerre in the top division. Northwich obviously needed the money. They ran out of balls after yet another was booted out of the ground; terracing was barely half-a-dozen steps high. Peter Murphy came close to a booking when he wouldn't stop complaining that one ball was too flat.

United were cruising at two-nil after Hawley scored his first United goal and Kevin Gray thumped home a header, but two Northwich goals in six minutes cost United two points. The San Siro, I feared, might have to wait.

Next up was a trip to Forest Green on the edge of the Gloucestershire town of Nailsworth. We drove through pretty villages and green-leaved lanes, then up a hill on a road which petered out just past the ground. I only spotted it because the Carlisle coach arrived just as we did. With the main entrance no wider than a driveway, the coach had to drop the players off on the road and we had to wait while they crossed in front of us.

Next door a neighbour was charging £3 to squeeze cars into his drive. We drove on and parked at a school for £1, the money going to a playgroup. Forest Green was that sort of place, quintessentially quaint.

Andy Preece scored 19 minutes into the game but just as United were getting into their stride, Tom Cowan clashed heads with a forward. His opponent stayed down longer (they usually did after a Cowan close encounter) but Carlisle's left-back had to go off for stitches. Preece dropped back and forward momentum stalled.

The half ended tamely. Conference grounds might be able to accommodate United fans, but their toilets can't. Whilst I queued outside the Gents, the PA announcer made the Forest Flutter draw. "The winning ticket is 01334," he said. I had a ticket in my pocket. I pulled it out as he read the number a second time: 01334.

The Bloke Behind Me also had a ticket. He shook his head. So did I. Poker faced, I didn't let on I'd won the raffle until I retook my spot on the terracing and told Sam. We collected the £140 winnings at the end of the game, which United won with some ease. "You've taken the three points and now the raffle," the Forester sighed as he handed over the cash. I felt a tad guilty so handed back £25 to buy a brick in the wall of the new ground Forest Green were planning to build.

United hammered Farnborough 7:0 at Brunton Park and were set to win at Halifax after two late goals from Hawley and Preece, but just as the Rev Man launched into a chant of *"CHAM-P-O-NEE!"* Halifax equalised. The Conference was proving a harder than expected nut to crack.

The following Saturday's game against Burton was live on Sky at lunchtime. United really were the big fish in the pond. *The Non-League Paper* would often have their game as its front-page lead. It was quite something to see that in a Harrogate newsagent on a Sunday morning.

Burton was a dire nil-nil. Next up at Brunton Park were Tamworth, when the first half was little better than Burton, but Hawley and home debutant Simon Grand scored in the second and the unbeaten run continued. Tamworth was the first in a six-game winning run. United were too fit, too quick, too good for the part-timers.

At Leigh the official attendance of 1540 was, apparently, the number of Blues in the ground. Leigh's supporters had entered through turnstiles that weren't usually opened so they weren't included in the count. A rugby league scoreboard in the corner still read *Leigh 30 Whitehaven 16*. Leigh would need the scoreboard in a second half when United scored five.

According to Darlington Blue Andy, who'd seen every game, no team had come close to United's level. "If we beat Barnet and Hereford *(first and third)*, it's all over," he said.

A draw at Exeter meant that United were unbeaten in their first 13 Conference League games. The 14th was against leaders Barnet at Brunton Park in front of 9,200, not a bad attendance for a fifth-tier game. United had plenty of chances but Barnet's finishing was better. Carlisle lost 1:3.

They recovered to beat Hereford by the same score the following week. I was enjoying the season. So too were many other Blues. There were nearly 7,000 Blues for Hereford, making the average for the season so far well over 6,000, and that included a televised game.

Carlisle beat Dagenham thanks to an eighty-eighth minute Karl Hawley winner and knocked Bristol Rovers out of the FA Cup before York away. Given what you've read before in these pages, you can guess what happened there.

Sam's mate Steve, a York trainee, was on the turnstile but was too honest a lad to let one or both of us sneak through. Dad Ian said Steve felt bad about that, but United's Peter Murphy would have felt worse. He'd been looking every inch a class act until he lost his cool after 20 minutes. Murphy was sent off for elbowing an opponent and United lost 1:2.

United went out of the FA Cup at Bournemouth, but only by a goal to a team two tiers higher. The next league game was at Accrington. United went behind but attacking the travelling support in the second half, sub Andy Preece scored twice. That was a good away trip. Tamworth wasn't.

It didn't start well. I'd sent off for three tickets, but on the Thursday they still hadn't arrived. I phoned the club who said they'd sent them off on Tuesday. They hadn't come on Friday and we had to leave before the post on Saturday. Luckily (thanks for small mercies) the game wasn't all ticket.

A couple of hundred unsold tickets were returned to Tamworth via the club coach, which meant we'd pay twice to watch the game. Sam and Leechy should've paid full adult price at the turnstile. They were 16 now after all, but I had no qualms about sneaking them in as Under 16s. It was costing enough to watch the game as it was.

The mystery of the missing tickets was cleared up the following Thursday, when the tickets eventually arrived. Someone had written on the envelope, *'Twice delivered to the wrong address.'* So thanks, Postie, you cost me £22 (one £10 adult, two juniors at £6). Add that to the £20 on the gate, and Tamworth away was an expensive £42. It wasn't worth it.

Like so many other teams, Tamworth raised their game. For all Carlisle's possession and superiority, they failed to make much of an impression on a Tamworth defence led by Matt Redmile, not so much Sunday pub team player as landlord. Athlete he wasn't, yet he headed the only goal.

Simpson came on for Preece, who'd taken offence at something a Tamworth fan shouted from the shed behind the dug-out. Preece angrily remonstrated with the home support. It was pretty clear he'd been racially abused. Stewards intervened (eventually) and removed the offender, but not one of the twenty strong police to our right budged an inch. They were there to keep an eye on us. Barnet won again and went 13 points clear of United. Tamworth left a bitter taste.

United beat Woking, drew at Morecambe on Boxing Day and again with Aldershot two days later. United's point-saving goal was scored in the 89th minute by Glenn Murray, his first ever. Fifteen seasons later he was still scoring in the Premier League. Murray's second came early in the next game, the return holiday fixture with Morecambe. United led 3:1 but only drew. There were boos at the final whistle.

Far worse was to follow.

Back in November an advert in the Dagenham programme invited residents in the vicinity to drop in at Foxy's Function Suite to see plans for flood defences. The Environment Agency's headline was an eye-catching *'Carlisle is at risk of flooding.'* Five days after the 3:3 draw with Morecambe, the risk became reality. On the night of Friday 7th January, Carlisle flooded.

Three people died on Warwick Road, the epicentre of the floods. Water nearly reached the Waterworks crossbar. Levels were at five feet in the Main Stand and up to ten in the East Stand. "Everything under those levels was more or less destroyed," chairman Andrew Jenkins said. Not only that, but a layer of silt covered everything. Computers, physio equipment, washing machines, desks, carpets. Club offices and the Neil Sports Centre, which had just had a major refit, were badly damaged.

Some said it would be a year before Brunton Park could open again. Remarkably, after just a month, United returned. Supporters volunteered to help with the clear up, led by Story Construction.

United played a FA Trophy tie at Workington where they beat Redditch 3:1 and were going to use Gretna, but more bad weather (frost this time) meant that there was only one other scheduled home game while Brunton Park was out of action: the next round of the FA Trophy against Barnet, which was hosted by Morecambe. Fifteen hundred Blues still made the journey for a game in a competition which, let's face it, hardly had the pulse racing.

United's only league game during those five weeks was a draw at Scarborough. The first at home after the floods was against Gravesend. On Warwick Road there was a builder's board in every window. One warned that the house had no floorboards. We could hear the sound of a hoover (or pump) in one house. In Thirlwell Gardens two water-pumping pipes stuck out of a back window. In the ground itself the blue carpet surrounding the pitch had gone, and the cushioned seating was peeling off lower rows.

The pitch however, seemed in remarkably good nick. It cut up but that was more because of the day's rain. At one point it came down not so much heavily as horizontally, reaching us in our seats two rows from the back of the East Stand.

The game, a 2:2 draw, wasn't great. The final whistle was met by a cacophony of boos, and the message board was full of demands for Simpson's resignation. United dropped to third and their form (just two league wins in 10) got worse. United lost at Dagenham and twice in quick succession to Stevenage. It was a miserable time in and around Brunton Park.

Before a night game against Leigh in March, United were tenth in the table. We could've stayed home to watch Chelsea v Barcelona in the Champions League. Carlisle v Leigh in the Conference League didn't have quite the same ring to it. This was a school night too. Sam and I wouldn't be home until midnight. The crowd, a handful over 3,000, was the lowest of the season for a league game at Brunton Park. But it was one of those occasions where Carlisle needed us as much, if not more, than we needed a fix of live football under the lights. It was our duty to be there.

United's loss of form had been in part, I thought, down to the realisation that they wouldn't catch Barnet at the top of the table. That meant the rest of the league season was pretty redundant until the play-offs. Everyone switched off. Simpson's team selections and tactics weren't quite right; players' performances weren't what they were at the start of the season; complacency set in and confidence suffered.

Andy Preece's departure (to manage Worcester) coupled with injuries to Gray and Cowan didn't help. The after-effects of the floods wouldn't have either but United couldn't hide behind those setbacks. They had a big enough squad to cope.

Thank goodness then, for Leigh RMI. They weren't the same eleven as the team United hammered 6-1 in October (the *News and Star* revealed they'd used 51 players already that season) but they were as good as relegated. If United were to kick start the season, here was the perfect opportunity.

We arrived with over an hour to spare, so we walked around the ground, having a knock-about on the training pitch with a plastic ball we found. We netted in both goals. "I wonder how many famous names have scored in these?" said Sam. It looked like United had been practising their shooting, as one of the goals was in the centre circle.

If they had, it worked. United won 3:0. I finished my report with a confident, "The season restarts here!" It was a good call. Leigh was the first of six wins in a row, the first five without conceding. United must also have worked on their defence in training. Cowan and Gray returned to the team and had a new centre-back alongside them, young Danny Livesey from Bolton.

Another new signing Adam Murray came into midfield. The 24-year-old had lost his way after playing for Derby in the Premiership aged just seventeen, while up front Derek Holmes, a chunky Scot brought in from Bournemouth, filled the gap left by Preece. The team had a new, revitalised look about it.

There was another new ground for us too: Canvey Island on Good Friday, the most unusual place I've been to watch United. Stretching a point, it was probably the closest United would ever get to playing a league game overseas, well, over water anyway, because Canvey is on the Thames estuary and can, as the name suggests, be cut off from mainland Essex.

The Thames was the other side of a flood wall behind the away end. Rob said there was a World War Two munitions ship sunk in the estuary. The vessel had to be checked every six months to ensure its cargo was still stable. If the explosives were to go off during the afternoon, the ground would be under water.

Had we remained on the flood barrier wall, we'd have seen most of the pitch without having to pay, certainly all three of United's goals, which were scored at the far end. United eased into a two-goal lead before Canvey had two players sent off and conceded a penalty, converted by Chris Lumsdon. With United in action again on Easter Monday, the second half was little more than a training session.

The strangest game incidentally, that I've watched at Brunton Park, simply in terms of who United were playing, was before the start of the memorable 83-84 campaign, which began with a remarkable friendly. United's list of pre-season games read: Workington, Queen of the South, Zimbabwe and Clydebank. Yes, you read that right: *Zimbabwe*. They were on a mini tour and also played Port Vale and Coventry. The only goal of the game was scored by Alan Shoulder which, as far as I am aware, gives United a 100% record at international level.

The weird Easter weekend continued with one of the strangest goals I've seen. Halifax were the visitors for a late afternoon kick-off (this was United's third live game on Sky.) To the list of credits at the end of the season should be added that of Halifax keeper Ian Dunbavin. A goalless, uninspiring game was limping to its finish when Dunbavin was struck by a moment of madness or magic, depending on your hue of blue.

Sub Glenn Murray chased another long ball into the Halifax box. Dunbavin gathered it with ease before Murray bumped into him. There was nothing malicious in Murray's challenge but Dunbavin didn't like it and kicked out at Murray.

"Penalty!" I roared. It should've been but the referee gesticulated to Murray and Dunbavin to get on with the game. Dunbavin didn't comply. Maybe he was trying to waste time, maybe the mist came down, but he continued to walk towards the referee, *carrying* the ball out of the box. Well, what else could the referee do but blow for a free-kick against Dunbavin for handball?

Dunbavin complained about that too, dropping the ball behind him. Murray picked it up, placed the ball for the free-kick and passed to Magno Viera, who knocked it into an unguarded net. Dunbavin had gifted United the points. They leapfrogged Halifax into third place and completed a club record five wins in five without conceding.

United beat Farnborough in their next game to go second, hammered York 6:0 and only slipped to third after losing to Exeter in the last game. Hereford pipped Carlisle to second behind Barnet. United would play Aldershot over two legs in the semi-final. They lost the first at Aldershot 0:1 on the Monday. Four days later it was back to Brunton Park for the second.

A colleague, a non-football fan, told me why even he kept an eye out for Carlisle's results: "It's the same as when drivers slow down to look at a road traffic accident."

Similarly, when asked if he wanted to come to the Second Leg, Leechy replied, "Of course. It's Carlisle. There'll be drama." There was.

Nine seconds. Nine seconds! That was the distance between United and the Play-Off Final. In the fifth and final minute of added time, Aldershot won a corner at the Waterworks End. Their keeper charged forward. "Jimmy Glass!" I feared. "It's pay-back time." The kick was from the same corner too.

The ball was cleared but only as far as their man on the edge of the box. The keeper didn't know whether to stay up or charge back to his own box; United didn't know whether to pick him up or not. With nine seconds remaining, the confusion caused by the keeper was all it took to distract United's defence. The ball was crossed back in, and an Aldershot player rose at the near post to head into the top corner.

I looked at my watch: 49 minutes 51 seconds. United had been only nine seconds away from the Play-Off Final. The lads who'd gone down to the front in readiness for a pitch invasion didn't know where to go now. A fan in front was in tears. He should've known better. He should've expected it. I did. This was Jimmy Glass pay-back.

So the aggregate scores were level. United played thirty minutes of extra time but they must have felt deflated. We did. The impetus had switched to Aldershot, whose fans kept up an impressive noise. We tried but our roars were intermittent. Every one of us nursed a wound. We'd been just nine seconds away from a pitch invasion, from a party celebration, from the Play-Off Final.

Extra-time was, after the ninety (five) we'd just witnessed, an anti-climax. United's performance until then had been their best of the season. We didn't award less than eight to any player. The atmosphere at the start was something else too, with nearly 10,000 Blues making one hell of a noise.

The players were up for it. The first loose ball had three of them diving in to win possession. Livesey's header from a corner levelled the tie on 13 minutes, Billy's volley after a McGill run and cross put them ahead after 35. Even the official Aldershot website acknowledged United's first half football was a delight. They gave little away second half until nine seconds from the final whistle.

Despite efforts to convince myself otherwise, I knew that with their tails up, Aldershot's feet were in the Final.

Three penalties into the shoot-out and that was one kick away from confirmation. They had convincingly converted all three, United just one. Aldershot had gone first, and although Lumsdon dispatched United's opening penalty, McGill then Glenn Murray saw weak kicks saved.

McGill looked in tears. Kevin Gray had to help him back to the centre-circle; Murray trotted back. He, like we, seemed resigned to defeat. Aldershot had four, yes, four chances to end United's seasons. Two attempts to score, two attempts for their keeper to save. It was all over.

"We were three-one down at Wembley, remember," Sam said. I'd thought that too but hadn't said anything. It was no use. This was pay-back time after all.

Aldershot's fourth penalty taker went for power not pace, the ball whacked against the crossbar, banged down into the ground and away from goal. We couldn't see it at the time but Mattie had made a great save, touching the ball onto the woodwork. I'd said that Mattie would save a couple. Not that it was going to make much difference. Aldershot still had three chances to win.

Magno Viera strolled up to the spot, put the ball down and coolly slotted it to the keeper's left. The goalie, Nick Bull, was a good one. I expected him to save the next if, indeed, Aldershot needed that extra chance. They still had two bites of the cherry.

Aldershot's fifth penalty-taker would prove their hero. I was sure of that too. I didn't even give myself the luxury of imagining a miss. The last seconds of United's season were in front of me. The kick was low to Mattie's right. Mattie dived that way - and saved! United had a chance now. Oh yes, United could level the shoot-out with the last kick.

Peter Murphy was United's fifth penalty taker. "Peter Murphy does not miss penalties!" Sam yelled. "This is in!" He was right. Bang! Goal! Sudden death! And there was no doubt whose play-off hope's corpse was on the slab now.

Okay, their man scored Aldershot's first sudden-death kick, but Chris Billy was taking ours. He's the Harrogate Blues' hero. 'Chris Billy? Don't be silly!' was the slogan for the banner the lads had planned, as in 'Thierry Henry, don't be silly, you're not as good, as Chris Billy!' He didn't miss and Aldershot had to go through it all again.

There was nothing wrong with their next penalty, aimed inside Mattie's bottom-left. It was well-placed and looked from our vantage point well-struck. But Mattie threw himself to his left, stretched out his arm and his hand turned the ball around the post. Three saves from three kicks!

Many fans (the younger ones who'd lost count of the score) really did think it was all over. Cleverer, calmer Blues (oh yes, we were confident again now!) knew otherwise and jeered them off. Sam turned to me. "United's next penalty taker is Danny Livesey!" he roared, victory all over his face. "He's been 10 out of 10,

United's Man of the Match!" Livesey had already won Sam £20 by scoring the first goal. "He won't miss!"

Livesey's nerve had to hold while the invaders retreated, but Sam had a point. Livesey had been magnificent. He hadn't put a foot wrong. And he wouldn't, he couldn't, surely not, start now. Danny didn't hang about. He ran up, struck the ball, kept it low to the keeper's right. Bull dived to his left and before the ball hit the net, Livesey was wheeling away towards Mattie Glennon, pursued by a second wave of invaders.

"We'll meet you back here!" Sam yelled at me as he and Leechy pushed past to join the invasion. Sam stopped long enough to hug me and then he was away. "I'd never run so fast in my life!" he said later. He got to hug Livesey ("All he said was, 'Fucking Hell!'"), then slap Billy and Magno on the head; he even grabbed one of the drinks bottles United had left in the centre circle.

We joined them on the pitch, gathering in front of the Main Stand, with only a mean, parting shot at Aldershot's supporters ("You're not singing anymore!") before we continued to party. United's players didn't appear but I didn't mind. Let them go bananas in the changing rooms. Heavens! They deserved to.

We were almost back off the pitch when the players did show up in the Directors' Box. Sam was off again, over the Paddock wall and up the terracing, where he high-fived Magno, Simmo, Murphy. "I asked for his shirt, but he said needed it for the final! Viera was joining in with 'One Mattie Glennon' too!" Sam reported.

This time we did leave the pitch, waltzing down Promotion Walk, the back lane of the Warwick Road houses, most of which are still empty after the floods. The car park was chocker, but over four hours earlier, we'd been given the best get-away spot.

"A good omen," I told the attendant. A good omen indeed. We didn't arrive home until after one in the morning. It took a while to get to sleep and I was up at five, still buzzing.

Eight days later and we were at the Britannia Ground, Stoke, for the Play-Off Final with a new soundtrack (to the tune of *Que Sera*): *"Danny Livesey, he scored the penalty, that took us to Stoke City, Danny Livesey!"* For the fifth time in the season, a Carlisle game was live on Sky. Blues outnumbered Stevenage supporters three to one in a crowd of nearly 13,500. Traffic congestion meant the Stevenage team had to walk the last half mile to the stadium.

File this under another of those games 'Endured Not Enjoyed', not until the final whistle anyway. United started stronger again and took the lead when two of the season's top performers, Cowan and Murphy, combined for the goal. Cowan crossed from the left, Murphy headed in.

United came under most threat when teenage sub George Boyd came on in the second half, but they had the best defence in the Conference (only 37 goals conceded) and Stevenage didn't create much, not that it seemed that way at the time.

Their manager Graham Westley (who usually did see most things differently) claimed that United's goal "led a charmed life in the second half" but a neutral newspaper reporter disagreed: 'Stevenage were pedestrian while Carlisle justified the Eddie Stobart logo on their shirts with a juggernaut approach.'

Right at the end of the game, with Stevenage's keeper up for a time-added corner, Carlisle broke and Viera had an open goal. I'm not sure if he realised the goalie was behind him. I didn't and was just hoping he'd waste more time by heading to the corner. He was brought down in a challenge and the referee awarded United a free-kick.

I was bemused when Lumsdon, instead of going for goal, whacked the ball into touch. He'd asked the referee how long was left and been told that the next time the ball went dead, that was it. So Lummy lumped it into the stand opposite and United were back in the Football League.

Arrivederci Canvey.

8

Mansfield Revisited

The 2005-06 season started for us at Wrexham, United's fourth league game. Before kick-off Rob and Sue entertained us with tales of their trip to Istanbul for the Champions League Final, which sounded almost as exciting as the play-off semi with Aldershot.

United had begun with a win, draw and defeat. Simpson kept most of the players from Stoke. Mattie Glennon and Tom Cowan were the two regulars who'd moved on. He'd replaced them with keeper Anthony Williams from Grimsby and Spaniard Zigor Aranalde from Walsall.

Their record in the second half of their relegation season had been play-off form, and what with the confidence and momentum a promotion brings, they'd been far more used to winning than losing for a year and a half. I was confident United would do much better than their previous six seasons in the fourth tier, now renamed League Two.

Outside the Racecourse Ground an old boy was collecting for Parkinson's. He told us how excited he'd been many years earlier to see Carlisle run out "with a chap who had a real fox on a lead." United hadn't won a league game at Wrexham in 67 years.

I didn't have anything like the nerves I suffered at Stoke, but the hairs on the back of my neck still rose with the first cries of *U-NI-TED!* Come the end of the match my throat hurt and my arms ached (it's not only players who need to rediscover match fitness at the start of a season.) For 18 minutes without a pause, 500 Blues had driven the team on with: *"PAUL SIMPSON'S BLUE AND WHITE ARMY!"*

It was a game to get excited about. At half-time Rob observed that the score could have been 3:0, 0:3 or 3:3, as there'd been so many chances either end. Wrexham very nearly scored in their first attack. Danny Livesey (*"HE SCORED THE PENALTY..."*) who'd been watched at every game by Premier League Sunderland, according to Rob, caught a striker as he lined up to shoot.

Before the referee could blow for a penalty and red card the defender (it looked like a foul to me), another Blue, unable to stop his covering run, inadvertently nudged the ball past Williams towards goal. I was sure the ball was rolling in, but it hit the post, rebounded onto the goal-line where Williams gratefully dropped on it. In all the excitement the referee seemed to have forgotten to blow for the penalty.

On another day the ball would've rebounded off the post and gone in, or the referee would've called play back, awarded Wrexham a penalty and sent Livesey off. I had a sneaky feeling (one that I had to immediately supress for fear of tempting the fickle Football Fates) that it was going to be Our Day.

That seemed more likely when a Wrexham defender chose to lunge into a melee both feet first and was ordered off. Adam Murray curled the free-kick round the wall, the keeper parried, Brendan McGill netted the rebound and noise levels in the stand above reached new heights. When United had another free-kick a little later, their keeper had to run out of goal to scream instructions to teammates in the wall as they couldn't hear him above our chants.

In the last minute Wrexham's pressure told on Kevin Gray, who climbed on a defender's shoulders in the box. Penalty. The kick was low and pretty straight. Williams dived to his right, stuck out a foot when he realised he was going the wrong way, and made the save.

United had seven points from four games. That was already two more than they'd managed by mid-December the last time they were in the Football League. Maybe it wasn't just Our Day; maybe it was going to be Our Season. United lost to a last-minute goal the following Tuesday but it was to Championship side Burnley in the League Cup and Carlisle played very well. Plenty of Blues travelled again to re-remix a terrace classic: *"IF YOU STILL HATE BURNLEY, CLAP YOUR HANDS!"*

Our ranks had swelled to over 1200 for Bury away at the start of September. Simpson's credentials were underlined again when he replaced injured striker Holmes not with like-for-like sub Glen Murray, but striker-cum-winger Raphael Nade, brought in over the summer to replace Viera, who'd returned to parent club Wigan.

Nade, once described in a United fanzine as 'a cross between an excited red setter and a collapsing ironing board' was, Simpson admitted, going through a crisis of confidence. It showed. Raphael had struggled to keep his feet let alone the ball, and we anticipated a parting of the ways of man and leather as he raced onto McGill's pass.

But Raphael kept his feet, kept the ball, kept going and, when the keeper challenged, lifted it over him with grace and precision. That was, alas for the lad, as good as his career got. He barely lasted half a season before a loan to Weymouth, free transfer to Ebbsfleet and return to France.

Simpson's managerial magic had however, worked again. Nade's goal at Bury was the only one of the game and took Carlisle to the edge of the play-offs. Departing Gigg Lane we were confident United would continue to climb the table. *"TELL ME MA, ME MA, TO PUT THE CHAMPAGNE ON ICE, WE'RE WINNING PROMOTION TWICE, TELL ME MA, ME MA!"*

Last word on Nade to Rob: "A shit version of Johann Smith, who was a shit version of Cleveland Taylor, who was a shit version of Rod Thomas. Like nested Russian dolls." You don't need to have seen all those to get

Rob's gist. Nade only scored one other goal, which came in November against Oxford. A new striker came off the bench in that game. He would have rather more of an impact on United's fortunes.

Before then United continued their winning ways. They beat Macclesfield at home and went to Cheltenham with a chance to go top. The last time we'd cheered United on at Cheltenham, United had been in free-fall, bottom of the league and going nowhere but the Conference. What a difference Simmo and 18 months of success had made.

United started the game full of confidence. Cheltenham scored against the run of play, Hawley equalised then put United ahead, before a lip-smacker of a third. Cheltenham didn't clear the ball properly, it fell to Zigor *("WE LOVE OUR SPANIARD!")* on the edge of the box. WHAM! He caught the ball waist high, and despite the keeper knowing what was coming, he couldn't do a thing to stop the shot, a mother-in-law of an Exocet, as in, "You know she's coming, but you can't do a thing to stop her!" as a mate once said pre-political correctness. Only Grimsby's victory prevented United going top.

Carlisle however, lost the next four. Nevertheless, the whole club was on the up, even if the team in early October wasn't. Many of the houses in Championship Walk remained empty after January's flood, but Fred Story had been busy around Brunton Park. A new club store had been built, there was a statue of club legend Hugh McIlmoyle outside, programme sellers had kiosks and the concourse bars were named after United icons.

A Friday night defeat at Oxford ended United's worse league run of the season. They won four of their next five. In mid-November, a month after losing at Oxford, they met again at Brunton Park. It was an historic occasion for the Harrogate Blues because Sam drove me to the game. He'd passed his test 10 days before. Matchday would be that bit sweeter; I could have that second pre-match pint.

The Oxford game was special for another reason. Carlisle were cruising at 2:0 when Simmo brought off Derek Holmes and gave a United debut to the substitute striker, Michael Bridges. Usually someone of his calibre was either a young pro at the start of his career or an experienced player on his way down. Bridges was neither. At 27, he was at his peak. Bridges at Brunton Park wasn't so much a case of stars aligning as the paths of different planets colliding, the bigger planet slipping into the smaller one's orbit.

Bridges was only 18 when he'd made his Sunderland debut in the Premier League. Less than three years later he was sold to Leeds for £5 million. He scored 21 goals in his first season as Leeds finished third and qualified for the Champions League. Early in his second season at Elland Road he was seriously injured against Besiktas. He dislocated his ankle and was told he would never play again. Having proved that prognosis wrong and recovered, two more injuries followed: a ruptured Achilles and damaged tendons in his knee.

The ankle injury prevented him playing for two years and in the three seasons that followed, Bridges failed to get much game time at all at Leeds, Newcastle, Bolton and Sunderland. He scored just two goals and you could almost hear the sigh of relief from Bristol City, his last club, when he was loaned to United. A few weeks later he was allowed to sign on a free.

All this for a player who seemed to have the football world at his feet as a 21-year-old and who, a Leeds mate told me, had the best touch of any Leeds player he'd seen. Bridges looked a class act in the half hour he played against Oxford, nearly scoring with a header and a long-distance drive. "He's a second ahead of those around him," I wrote, "just like Hawley," which was quite a compliment to the striker (Hawley, that is.)

United won 2:1 to stay fifth in the table. "We are currently the fifth best side in the League but safety is still my main priority," said Simpson afterwards. It was ours too. As Sam said, with 30 points in the bag, they were only seven wins from safety. If United could keep Hawley and Bridges, they'd be clear of relegation by Christmas. Bridges was sub again for the next league game, a single goal defeat at home to Wycombe. He started up front in the next at Rushden. United won 4:0 and Bridges scored.

Peterborough the following Saturday brought up the half century of away grounds Sam and I had been to together to watch United. The 600 Blues included a drummer in front of us, who banged his drum with such gusto that midway through the second half a stick broke and the top end flew up the terracing behind us. Drummer Boy was aided by one very drunk Blue, who lurched beside us until his mate propped him against a crush barrier. He came to life towards the end of the game, as did United.

A goal down, Simpson moved Bridges from the left to the middle. That made the difference. United had more cut to their thrusts. Peterborough conceded free-kicks and Lumsdon's accurate deliveries put their defence under pressure. With 11 minutes left, United equalised: Lumsdon whipped the ball in, picked out Hawley's near post run, and Bridges finished it off with a header. The point took United third.

Once Bridges was in the starting line-up, United had an unbeaten run of seven games, winning five. He was cup-tied so didn't play at Tranmere in the LDV Trophy. We'd been to Oldham for the First Round, which United won on penalties 5:4, the best of which was a cheeky chip down the middle from centre-back Simon Grand.

He scored again in the shoot-out at Tranmere who, like Oldham and Round 2 opponents Blackpool, were a division above United in League One. It was another long, cold night; longer than Oldham because the first 20 (repeat, twenty!) penalties were all converted. Carlisle keeper Kieran Westwood went ahead of four outfield players and scored. His Tranmere counterpart was the first to miss the target, by some margin, and although Grand had cramped up, he managed to hobble to the spot. His successful kick gave United an 11-10 victory.

United's form, Bridges' arrival and the possibility of another LDV Final (United were in the quarters) made

Christmas a good time to be a Blue. On Boxing Day 11,200 watched the Darlington game, the biggest Brunton Park crowd for 10 years since the championship celebration against Lincoln. United went ahead with another penalty, this one from Lumsdon, but conceded a soft far post header.

On New Year's Eve against Rochdale, Leechy, whose 18th birthday was on Christmas Day, had his first legal pint from the East Stand concourse bar. Sam had discovered a fake £10 note in his change from the Ticket Office. He'd taken it back but been told to buy a programme and get rid of it that way!

Bridges rounded the keeper to score the winner. After the final whistle Kevin Gray got the players together in a huddle on the pitch; it's unlikely they'd have been discussing who'd be i/c the kitty at First Footing. We arrived back in Harrogate to a surprise party for Sam, 18 on January 1st. It was a Happy New Year all round.

United started 2006 as they'd finished 2005. They won at second-place Grimsby, put four goals past Bury and bounced back from a first defeat in eight league games at Shrewsbury by banging in five at Boston, where Bridges scored a hat-trick. United went second and stayed there after a draw with Cheltenham. In the LDV quarter-final United beat Kidderminster.

The month ended with a trip to Macclesfield on, unusually, a Sunday. The game was declared a Fans United Day to help Macclesfield pay a fine from the Football Association relating to the building of their stand. Most United fans took the view that Macclesfield's inability to balance their books meant they'd been able to buy better players to keep them up the season United went down.

At £13 for me and £20 for the lads (I treated Phil, the latest Harrogate Blue to celebrate an 18th birthday with United), I reasoned that Macclesfield had received enough of my money already. I wasn't throwing any coins in their buckets. The attendance was over 4,100. More than half were Blues.

My pre-match build-up was running a 10k near Leeds. Just before the start of the race I chatted with a friend who moaned about declining standards at his school. "Cheer up!" I said. "We're here to enjoy ourselves! Anyway, if you think you've got it bad, think of me standing on an exposed away end at Macclesfield this afternoon when we're three goals down!"

That was added in jest, of course, because United were flying and a win would send them top. My flippant reply didn't sound so funny when United *were* three-down at half-time. The Macclesfield defeat was the exception that proved the rule. United didn't lose another league game until the end of April, a run of 13. They put five past Chester and Rushden before heading to Darlington. "Get there early," Bryan said. "I think all the car park tickets might've been sold in advance."

We did and they hadn't, but an hour-and-a-half before kick-off the stadium's bars were full of Carlisle fans. We sat in the car and read the programme and papers to while away some time. *The Times* had this headline: *Poor Team Lifted by a Striking Trio*. It was a review of an opera's first night. Darlo's manager Dave Hodgson (no opera fan, I suspect) had claimed that was more or less the case for Carlisle. Take out Bridges and Hawley and Carlisle weren't much of a team, he claimed. You would've thought a manager of one of the league's lesser achievers would avoid winding up the opposition.

Over 3,500 Blues journeyed to Darlo. There were rumours, according to Bryan, of cars turning back on the A66, so rammed were the jams. Kick-off was delayed, as it had been before when the Reynolds Arena struggled to cope with a United-size crowd. Carlisle would never have a better chance of ending a 15-game winless run against Darlo. It was about time fortune smiled on United. And smile it did just before the break.

Livesey read the drop of a loose ball quicker than his marker and lofted the ball goalwards. Gray went up with the keeper, won the duel and Carlisle led. With the big screen to the right of us, we enjoyed an immediate action replay. Livesey's boot was high. On another day there might've been a free-kick against him but fortune favours the brave, and let's face it, when you play three strikers (Bridges, Hawley and Holmes) away from home, a team makes its own luck.

They did that again on the hour. The ball was passed back to Darlo keeper Russell; Holmes followed it and I followed the ball's bounce. I had a feeling it might just deceive the Darlo keeper. The pitch was sticky and the ball was bobbling. Russell swung his right boot, made the faintest of connections, slicing the ball behind him. He frantically scrambled back to his goal; Holmes calmly lifted the ball over Russell's despairing dive.

He came to a halt in front of us, arms raised. 'Goals like that only happen when you're top of the league, when you're, oh sod it! Let's say it: Champions Elect!' I wrote afterwards. If that was pure comedy, the next goal was pure class. Bridges had yet to make his mark on the game. Darlo would've done well just to leave him alone, to let him have a (rare) off day. But he was then taken out on the touchline.

The referee played advantage but Bridges wasn't happy. Three or four passes later he received the ball on the edge of the box, still angry. He took one touch, then with a simple step-over, he sliced between two defenders and made space to smack the ball into the far corner. "One of the best goals I've ever seen!" enthused Sam.

Game over. Glenn Murray and Grand scored goals four and five. "I laughed all the way through the second half!" posted one fan on the message board.

"FIVE NIL TO THE CHAMPIONS!" we roared. The stadium PA tried drowning us out on the final whistle but failed. *"AND NOW YOU'RE GOING TO BELIEVE US, THE BLUES ARE GOING UP!"* The players came over to applaud us, got in their huddle, and applauded us some more. On the way out I high-fived Parky before starting another *"5:0 TO THE CHAMPIONS!"*

United were still on course for the League Two double: the title and LDV Trophy The semi-final was over two legs against a Macclesfield team who'd inflicted United's heaviest defeat of the season three weeks earlier. That said, they were mid-table, well below Carlisle. With this being the sixth semi-final in 13 seasons, many United fans weren't too excited. The crowd of 5,700 was below the league average and the Warwick was closed.

Macclesfield went ahead after nine minutes before Karl Hawley equalised. Hawley wasn't the sort of striker to pick the ball up 30 yards from goal, beat a player or two and score (like cup-tied Michael Bridges); his success rate owed much to his speed on the turn, the accuracy of his shooting and his big backside, a battering ram into a defender's mid-rift.

Peter Murphy, who had a habit of getting important goals, scored with a ninetieth minute header, helping Simon Hackney's corner over the line. His goal was that simple it made a mockery of what had gone before, when United laboured against an average defence. But the tie wasn't over, not by a long way. What's more United had never won at Macclesfield and I knew we'd be in for a nervy ninety-plus minutes in the Second Leg. Two of United's four LDV ties that season were won on penalties and I predicted another shoot-out at Moss Road.

It took two-and-a-hour hours to drive 87 miles through rush hour traffic and rain to spend three-and-a-half hours stood on that exposed terrace in more rain at a ground which, as we Blues observed, wasn't the most salubrious: *"It's got a door and a window, my garden shed is bigger than this!"* The alternative was a comfy night in watching the Champions League. So of course, there was no alternative. Carlisle, not for the first or last time, took me out of the comfort zone and up to the edge.

Three minutes gone and Macclesfield were in front, not just in the game but the tie, for if scores were level at the end of extra time, away goals counted double. Before long it was two. Macclesfield were first to every second ball. "They want it more than Carlisle do," sighed Sam, but right on cue, United scored. Hawley cut inside, shot and former Blue Dave Morley (once described as "a Premier League midfielder" by Roddy Collins) stuck out a foot and deflected the ball past his keeper.

There were no goals second half so the game went to extra time and with just 15 minutes of the tie remaining, penalties looming large and United attacking the home end, they won a corner. Adam Murray had a shot blocked, the ball came back to McGill who struck it well, very well. It beat the keeper and cleared a defender on the line, only to hit the bar and bounce out, but a Blue got to the loose ball first, hooking it back in and OH! YES! GOAL! GET IN!

We didn't know who'd scored until Sam calmed down enough to phone Leechy. The name flashed back over the wires: Simon Grand. To his cheeky spot-chip at Oldham and the decisive penalty at Tranmere, add the semi-final winner.

Macclesfield had less than 10 minutes to score twice. All United had to do was keep the ball, whack it downfield, mess about in the corners. I counted down the minutes. Two to go, 90 seconds, one, 45 seconds... Instead Adam Murray crossed, their keeper caught the ball, cleared, and a fresh-legged sub tore past Arnison, crossed low and someone slid it in. Even the scorer didn't look convinced that his goal would make a difference. The referee would surely blow as soon as the game re-started.

But the re-start was delayed because the ref insisted Livesey and an opponent go off for treatment (they clashed heads), which meant one of United's central defenders was off, and that wouldn't be a good thing if there was added time to extra time, which there was going to be, 30 seconds at least, because Macclesfield's manager threw on a sub.

My watch showed 16, then 17 minutes had gone. Macclesfield launched the ball forward, it evaded everyone, the referee either signalled for Westwood to hurry up, or to gesture that it didn't matter which side he'd take the kick from as he'd blow up straight away. And blow up at last he did! PHEW! Game over, semi-final won, and Cardiff (to play Swansea) here we come!

After beating Lincoln 1:0 on the Tuesday before Sunday's Final (Bridges scored), Bryan phoned. "United are up, Tim." That wasn't like Bryan. I'm usually the ridiculously optimistic one, but he repeated, "No. They are up." By the day of the final, United were six games into a run of seven straight league wins. They topped the table and only needed 11 points from the last seven games to guarantee promotion, and that was assuming Orient won all their remaining six matches.

Games like the Cardiff Final were the reward for wild, wet and windy nights on the puddled terracing of Macclesfield. Even the drive to Cardiff was pleasurable. An early Sunday morning departure meant the roads were empty, my passengers slept, so there was just me and all that glorious anticipation, mounting excitement and, once in Wales, banks of daffodils lining the verges. Oh happy day!

There was a spring in our step and comfy seats in a city centre coffee shop to sink into. We were only two minutes from the ground, yet there we were, sipping in comfort. That wouldn't have happened at Wembley. Some Swansea fans were also in the coffee shop, including a family on the level below. We shook our United flags and they waved theirs at us. "This is a home game for you," I said.

"No it isn't!" she replied. "We don't think of Cardiff as home." Swansea and Cardiff don't get on. More of that anon.

United had 13,000 of the 42,000 fans in the Millennium Stadium. Our seats in the stadium were as good as the ones in the coffee shop; at £44 they had to be. They were top of the Middle Tier, backing onto private boxes. I had loads of legroom. I was worried however, that we would be with non-singers. Fortunately I spotted *Kirkpatrick 16*, an away day regular, a few rows to my left. He and his mates were up for a chant despite grief from the day-trippers in front.

Swansea were top of League One and easy on the eye, not least because they had Lee Trundle, while United were without talisman Bridges. Trundle scored after two minutes, controlling the ball on his chest and volleying as it dropped. Some goals against your team are so good you just have to shrug your shoulders and applaud. That was one of them.

Carlisle played well. Just before half-time Zigor's long throw was flicked on by Holmes and Andy Murray, timing his run, headed the equaliser. It was United's first goal, bar shoot-out penalties, in their four Final appearances.

Trundle, inevitably, set up Swansea's winner for Akinfenwa, flicking the ball through despite having his back to goal. United had a case for a free-kick against Akinfenwa, either for handball or a foul on Gray. It's not often Gray was out-muscled, but Akinfenwa was, even then, a big lad. Swansea's celebrations featured Trundle holding a Welsh flag painted over with 'FUCK OFF CARDIFF'; he also donned a t-shirt of a Swansea fan pee-ing on a Cardiff shirt. I should tut-tut here, but Trundle loved his club (and hated their rivals) like a fan.

Although winning at Cardiff would've been wonderful, the following Saturday United had a more important fixture against Grimsby, with 11,000 inside Brunton Park to watch first v second. It wasn't a great match, the wind saw to that; we'd driven through a blizzard on top of the A66.

United were clearly the better team, and if Grimsby, who didn't offer much, were the next best in the Division, United deserved to be worthy champions. Grimsby's main threat was striker Michael Reddy, but Livesey had him in his back pocket, so much so that the forward raked the back of Livesey's leg after one tackle. The injury forced Livesey off, but Murphy dropped back and dealt with him just as successfully.

And that was the thing about United, they'd a strong squad. Adam Murray, who came on as sub when Livesey went off, had a great spell, first on the left, then on the opposite flank after Simmo unleashed Simon Hackney. They were also a squad who could scrap better than the rest. Billy and Lumsdon didn't play that well against Grimsby, but they'd win the ball back. They were tough tacklers, hard workers, horrible to play against.

And then there was Michael Bridges. He was different class and once again the difference. Hawley had a mare, his afternoon summed up by an awful piece of control after Westwood's goal-kick bounced right through to him. Hawley could have hit the ball first time, or at least controlled it before striking for goal, but the ball simply bounced off his boot to the keeper.

Minutes later Bridges was in a similar position thanks to Zigor's long ball. The keeper rushed out of goal, but Bridges wasn't fazed, lobbing it over him. The finish was that accurate the ball didn't bounce until it was over the line.

After the final whistle the players got into their familiar huddle before turning to clap the 10,000 Blues, who left triumphant. Back in Harrogate Diane and I treated ourselves to a night at the opera. The singing wasn't any sweeter to these ears than the sound of the East Stand in full voice at the end of the game.

It was a Big, Big Win. United pulled six points clear of Grimsby. They only needed six more from six games to secure promotion. One of those came at Bristol Rovers on Easter Saturday; Notts County were next on the Monday.

United needed Bridges against County, who took an early lead before United equalised in first half added time. Bridges' volley was a lovely strike but the keeper had the shot covered, getting two hands to the ball only to spill it. The ball bounced out of his hands, off the post, and in.

United improved but not enough to score again in the next 45. But at the back of my mind was the sneaking feeling that United would, well, sneak one. That's what happens when you're top of the league. Into added time and Hawley cleverly back heeled the ball to Bridges, who'd checked his run to Hawley's right, throwing off two defenders, leaving him unchallenged to slam the ball low into the goal.

It was United's 13th league game unbeaten. They won because of Bridges. He was the difference between

United and every other team in the division. That wasn't to belittle the efforts of the rest of the squad. Bridges however, was special. His winner sparked off wild, wild celebrations. "That's why we're going up!" we roared.

Indeed, had Orient and Grimsby not drawn with each other, United would have been up with that goal. It would only be a matter of time. Results in 12 games would have to go against United to prevent promotion, and that included four United defeats.

On the journey back Sam sent a text to his football manager, who'd earlier asked if he could play in the following weekend's cup final. Sam replied read: *Sorry, but I've supported Carlisle for 14 years and I want to see them go up at Mansfield next Saturday. I hope you understand.* He probably didn't but thousands of Cumbrians would.

Two years to the Saturday after Mattie Glennon's last gasp penalty save meant a stay of execution, United returned to Mansfield needing a point to win promotion. They crafted several quality chances as they attacked a packed away end first half but went off the boil in the second. Then Mansfield scored. That wasn't in the party plans. Mansfield could've had more. A sub blasted over with only Westwood to beat then nearly forced Ziggy into an own goal.

Simmo threw on forward after forward. United finished with five up front: Hawley was shifted to the right, Hackney came on the left, with Bridges, Glenn Murray and even Simon Grand down the middle. Time ticked on, past the announcement that "the fourth official has indicated there will be a minimum of three minutes added" and past the first of those.

Westwood rolled the ball out of his box and thumped it downfield. Glenn Murray got his head to it, flicking the ball through to Hawley. He shot, the keeper saved, the ball rebounded to Hackney who seemed to have an open goal, only to slice the ball horribly; then Bridges shot, the ball flew across goal again, the keeper saved again, and now it was with Hawley. He shot a second time, and this time the ball beat the keeper, hit a defender on the knee, and ricocheted into the root of the net!

United had done it! Yet another late, late goal. When things go your way, they go your way. Why had I ever doubted that United would score? Over the ninety plus minutes Hawley had been hapless, but now heroic. His 26th goal of the season had won United promotion.

Or had it? No sooner had Mansfield kicked-off than Lumsdon climbed all over the back of an opponent and conceded a free-kick inside the Carlisle half. United cleared the ball, but it was crossed in again. United cleared that too, the players (and ref) following the ball out. As he ran, the ref spread his arms wide and blew. United were promoted! Let the party begin!

The players came over, clapped us, clapped each other, danced and hugged. I couldn't stop smiling, grinning, beaming! The players went off, then returned. Most Blues had stayed. Hawley went over to speak to his dad, missing the team photo which appeared on the front page of *The League Paper* next morning. Kieran Westwood came near us to kiss his girlfriend, and Sam threw him the Carlisle flag he'd bought for Cardiff. Kieran kept tight hold of it.

We saw Rob Lees, Skipton Tim and other friends Dougie, Paul Mooney and son, Blues who'd followed United for years, and for whom this moment made up for all the hard, heartbreak times. Knowing there would be no quick getaway, Sam and I waited by the team bus to get some photos on his mobile. No player turned us down. I cocked up one of Sam with Bridges, the last Blue out. "Old people and technology!" he sighed to Sam.

It was a great way to end the day, a great way to end the season and it wasn't over. There was a championship to be won and another party, hopefully with trophy presentation included, at Stockport in a fortnight. We'd already got our tickets.

I missed the Torquay home game a week later as I was on the staff team football tour to Mallorca. United carelessly missed out on the trophy presentation by losing for the first time in 14 games, which must have frustrated most of the 13,500 crowd, the third five-figure attendance in a row. The result mattered more to Torquay; it saved them from relegation.

Carlisle won the title at Rochdale on the Tuesday in a re-arranged fixture and would receive the trophy after the last game at Stockport, but it would be presented back at Brunton Park, the reason being that Stockport faced relegation if Oxford won and they lost. Edgeley Park would be no place to party. It would be like a wedding reception and wake sharing the same venue.

That made for a strange atmosphere. Pubs around the ground were packed beforehand with amiable United and County fans. Their overspill filled the street. Programme inserts from the police warned that any pitch invasion from either set of supporters would jeopardise celebrations. We had no wish to see County relegated. They were a northern club after all; if they stayed up, southerners Oxford would go down.

The game ended scoreless and Stockport survived. Simpson came on for the final five minutes, the last of his 798 professional games in a career spanning two decades. As we left the ground fans in the home end leant over the wall to shake our hands. We headed back home rather than up to Brunton Park for the presentation. We didn't mind. There would be others in the future.

9

McDonald and Ward

Two successive promotions made it inevitable Simpson would move on. It was just a shame, from most Blues' perspectives, that it had to be to Preston. In doing so, he lost some of the goodwill he'd built up over two-and-a-half very successful seasons.

That seemed harsh to me. Simpson, like other heroes Simon Davey and David Reeves before him, couldn't be blamed for furthering his career and earning more money at Deepdale. Besides, I didn't have a thing about Preston. I used to watch them occasionally when I lodged in my student days at Garstang. Deepdale oozed history. There was a lady as old as the ground who used to ring a handbell at random moments during the game.

Just as Simmo was always going to move, so too was Bridges. He'd been too successful not to attract attention from bigger clubs. He was sold to Hull for £350,000 at the end of August. It was great business for United, who'd signed Bridges for nothing in the December. It was a privilege to have watched him.

In the space of a few weeks United had lost their championship-winning manager and best player, yet in the short term at least, it didn't seem to make a difference. Carlisle's new manager was Neil McDonald, who'd coached at Preston, Bolton and Palace. He'd been at Carlisle as a schoolboy before joining Newcastle, playing for them and Everton in the top tier.

Initial impressions suggested McDonald was going to improve United. Not that there was much wrong with them after two straight promotions, but the style of their play was as good as anything under Simmo.

"It's just like watching Brazil!" we sang during a 2:0 win against Cheltenham. And it was! Not the underachieving Brazil of that summer's World Cup, but the 1970s Brazil of Pele, Alberto, Rivelino. United's one touch football and short passing, possession game really was that good. McDonald had taken Simmo's squad to a higher level. To see Kevin Gray happy to pass the ball across the back line when challenged rather than lump it forward said everything.

The third Saturday in September marked a Big Day for United and a Big Day for Sam. Two years on from a league game at Forest Green Rovers, we travelled with nearly 2,500 Blues to see United at Nottingham Forest.

On the way, Sam picked up the keys to his room at Leeds Met University. We took some of his belongings with us. The next day he would move out of home and into student halls. The house didn't seem the same.

Such however, is life. Things don't stay the same, thankfully. If they did, United would still be in the Conference.

Come kick-off, the attendance was close to 20,000. We Blues had the lower tier of the away end; the noisy Forest boys the upper. I hadn't been in a ground before where that was the case. With more of their singers and shouters in the single tier to our left, the home support made a good noise but no better than the Blue Army.

At times I couldn't be sure who was doing the singing, only a glance to my right at the Forest boys to see if they were out of the seats in the corner told me. And as soon as we saw that they were standing, then we were up out of our seats raucously replying.

If one thing was certain, we'd agreed before kick-off, it was that Grant Holt would score. The penalty he'd won at Rochdale had effectively sent United down to the Conference. Holt would be booed throughout then score, of that we were sure. Holt did net early on but his joy was short-lived; he was off-side. Our joy lasted longer.

Holt's strike partner Junior Agogo was more of a handful. A little later he and Murphy tangled on the edge of the box. Although it was at the far end, it looked like six-of-one, half-a-dozen of the other. The referee seemed to think so too, and let the tussle continue. Not so the linesman. He waved his flag and the ref gave a penalty. Murphy was incensed. The Forest boys above us were delighted.

Cue Grant Holt. "Not again!" I fumed. I couldn't block the roar of the City boys above.

Sam however, remained calm. "What goes around comes around," he said.

"But this is Grant bloody Holt!" I argued.

Sam wasn't to be swayed. "What goes around comes around. He'll miss."

Kevin Gray was booked for showmanship, picking the ball up to delay the spot-kick. Holt aimed for Kieran's left, Kieran dived that way and dropped on the ball. He didn't catch it first time but held it at the second attempt. Holt hadn't scored! A penalty save is as sweet as a goal and our celebration, in the sight-line and ears of the Forest boys, was loaded with three, four extra sugars!

Holt's game went from bad to worse, and he was subbed off in the second half. United went from strength to strength. It was more of the Beautiful Game: passing to feet, give and go. The finishing wasn't as good as the build-up but we weren't too bothered. A point at the leaders, thoroughly deserved, meant United's unbeaten league run was now six games. The draw felt like a win. A great atmosphere, quality football (even Forest manager Calderwood said it was "bloody good entertainment") and that unforgettable penalty-save moment.

United were more than holding their own in League One, the team improved by the signing (on loan at first) of Paul Thirlwell. Northampton away was more fun again. Sixfields is in a dip, which means you can see into the ground from the bank behind the home end. Some local youths watched the game from there, the best vantage point being on the roof of the bus shelter. When Northampton played Manchester United, fences went up to keep folk from viewing for free.

Inevitably the temptation to run and roll down the bank proved greater than the spectacle below. During the second half the urchins' fun and games proved as entertaining as the action on the pitch. Sam and I had done the same earlier, scrambling down the bank, then racing each other up it. We ran down again to meet the players off the coach, including Paul Thirlwell, who'd signed permanently. "So you were the two fans running down the bank!" he said as he handed over the complimentaries. United players had watched us for a change.

United lost 2:3 but stayed mid-table thanks to their win-at-home-lose-away form. The following Saturday we gave Steph Thirlwell a lift to the home game with Crewe. She told us that Paul had offers from Hull, Burnley and Sheffield Wednesday, but he chose United.

She also said he'd turned down the chance of an extra day-off over the vacant FA Cup tie weekend (Carlisle had gone out in Round One) as he didn't want to seem a special case when the rest of the team returned to training and he was a day late. That commitment denied Steph the long weekend in Dubai they'd planned.

Another strong signing in the 2006-07 season, and a player making his league debut in the Crewe game, was Blackburn loanee Joe Garner. "A spiky youngster and far more impressive than cumbersome Danny Graham," I wrote. If Garner were a plant, it would be a nettle, nasty and nippy if you got too close. He would top any list of those opposition players who are irritating in the extreme, but whom you'd love to have in your team.

A few years later Garner came back to play against United for Preston. Within minutes our appreciative round of applause had turned to abuse, as Joe dived, feigned injury and whinged at the referee. He was horrible. Sam once met him on a United night-out in Leeds. He said Garner was quietly spoken, friendly, just a decent lad. Quite the opposite of his on-pitch persona but a perfect example of a player for whom winning is everything. Little wonder he went on to have a long and successful career.

With eight games to go, the season was meandering gently to its close, but then United hit a purple patch, winning five out of five to be a mere point behind Oldham in the last play-off spot. After the fifth of those victories at Rotherham, the walk back to the car between the scrapyard and railway line seemed almost picturesque. What was stopping United making it six, seven, even eight?

Bristol City, second in the table and a win away from promotion, were next. Heading out of Harrogate, I spotted something roadside as we drove out of Harrogate. "That was a dead fox," I said to Sam, the worst possible omen.

Brunton Park had the big game feel. Bristol fans had arrived early and in force. The Premier Inn beer garden was packed with them and there was a 'Carpark Full' sign at the entrance to the Riverside. Brunton Park was busy too. Carlisle's biggest gate of the season, 10,000 plus, was ready for action, as were United.

The early play was up the Waterworks End. Westwood might just as well have been in the Warwick with us. After just four minutes, Danny Graham nodded past the keeper but two minutes and 37 seconds into first half added time (the referee had only indicated two minutes), United conceded. Bristol went into the break on the up and came out with a spring in their step. They took the lead and added a third.

Season over? Well, no. Oldham had lost too, which meant United were still one of three teams after the last play-off spot. Another was Swansea, who United were playing at Brunton Park the following Saturday. And we thought this was going to be a stress-free end of season.

Brunton Park hosted 10,000 again. Behind the Waterworks goal among the Swansea flags were two from the Harrogate Jacks. I remembered one from the Cardiff Final and (some coincidence this) in a cover lesson at school a few days later, I met the lad whose dad had them made. The boy was called, not surprisingly, Jack.

Forty seconds after kick-off, Swansea scored. Lee Trundle, the player with the quickest feet in the division, had his back to goal but PING! He spun and his left-foot strike was in the top corner before Westwood had time to blink. For the rest of the half Swansea played United off the park. Trundle and Andy Robinson were the two most talented players in the division. I told a Swansea fan that afterwards; he was particularly chuffed as it turned out he was Robinson's brother.

United hung on and came out for the second half a different team. Throughout the campaign, they'd played some really good give-and-go, pass-and-move football. They did so again. MacDonald abandoned the defensive 4-5-1 formation and threw American Johan Smith up front alongside Garner. After four minutes Lumsdon's through ball had Smith snapping at a defender's heels. Suitably unsettled, defender and keeper hesitated, Smith nipped in, rounded the goalie and scored in front of us in the Warwick.

That was the best and worst thing to have happened for the United striker. Smith was full of confidence thereafter, but the blinkers were on. Midway through the second half, United's slender play-off hopes disappeared. That was the moment Smith, with only the keeper to beat, and Chris Lumsdon free to his left, decided to go for goal himself. The keeper blocked his shot.

Smith, who had not learned the meaning of *No 'I' In Team*, had blown United's best chance of winning the game and in so doing, it appeared, blown our dreams of the play-offs, of a game at the new Wembley, of promotion to the Championship.

Still United attacked. Derek Holmes came on and United were playing with three attackers. A draw, after all, wouldn't do. It wouldn't do for Swansea either. Oldham were two-up at half-time, and if they won, both teams' play-off hopes would disappear.

Frantically United and Swansea went at each other. "Someone will score before the end," I said. Swansea did just that. The goal, two minutes into added time, was disputed, as the scorer Darryl Duffy seemed to have bundled a cross over the line with his hand. Ziggy and Kieran thought so, arguing furiously with the referee.

In the context of the game, it mattered, but not to United's play-off hopes. Lose or draw, United were out of contention for the play-offs. The season was over. Carlisle's wannabe hoolies came on to confront the Swansea fans, before a couple of police dogs barked and sent them scurrying off. They weren't well received by Blues who'd stayed put.

Pitch cleared, United's players came out to take their bows. They deserved our applause, and we deserved theirs in return. The season had been a team effort: the players giving their all on the pitch, and off it, we Blues singing our hearts out .

As detailed earlier, the following season (2007-08) ended abruptly with that Jonny Howson goal in the Semi-Final Play-Off, the worst end to a season I've known and that includes the relegations. At least we could see them coming. The pain's gone now and looking back at the four and a half seasons before Howson, United had the most successful spell in the four decades I've followed Carlisle.

To maintain their upwardly mobile momentum, United splashed out £140,000 to buy Joe Garner from Blackburn, breaking the club's transfer record. The season started with a draw at Walsall. Two days later and out of the blue, Neil McDonald was sacked. It was as much mystery as shock. Fred Story simply said the United board had lost confidence in the manager.

McDonald said he hadn't seen that decision coming (we hadn't either) but nothing else. McDonald could come across as arrogant, we'd heard. If that was the case, maybe Story simply didn't warm to his employee. I never met McDonald so couldn't say. I did enjoy watching the football he had United playing. His would be a hard act to follow. Assistant manager Greg Abbott took charge of the team while Story and the Board searched for a new manager. McDonald's departure didn't impact on results. United won four and drew two of the eight league games under Abbot.

We left earlier than usual for the Tranmere home game (one of the two defeats under Abbott) because we had an invitation to meet youth team manager Eric Kinder and Greg himself. I'd written to Kinder about a Sixth Former at the school, Jonny Webb, who'd captained England Schoolboys. I'd never contacted Carlisle about a potential player before, but with Jonny picked for England, he was a bit useful by any standard.

I thought the club might send a scout to a school game; I didn't expect a phone call and invitation "to have coffee with me and Greg." I stressed I hadn't even told the lad I'd written to Carlisle, but Kinder said it was a way of thanking me for telling them about Jonny.

He took us on a tour first. We walked down the tunnel to pitch side, where he asked me about Jonny (in between dodging the spray from the sprinklers.) I told him he was a really nice lad and obviously a very good footballer, but he was bright too and his parents were keen on him finishing his A Levels. We then returned to the coaches' office, where we met assistant manager Dennis Booth, Greg Abbot and chairman Andrew Jenkins. "Is he the one who's trying to find out my team?" Greg said of Sam, who'd asked Eric yesterday if Paul Arnison was starting (he was).

The club was keen to get Jonny to play, even suggesting he could continue with his studies and come up for youth team games at the weekend. I kept emphasising that I hadn't even told Jonny's parents I'd been in touch. When I did they were flattered but Jonny was already in contact with Leeds.

He signed a professional contract with them and made his debut as a second half sub in a FA Cup win at Northampton. He slotted in at the back alongside Ludo Michalik, who'd go on to play for Carlisle; also in the team was Jonny Howson. That alas, was as good as it got for Jonny. A hip injury got worse. He didn't play again for the first team and, at 22, had to retire from football altogether.

Greg's two months in charge had gone pretty well. His last league game was at Hartlepool in October on the same day a permanent appointment was announced, John Ward. 'It's an exciting appointment,' I wrote. 'Ward has a good reputation in the lower leagues, especially after recent success with Cheltenham.'

I remembered Ian Blackstone, a friend from Harrogate, an ex-York and Scarborough pro, telling me Ward was the best manager he'd had, not least because all their pre-season training was done with a football. "And I'd never been fitter," Blackstone added.

The surge of optimism on hearing the news as we drove home from Hartlepool dulled the disappointment of two points dropped. Hartlepool had equalised after 85 minutes. In added time Danny Carlton skied over the bar at the far post from a couple of yards out. He and we missed out on a bonkers celebration at the away end.

The instant impact of a new manager bounce took United higher than the East Stand roof. In Ward's first game in charge, against Millwall at Brunton Park, United scored four before half-time. Afterwards Millwall sacked their manager Willie Donachie, father of Danny, he of track/shell suit fame.

United lost at Yeovil but beat Gillingham, went third and won again at Southend to top the table at the end of October. They stayed there after the famous 3:1 win over Leeds and were never lower than fifth from then on, even after a poor performance in a 0:3 defeat at Bristol Rovers, made worse for us when our complimentaries (with two more promised for my nephews) failed to make it from changing room to ticket office. Paul Thirlwell phoned after the game to apologise.

He was dropped for the next game, home to Hartlepool on New Year's Day, a 4:2 win. I don't think his omission from the team was linked to the ticket mix-up. We saw him in the carpark, where he apologised again. He didn't say he wasn't playing. Steph told us later that Ward had not explained why.

Paul was back in the line-up, replacing suspended Mark Bridge-Wilkinson, for the next game against Port Vale, where recent history (the previous season's encounter at Brunton Park) repeated itself. United had trailed nil-two at half-time and won the game with three goals after the break. The same come-back scenario played out again, with United's recovery sparked by Luke Joyce in his first appearance of the season. He'd replaced Paul at half-time.

I feared he had been made the scapegoat for another poor first half-performance from the whole team. He had, in fact, suffered a recurrence of his calf strain. Steph confirmed that afterwards, but I was reluctant to text her the good news that United had pulled a goal back early in the second half as the scorer was Paul's replacement. That's what comes of getting too close to a player. You lose perspective. I should've been 100% happy that United had scored, but part of me felt for Paul. Joyce also set up the first of Hackney's two goals that won the game.

Thirlwell's injury meant we were unlikely to get complimentaries from him for a while, but we might from the hero of the hour (well, forty-five minutes) Luke Joyce. One of the lads on Sam's PE course was his best mate. Sam sent Luke a congratulatory message via Facebook, to which Luke replied, offering complimentaries.

United's home form in the 2007-08 season was very good; they won 14 league games in a row. That contrasted sharply with away form. In January at Oldham with United two down, the Blues demanded: "Wardy! Wardy! Sort it out!"

After the game you could almost hear my fingers thump the keyboard in anger as I typed (in bold): 'United will not win promotion this season. There, it's written! In black and white, as bold a stat as this: five successive away defeats and no goal in any of them! We've endured losing sequences longer than this, but what makes the run so much harder to bear is the fact, yes, *fact* that this United team is not one which should lose five games in a row. For goodness sake, they've won eight on the trot at home!'

It didn't take a genius to work out what was wrong. United played 4-4-2 at Brunton Park and attacked; away from home, it was 4-5-1 and defend. 'Unfortunately, on the evidence of his management thus far,' I fumed, 'John Ward is a long way from being a football genius.'

I had to admit however, that maybe he was a little closer to that accolade after United dropped just two points from the next 10 games, at the end of which they were up to second, where they remained despite the unbeaten run ending to Forest on a Tuesday night in front of nearly 10,000. No one booed at the end. If United had to lose, at least it was to a decent team. The Forest players were reported to have commented on the United fans' reaction; they were more used to being jeered off the park when they lost at home.

Whether United would get a similar reception against Yeovil on the Saturday was less certain. They were a goal down with only 14 minutes to go. At which point Leechy deliberately turned away from play. We'd blamed him for the scoreline; United had a poor record when he came to games. He'd offered to go outside if United were still a goal down in added time but did the noble thing by facing the back of the Warwick instead as Mark Bridge-Wilkinson lined up to take a corner.

He swung it in, Peter Murphy stooped to head, the ball took a couple of deflections and suddenly there it was, popping past the Yeovil keeper into the net. GOAL! Thanks Leechy! Ninety minutes passed and Ward subbed on young striker Gary Madine. Bridge-Wilkinson looped a free-kick into the box. The ball held up in the wind and fell Madine's way. He had his back to goal but still might've been tempted to go for a header. Instead, he did the sensible thing, chesting the ball to Scott Dobie, who swung his right foot, connected and YES! It was in. Another three points.

Five clear with a game in hand over Doncaster and just four to go. 'United weren't just back to winning ways,

but well and truly on course to the Championship!'
I wrote, my prophecy of doom after Oldham long
forgotten.

That gap increased to six after a draw with champions-
elect Swansea. The point mattered more than the
performance. In fairness, Swansea were the better
team. Were Doncaster to lose to Swindon on the Friday
night, United would go to Elland Road a few hours
later knowing that a win would more or less secure
promotion. "How sweet, oh how sweet, would that
be!" I wished.

I never got to enjoy that. Doncaster beat Swindon and
Carlisle lost at Leeds, then again at home to Southend
to a last minute-goal. They'd been poor against
Southend in the first half but fluked an early equaliser in
the second and were beginning to look the better team,
when David Raven slid in for a challenge on Nicky
Bailey.

He'd already upset home fans with a five-star writhing-
in-agony performance to get Bridge-Wilkinson booked.
When Bailey came back on, he flattened Hackney
straight away. He was booked but should've been sent
off. Raven's challenge on Bailey didn't look that bad,
but the referee couldn't wait to get his card out. Raven
was off. Bailey went right up there with Paul Huntington
in our list of unpopular opponents.

United's swagger became a stagger then a stumble.
Southend's last-minute winner would've been a sickener
in any game, but in the context of United's promotion

push, it was two fingers down the throat. At least Doncaster didn't win, so United were still two points ahead with two games to go. Next up was a tricky trip to relegation threatened Millwall, a place where teams needed that extra bottle.

I followed the game via the radio, messageboard and texts from Sam, who was just as nervous in Leeds. Doncaster were at home to relegated Luton. After 34 minutes Doncaster went ahead, the goal taking them second above United on goal difference. Just before half-time things got worse: Millwall scored. Soon after, Livesey conceded a penalty, was sent off and Millwall added their second from the spot.

Reaching for the straws, I could still dream, for if Luton equalised and Forest didn't score, United would be second again. But on 84 minutes Doncaster scored another, then Forest grabbed a late winner. It was a worse-case scenario. United were fourth behind Doncaster and Forest.

The last game was at home to Bournemouth. United drew; a win wouldn't have promoted them anyway. Forest pinched the last promotion place. Doncaster would play Southend in the play-offs and United would meet Leeds. And you know what happened next.

It was United's best season for 22 years in terms of where they finished in the League. I made it to 35 games and Sam 38. Looking back however, even now, I can't help but feel United blew it, both at the end of the regular season and in the Play-Off semi-final. The run of five consecutive away defeats still rankles. Ward took over when United were fourth and they finished the season in the same position. Fourth of twenty-four is good, don't get me wrong, but one more win would've won them promotion. One more win, a season at least in the Championship, and the last 15 years would've been very different.

That said, there was every reason to be realistically optimistic at the start of the 2008-09 season. United only lost two players: Garner to Forest for over a million and Westwood to Coventry for half a million. Returning to Brunton Park were Richard Keogh from Bristol City (seven decent games on loan in 2007-08) and, even better, Michael Bridges, signed on a season long loan from Hull. Bridges' two seasons on Humberside hadn't been productive. He was injured (again) and other players were preferred in the line-up when Bridges was fit. He only started nine league games in two seasons and spent much of 2008 on loan at Sydney FC, Australia.

The season opened really well, with four wins and a draw. Even Danny Carlton scored, twice, on the opening day at Bristol Rovers. The striker hadn't managed one the previous season. United's winning sequence however, was the falsest of dawns. United lost at Scunthorpe, home to Leeds (double the pain) and on the final whistle after a fourth straight defeat, the man on the Brunton Park PA played *Help!* by the Beatles.

Ward was taking a lot of the flack, some of it deserved. He continued to play Carlton rather than Bridges, giving support to the rumour that Bridges was the Board's signing, not the manager's.

It was six defeats in seven before we travelled to Colchester. Their new ground is on the outskirts, tucked just inside a by-pass, a long way from the town centre. We went in search of a pub. It was quite a quest. First we had to find someone to ask. Not easy. Eventually we spotted a local who said a pub was half-an-hour's walk away. We weren't far from the rugby club however, so we crossed a pitch towards it, only to incur the wrath of a jobsworth who came on to the balcony and yelled at us to get off it.

We weren't allowed in, of course. Two pucker rugby club officials said there was a pub "straight down the road." We passed the car-park attendant, exchanged pleasantries, and headed "straight down the road." No pub. We turned round and headed back. But not through the car park. The attendant wouldn't let us in so we cut through a hedge and walked back across the pitches. Welcoming place, Colchester.

It wasn't a great start to matchday. We did receive three free tickets from Luke and with one good turn deserving another, we gave the extra one to a random Blue, making his day, he said gratefully. That, alas, was as good as the Feel Good got.

United were two down after 13 minutes and three behind by the half hour. Final score 0:5. Back home I fumed: '*Ward said of one of keeper Ben Williams' clangers, "I feel for him, but I don't feel sorry for him."*

My sentiments exactly. I feel for you, Mr Ward, but not sorry for you. You had to be there, it was your job. I didn't but I was and wish I hadn't been.'

They lost again on the Tuesday, at home to Hartlepool. 'John Ward might just have written the shortest suicide note in football history this evening, printing the names C-A-R-L-T-O-N and J-E-F-F S-M-I-T-H on the team sheet,' I vented. 'Picking them is the equivalent to falling on your sword.'

Ward tetchily refused to answer questions about his future. Asked whether he'd lost the dressing-room, his denial was barely audible. Luke reckoned Ward could be gone by the end of the week. He didn't want Abbott to take the reins, because he'd just broken into the team. "It's not that Abbott doesn't like me, but he loves Thirlwell, Lumsdon and Bridge-Wilkinson."

'They're the lucky ones,' I noted. 'No one at Brunton Park has love for Ward anymore.'

His end was nigh. In November United conceded an early goal again at Stockport, then two more. Ten league games, one draw, nine defeats. United had plunged to one place above the relegation zone. Ward disappeared quickly down the tunnel on the final whistle. That was the last we saw of him. On Monday morning he was sacked. United's Board had bitten the bullet. Ward's assistant Greg Abbot took his place.

10

Greg, Gary, Goodison

United's results improved under Abbott. Michael
Bridges came back into the line-up; Ward had only ever
used him as a sub. After a 3:0 victory over Huddersfield
on Boxing Day, I wondered whether Ward would still
have been in a job had he played Bridges. He almost
deserved the sack for denying Blues the rare opportunity
to watch someone of his genius.

Abbott borrowed keeper Tim Krul from Newcastle,
who starred in a four-game unbeaten run (10 points)
starting with that Huddersfield victory. Remarkably
Abbott never recorded three successive league wins in
his time in charge, which was to last nearly five years.

Krul kept three clean sheets in a row and had a blinder
at Elland Road. Little wonder he went on to play in a
World Cup quarter-final. He seemed to fill his goal and
bossed everything in the box. Krul pulled off one great
save by throwing his huge frame to block a close-range
header, by when United had taken the lead. Danny
Graham steered the ball through the legs of Ankergren

and I found myself dancing in the aisle and in the gangway behind.

The Leeds boys in the South Stand below tried to taunt us with, *"Two Nil and You Fucked It Up!"* with reference to the play-off semi-final. The lads behind had the retort: *"WEMBLEY! AND YOU FUCKED IT UP!"* Thank you again Doncaster. More to the point, Leeds were f-ing this one up too. Eight minutes later, United scored again in front of the Kop. Bridges seemed to have wasted his chance as Ankergren and a defender slid in to challenge, but the latter got more of the former than the ball, and Bridges was left to aim for an unguarded net.

"How did Bridges celebrate?" Bryan asked later, for the ex-Leeds man had said he wouldn't celebrate a goal against his former club.

"I don't know," I said. "I was too busy dancing in the gangway!" I hugged Sam, Grant and a random Blue pogoing past!

"But how bad will it be now if United mess this up?" I thought. I wasn't going to count any winning chickens. I wasn't going to look at my watch second half either, for it would be a long, long one.

Anti-talismen Andy Robinson and Lee Trundle came on as subs but still I didn't check the time, not even when the number of Leeds fans leaving prematurely suggested not long was left. *"CAN WE PLAY YOU EVERY WEEK?"* we taunted, and best of all, *"THERE'S ONLY*

ONE UNITED!" When I dared look at my watch it showed 47 minutes and there were only four minutes of added time. Victory now was ours to enjoy. I hadn't felt the cold at all and couldn't wait to gloat among the Leeds lobby at school.

United beat Milton Keynes a week later, second only to Leeds in the list of Clubs We Don't Like, before things took a U-turn for the worse. From the end of January through to the penultimate game of the season, United won just two of 20.

Desperate times caused for desperate management. Abbott signed Ian Harte, the ex-Leeds and Eire left-back. "Make sure their right-winger is slower than your grandma!" Leechy warned Sam, but Harte played centre-back on his debut in a draw with Northampton. He picked up the sponsor's Man of the Match award despite breaking a bone in his hand. He didn't play again until the last two matches of the season.

There was some respite from the sorry 20-game sequence on the away day to Leicester, which we'd penned in as the glamour trip of the season. It didn't disappoint.

Great football days are made of this: an easy drive to a Big Ground; picking up Bryan; finding the ground and a parking place with ease (albeit an expensive one, £6); a pub right outside the car park; a couple of pints outside in the sun with other Blues; being propositioned by lap dancers from a pub nearby (we weren't tempted tho pre match footie chat did for us, thank you);

chalking off a new ground; the friendliest steward of the season, a Brian Blessed lookalike, who directed us to seats together on the very back row; a cracking atmosphere amongst the 991 Blues; a great performance from United; and a great ending.

With Krul back at Newcastle, Ben Williams came into the team. He had a blinder. *'The reason they didn't score more than two was down to Williams' goalkeeping brilliance,'* I wrote, *'a phrase you won't have read before in any report of mine this season. '*

Bridges gave United the lead on the half hour; Leicester equalised before Mattie Fryatt, a former loanee at Brunton Park, put Leicester ahead in the 88th minute. *"Even when United play well, they still lose,"* I sighed. *Or to put it another way, as Leicester's bare-bellied Drummer Boy and mates very loudly did:* "One-nil and you fucked it up!"

"Premiership and you fucked it up!" we bellowed back. It wasn't much consolation.

*Into added time. Kavanagh spread the ball wide to left-back Michael Liddle. He crossed, Dobie got above and between two defenders, headed the ball down and OH YES! The keeper could only get a hand on it and the ball was over the line and in the net and we were bouncing up and down and I was grabbing the Bloke In Front as well as Sam and Bryan and OH YES! Football **is** (underlined, italics, bold) a Beautiful Game. Fact.*

Only the game wasn't over, for a chip into the Carlisle box dropped behind a jumping Blue to a Leicester player at the far post. From where we were we couldn't see what happened next, but from the sounds of it, his shot beat Williams. Keogh however, cleared off the line. Then they had a corner, that was headed wide, and with the goal-kick in the air, the ref blew.

The stress-free celebration began. Leicester's fans couldn't wait to leave. We wanted to stay. The players came over and we left the stadium with 20,000 others and a mighty spring in our step.

A jaunty jog post-match was rare, alas. United were in trouble, relegation bound come the last away game at Cheltenham. Looking at the bigger picture, it was a tribute to the meritocracy of football that we were travelling to a ground as small as Whaddon Road in the same season we'd been to Leeds, Leicester and Huddersfield. We knew which sized grounds we'd rather be visiting next season: Charlton, Southampton and Norwich or Barnsley were coming down from the Championship; Boston were coming up to League Two from the Conference.

It was only Harte's second game after that broken bone in his hand. He replaced Peter Murphy, which wasn't a bad move by Abbott. That decision was further vindicated when Harte scored.

"I can see him scoring," Sam said, just before Harte whipped the ball over a free-kick wall and into the top corner. The keeper didn't have a chance. ONE-NIL! The Great Escape was on! But put one foot into the comfort zone, lift your eye too high above the horizon,

and football's going to trip you up. United didn't concede a goal but did lose a player. Evan Horwood had been booked for picking the ball up and walking away with it to delay a free-kick, a stupid way to get a yellow card. He fouled again on the edge of the box and was off.

Horwood's dismissal came after 67 minutes. United hung on. Then after 81 they were down to nine, a Cheltenham header beat Ben Williams and was stopped on the line by a Carlisle hand. The referee had no option; he had to send the player off and award the penalty. The United player? Michael Bridges.

So United's most talented player, trudged off. It was his last act in a United shirt. He'd miss the final game of the season. He took with him United's hope of saving the game and, indeed, of saving the season. Williams dived to his left. The penalty went to his right.

Cheltenham nearly scored again in their next attack, the ball whizzing over Williams' bar. Another shot hit the foot of the post. They kept four players forward, and the keeper went up for their next corner. Cheltenham had to score to stay up. It was frenetic stuff; United would have their chance. They did.

The abiding image from the end of last season was Howson's shot rolling past Westwood. This season had one too. In the chaotic last few minutes, as both teams frantically raced against the clock to grab a goal and avoid relegation, Ian Morris, United's rangy loanee from Scunthorpe, ran onto Lewis Neal's through ball, skipped past the one remaining defender, took aim, shot – and the keeper saved.

A thin fluorescent line of police and stewards threaded onto the pitch and faced the United fans. But no one was in the mood to go on the pitch. Cheltenham were relegated and thoroughly deserved to be. If they couldn't beat a team as poor as United with a two-man advantage, they didn't deserve to stay up.

There is still the faintest flicker of hope for United. If they beat Millwall (yeah, right!) next week and Brighton don't beat Stockport; and if Northampton lose to MK Dons on Tuesday and Leeds on Saturday… But that's hope for you. Teasing, torturing. Because it isn't going to happen. This, after all, was United's eleventh consecutive game without a win, six of them 1:1 draws. United had been ahead in all six. How are they going to beat, of all teams, third-placed Millwall, who'll be doing everything they can to stay third and avoid MK Dons and Leeds in the play-off semi? Yet there is still a chance. There is still hope and that makes the agony of expectation even worse.

United needed help more than hope and needed that help to come from the two teams I wished ill on week in week out: Milton Keynes and Leeds. In midweek Milton Keynes did United a huge favour by winning at Northampton. A point for the Cobblers would've put them beyond United's reach.

So United needed Leeds to beat Northampton at Elland Road. If they didn't, even if Carlisle beat Millwall, they would finish below Northampton. United had to win and Northampton lose. Brighton were also in the mix. If they lost and United won, Carlisle would finish above them too, but Brighton were on a roll and at home to Stockport, who were safe with nothing to play for.

The odds weren't in United's favour, yet come Saturday I was full of optimism. I went on a United messageboard at 06.22:

And may I be the first to say...

U-NI-TED!
COME ON YOU BLUES!
WE LOVE YOU CARLISLE, WE DO!
C AND AN A AND AN R AND L, I AND S AND L
AND E! U-N-I-T-E-D, CARLISLE UNITED FC!
COME ON CARLISLE!
U-NI-TED!

My call to arms over the e-waves was answered:

Repeated loudly from Knaresborough all the way to BP this morning.
COME ON YOU BLUUUUEEEEESSSSSSSSS!!!!!!!!!!!

And from Loiner, a Leeds fan: *Good luck Carlisle, you can do it. Northampton will lose so just do your part.*

Another Carlisle fan, 'Rids', spoke for all true Blues: *"This season has been such a mixture of disappointment, anger and frustration. However, today I shall forget those feelings for 90 minutes and cheer my team on like it's a cup final. The next few months without the buzz/ nerves/butterflies on a Saturday afternoon will be so dull. This is why we are football supporters, this is why we love Carlisle United. Like it or not we're all hooked and we'll all be with them for years to come. They may be in a bit of a mess at the moment, but they are our mess. And I will certainly be there through thick and thin next year. Be Just and Fear Not!"*

Just to be on the safe side, Sam and I changed our pre-match routine. Rather than heading down Championship Walk (the back of the houses on Warwick Road), we headed straight down the Warwick. "Today it's 'Not Relegation Walk'," we agreed.

The Sportsman was busier than usual. The lads from the Warwick who drank there even started chanting. In all the optimism and excitement, I left my third woolly hat of the season in the bar, plus the programme. But in the club shop I had met Jimmy Glass (invited up to sprinkle some of his magic dust) and I'd remembered to take out the newspaper he'd signed, so everything was okay.

The Warwick was fuller than usual. A couple in front moaned throughout and didn't return for the second half. We'd seen them off with our singing and shouting. There were over 9,000 Blues and a few hundred from Millwall. The atmosphere was the best it had been all season, with all three sides of the ground loud and proud to get behind United (bar the miserable couple.)

United looked up for it and Leeds had started well too. From Elland Road Leechy texted Sam to say so. Things looked promising and a whole lot better six minutes in. Joe Anyinsah laid the ball back to Kavanagh. Distance and speed can be deceptive from the back of the Warwick. "He's too far out and the shot's going wide," was what I started to think, but before I'd got more than a couple of words in – BAM! The ball was in the back of the net.

Kav's strike was an absolute screamer. The replay on The Big Screen at the Waterworks showed just how hard Kav had hit the ball. He'd done that before, so it wasn't a surprise, just a delight! The keeper barely twitched before it was in and Sam and I were hugging each other. Soon after, Leechy called. Sam turned to get the phone out of his pocket, so I knew something was up.

"GET IN!" he shouted. Leeds had scored. A few seconds later the rest of the crowd heard. United were out of the bottom four. They dominated the half but didn't score again. At half-time we shook our heads. "Same old story," sighed Sam. "We needed a second when we were on top. The next ten to 15 minutes are massive."

Five minutes into those massive ten to 15 came the biggest moment of the match and, let's face it, of the season. United attacked down the right, the ball was headed out of the box and bounced invitingly in front of Paul Thirlwell. Given time, he said on Radio Cumbria afterwards, "I'd have put it in the carpark." Resisting his instinct to bring the ball down and pass it sideways, he thumped it goalward. And how.

From where we were the ball was in from the moment he connected. Like Kav's goal, the Millwall keeper didn't even get close to its slipstream. Paul wheeled away to his left, skidded on his knees in front of the Main Stand, and was lost beneath elated teammates.

The Paddock heard before we did. Murmurs turned to cheers, and Sam was answering his phone again. "Two-nil Leeds!" An hour gone, just 30 minutes to go. It was looking good, very good, for United. This was our day. Leeds scored a third, and the minutes gradually, gradually slipped by. I was wishing my life away again. It had to be done.

The teens gathered at the foot of the Warwick, spilled over onto the side of the pitch, ran on to it prematurely, and were waved off by Williams. It was game almost over. The whistle blew, the lads ran on, the players charged off, the police lined up in front of the Millwall fans, and United were safe. Season over. United were still in League One. We'd be watching our football next season at Charlton, Southampton and Norwich instead of Burton, Barnet and Accrington.

We didn't go on the pitch but jauntily jogged back down Warwick Road. My dad phoned and there were texts from Steph Thirlwell plus some of the staff football team on tour in Scarborough. I was never going to be there; United needed me more. It felt like we'd won promotion.

In the end, it had all been pretty painless. Not in the way that we'd imagined as we drove back from

Cheltenham, with the heart-breaking image of Morris's miss and the head-shaking reality of the league table merely prolonging the inevitable agony of relegation another seven days. No. It was surprisingly straightforward and stress free. It might sound oxymoronic, but well before quarter-to-five and the last minutes of the season, United were in the relegation-comfort zone.

Going back to the start of these memoirs, that huge swing of fortune, of emotion, of well-being with the world, depended on two kicks of a football: one from Graham Kavanagh, the other from Paul Thirlwell. If I were being pedantic, just one would've done; Thirlwell's, so far as the league table turned out, was academic.

I'd forgotten what a turbulent season it had been, no doubt partly because the last (and lasting) memory of it was that whoosh of relief that carried me all through the summer. The final line of the last of my 33 match reports said as much: *'It'll be an even better summer now. Roll on August. I'm going to miss United these next three months.'*

Despite being able to rewind vividly to key moments from games decades ago, football fans in some respect have the attention span of a goldfish. Millwall, the last game of the season, was so good all I wanted was to be at the next match and have the chance to feel the same again.

After seven seasons of excitement at the top or bottom of the tables, Carlisle were due a mid-table, (relatively) stress-free 2009-10. They got it. United's highest position was ninth in early September, their lowest 21st in mid-October. Once the season settled down, they were in little danger of either relegation or making the play-offs.

That isn't to say it wasn't a fun or exciting season; far from it for the Harrogate Blues. For one thing, United's cup runs were memorable in all three competitions. Off the pitch, *So Jack Ashurst* made a one-off return and I had even more of a vested interested in the club's fortunes. I was now a sponsor.

The lads from Athletico, the staff football team, had clubbed together and presented me with a 50th birthday present: sponsorship of Carlisle's young striker Gary Madine. The package included, the letter said, "Acknowledgement that you are Gary's sponsor in every home game of the season; the first Matchday magazine; home and away shirts; and a meet and greet session with all the players later in the season at Foxy's Restaurant."

I don't know how much the sponsorship cost. Sam had organised it, but they did say Gary was one of the cheaper players on offer ("we don't like you that much.") However much they paid, they had full value for money.

"Gary had an up and down season one way or the other," was the official line in the letter that came at the end of it, thanking me for sponsoring him. Gary's antics kept the Harrogate lads amused all season and beyond. He's probably still the only Carlisle player most of them could name.

In brief, here's Gary's season: on the bench at the start of the season; in front of The Bench and fined for being drunk and disorderly in September; loaned to Championship club Coventry City in October; back to Carlisle and into the starting XI; loaned out again to League Two Chesterfield in February; arrested for assault in The Beehive; back to Carlisle again; scoring at Wembley; finishing the campaign as United's main striker.

United's season was uneventful by comparison, at least in the League. They had a strong defence but were short up front. Their two top scorers were gone: Danny Graham had left for Watford, Michael Bridges returned to Hull, then briefly to Milton Keynes (I'll forgive him that, especially as he didn't stay long) before moving to Australia. United failed to replace them effectively but did find goalscoring riches elsewhere, not enough to make the play-offs, but enough to keep out them out of relegation's reach. The chunky nugget was Ian Harte and his 16 League One goals.

In December we did Gillingham away. Hannah was coming to the end of her first term at Millennium Performing Arts College in Woolwich, living within earshot of the Valley, Charlton's ground. It was tough leaving Hannah, knowing that we wouldn't see her as regularly as we did Sam, so picking her up to drive home for Christmas put us in a happy, holiday mood. Sam came too because, fancy that, United were playing just down the M2.

Priestfield used to boast the oldest stand in the country, but that was on one of the three sides that had been replaced by shiny new structures. The open terrace of the away end had gone too and been replaced by, er, well... It hadn't been replaced, not permanently anyway. The away fans' section was half of a temporary stand, and believe me, you didn't want to look between the gaps in the slats. It was a long way down. Even the locals weren't enamoured by the place. "They're going to knock the ground down and build a slum," muttered one we met.

It had been a few years since Hannah had been to a game with us; it had been 31 years to the weekend that I'd seen United away for the first time at the same venue. That game ended 0:0 and so did the 2009 one.

We were happy to have Hannah home for the holiday period, which was a cheerful one for United too. They picked up seven points from nine in the three December games after Gillingham. I was pleased for manager Greg Abbott. My opinion of him had changed after a game, not at Brunton Park, but Wetherby High School.

I'd taken a Sixth Form team there and was surprised (mildly excited too) by the referee, one of the teachers, wearing a Carlisle United training top. I asked him at half-time where he'd got it. "From that lad's dad," he said, pointing to one of his players. "He's the Carlisle manager."

I scanned the touchline for Dad without luck, but I had a chat with Greg's lad afterwards.

"He's trying so hard!" he told me. "It's really tough for him."

Son of Greg went on to say Richard Offiong (one goal in 19 games) had been signed more on the strength of video clips than scouts' reports because his dad was under pressure to sign someone, almost anyone, to play up front. Greg's son was quite emotional as he defended dad. It made me appreciate, which I don't often do, that Greg the Manager was just one part of Greg the Man, and his lad was telling me about Greg the Dad. I had more sympathy for Greg after hearing that from his son. It helped, of course, that United's results were improving; in the FA Cup Third Round United were drawn at Everton.

From the outside Goodison was as grey and grim as the skies, a huge box shoved between terraced housing and a school yard. A tight squeeze indeed. Everton had stuck a third tier on the main stand, but from the opposite side, it looked precariously balanced, the seats seemingly stacked steeper than 45 degrees. There wasn't much space on our side either, with little room in the concourse and the narrow stairs to the upper tier. I wouldn't have fancied making a hasty exit. Still, it was ten times better than the away end at Gillingham. At least we had a roof above our heads.

The chants were familiar, and whilst there was nothing wrong at all with *U-NI-TED... C-AND-AN-A-AND-R-AND-L...*, *WE ARE CARLISLE FROM THE NORTH... WISE MEN SAY* and *GLORY GLORY...* it was a pity we didn't try something new, though I thought I heard strains of *CAN'T HEAR THE EVERTON SING*, which some Ultras on messageboards had urged us to try. What was easy to hear however, was the Everton fans *not* singing. There was no contest at Goodison. It was all over bar the Blue Army shouting.

On the pitch Everton had the 3:1 beating of United. One reason United lost was because Everton's crucial second goal should've been disallowed after Mattie Robson was pulled back in the build-up. Everton should've been down to 10 because Fellaini, already on a yellow card, flattened Kav off the ball. The referee either didn't see it or chose not to.

United weren't outplayed. Indeed, there was nothing between the teams whatsoever, which suggested that either Everton played badly, or United played really well. I'd go for the latter and so would all Blues and most Evertonians. Two of the school's Sixth Formers were amongst the home fans and said as much.

James Vaughan put the home side ahead after 12 minutes (he was still scoring against United a decade later for Tranmere) but Clayton soon equalised and Everton only went ahead again in the 82nd minute. Their third was a penalty with the penultimate kick of the game. Phil Neville went up in my estimation because his first reaction at the final whistle was to turn and applaud the travelling support.

As Sam and I trotted down the East Lancs Road (closed to allow fans out; it had been a 30,000 plus crowd after all), we felt good. We'd come to Goodison, we'd seen United put in a cracking display, and although Carlisle hadn't conquered on the pitch, we had off it. The Feel

Good Factor lasted well into Monday morning, when it received a very big boost indeed.

At break there was a note in my pigeon-hole asking me to phone Sam's former primary school teacher about a 'sport resource.' I assumed she might want to borrow something from the PE Department. I gave her a call.

"Did you get my cryptic message?" she asked.

"Yes. What can I get for you?" I said.

"No," she replied. "I have got something for *you*. Carlisle played at Everton recently, didn't they?" My ears pricked. Yes, I said, go on. "Well, one of the Carlisle players gave Danny his shirt after the game."

Danny, remember, was Danny Donachie, her nephew and Famous for Fifteen Minutes as a United Sub. He'd given me his club shell suit and was now a physio at Everton.

"He thought you might like it."

"LIKE I?!" I yelled in delight. "LIKE IT? I'D LOVE IT!"

Next question: "Whose shirt is it?"

"I hadn't heard of him," she said. "Hold on..." she went and got the shirt. "Kavan-"

"KAVANAGH! Graham Kavanagh!" I said. "He's only one of Carlisle's best players!"

"Well, it's here if you want it," she said. So at lunchtime I ditched the lesson planning and ran to her house. She didn't know why Kav had given Danny the shirt, but I assumed it was because Danny had done some physio on him. Danny had taken the shirt home for his sons but they were Everton fans and didn't want it.

Needless to say, Sam was as excited as me to hear the tale and to get his hands on the shirt. Diane didn't really share our euphoria, but did say, "I suppose it's like Hannah getting one of Byonce's shoes!" Getting my hands on Gary Madine's shirt, promised me as his sponsor, wouldn't be as straightforward. More of that anon.

Our next away day was even bigger than Everton: that Johnstone's Paint Trophy Semi Final First Leg at Leeds. United won 2:1 and three weeks later reached Wembley after the shoot-out success at the end of the Second Leg, despite the Keogh penalty miss.

Keogh's performances and rapid rise to cult hero had helped galvanise the team. As with most of my favourite Carlisle players over the years, Keogh played every game as if his life depended on winning it. If a side has a player like Keogh, teammates respond. Those that don't (think back to whoever it was pulled out of the tackle that so upset Kevin Gray) wouldn't last long before being hauled to account.

At Southend, Paul Thirlwell left three complimentaries and we offered our spare to a Blue outside the ground. She said she already had a couple. "Who from?" I asked.

"Richard Keogh," she replied. "I'm his mum!"

"So you're the lady to thank!" I said, after a *KE-OGH* burst from Sam and me. She was a friendly mum and we had quite a chat.

"That was the first penalty Richard had ever missed," she told us (reference the Leeds shoot-out.) "He used to play centre-forward all the time." I wonder if Greg had known that when he was desperately searching for a striker? He was a messy lad too, she said. When he shared a Bristol flat "there were pizza trays everywhere!" Now he was living with his girlfriend, who fed him better. Maybe it was her we should've thanked for giving us the new slim-line, cult-hero model.

Southend's away entrance façade was only marginally more appealing than the back end of Gillingham's away end. Ramshackle at best, the modern automatic turnstiles looked ridiculously out of place. The ground was better inside: tidy, compact, with the home end opposite probably the smallest double-decker in the league. I counted only seven rows in each tier.

United blew a two-goal lead against a bottom-four team which hadn't won in 11 and played for over a quarter of the game with only 10 men, but it wasn't all bad. United's points tally rose to 48 (only two to safety and it was still March) and no one got injured or suspended. That mattered because the following weekend would see a return trip south for the JPT Final with Southampton.

The New Wembley dominated the skyline of north-west London, dwarfing the surrounding city scape of warehouses, soulless retail outlets and clogged roads. In keeping with the environs, the façade of the stadium was drab and grey too. It didn't look a football ground. Okay, there was the arch, but that seemed more an after-thought, a bit like a racing stripe on a Reliant Robin. We could've been heading for a call-centre.

Real estate in London was still expensive. We paid £10 for our spot on a side-street. There were a lot of early arrivals walking around the stadium but you wouldn't have known one end of the ground from the other. There's the Bobby Moore statue as a reference point but little else, bar two long queues from the walkway wall across the forecourt to two toilets which, graciously, had been opened.

Yes. Two toilets. So you get there in good time, as you have to, given the decision to build the biggest football ground in England in just about the least accessible place in the country, to find the longest queue for a loo you're ever likely to suffer in. It's a place of superlatives all right, and little colour. Escalators took us to the Upper Tier, with stewards at the top and bottom of each one, but their day-glow jackets were the only breaks to the drab interior.

Wembley's ticketing system was automatic of course, but just as many staff were employed the other side to search you. I had a Moscovite pat me down. There were a lot more stewards around in the concourse, and I must admit, given the glum faces the last time we were down

Wembley way, their cheerful demeanour was a big improvement. There were also troops of cleaners sweeping up as you ate and drank. It was almost as if Wembley Inc was worried we'd mess the place up.

It had a lot of food and drink outlets too. They had as much real-estate floor space as the toilets; there's no money to be made from the latter after all. At half-time I gave up queuing to get into one, so rather than scrum for a pee, I sat cross-legged second half.

At least the inside of the stadium was spectacular, albeit too red, and it didn't bother me that I was so high up, despite being far from the noisy hard core of United's support. There wasn't, alas, much to sing or shout about for United picked a bad day to implode.

It all went wrong from the 15th minute when Peter Murphy stuck up his hand to stop a cross. It was so obvious and inexplicable a handball that even the referee did a doubletake, as if he too couldn't believe it. Murph was booked (he could have been sent off), Ricky Lambert didn't miss penalties and United never got over the shock

The only consolations were that the 1:4 scoreline could've been worse and Madine scored, flicking Harte's late free-kick into the far corner. That brought his total of goals for the season (two) level with his number of arrests and it made his sponsor happy. As much as I left the stadium wishing a swift return with United, my overall impression was on the 'under' side of 'whelmed' by the new Wembley experience.

The season meandered to a mid-table finish. Even the visit of Leeds lacked some of its edge. Win or lose, it wouldn't make one jot of difference to where United would be playing the next season. What's more, as the game was during the school holidays, I wouldn't have any grief from the plastics on Monday. They'd have forgotten all about it come the start of term, if indeed, they knew the game was on at all.

That was just as well because United lost 1:3. Harte clapped the Leeds fans at the end before United's. Rumour said he had a Leeds tattoo and desperately wanted to return to Elland Road. "If that's the case, let him go," I muttered. "But we'll keep his goals, thank you."

The game ended with the pitch ringed by more police than I could remember at Brunton Park, but an invasion, given the result and United's poor show, was never going to happen. It was also unlikely that the two teams would meet again in the near future, which suited me just fine; I was sick of Leeds. This was the tenth game with them in three seasons.

'Sod off to the Championship!' I wrote at the end of the report, which is what they did. Leeds finished runners-up to Norwich and haven't been back to Bruton Park since.

A season which had been dormant for too long proved it was far from extinct with (and I quote the roar from the away section of Carrow Road): *"The best trip we've ever been on!"* Or to put it another way: *"Championship and we're taking the piss!"*

The Norwich fans' party had started loudly a couple of hours earlier, for we weren't long in the Queen of Icini pub on the riverside before the place took off. Let's face it, Norwich fans had plenty to sing about. They had lost 1:7 to Colchester on the first day of the season, sacked their manager, appointed the Colchester boss then whizzed through League One.

The pub rocked and both sets of fans joined together in a rendition of that popular football ditty *We all hate Leedscum!* We had plenty to sing about in Carrow Road too because Madine scored inside sixty seconds. Harte quickly added a free-kick and United won 2:0, gate-crashers at the party, grabbing the best beer before leaving with the most attractive girl. It was that good an afternoon it felt as if Carlisle had won the league. We left Norwich to their celebrations, looking forward to hosting our own promotion party in 12 months.

A week or so later I received a parcel from the club containing, I assumed as I opened it eagerly, Gary Madine's home and away shirts, as promised as part of the sponsorship package. Only it didn't. The shirts were the red away and white third-choice kits. Sam phoned the club to complain.

"Ah yes, Mr Pocock," the voice at the end of the phone explained. "I'm afraid we don't have the blue one. Gary threw it to the away fans at Norwich."

"No he didn't," Sam replied. "We were there and that didn't happen. Besides, United were playing in red."

I wrote to Chairman Andrew Jenkins. Almost by return of post I received an apology: "It is certainly not the treatment I would expect any supporter should receive, let alone one as loyal as yourself. In the present climate we should be falling over backwards to please and grow our supporter base."

Apology accepted. Jenkins had also investigated, at Sam's request, the lack of a Meet the Player gathering for sponsors. It was cancelled, he said, due to "the hectic Wembley organisations." He invited me to phone him at the club at the start of the following season and he would arrange for me to meet Gary.

"He is a young lad trying to find his way in life and he has my support in what is a difficult time for him," wrote Jenkins, who struck me as being a thoroughly good egg. A blue Gary Madine shirt arrived just a day or so later.

Early the following season I saw Jenkins outside the ground and thanked him for dealing with our complaint. Once again, he was profuse in his apologies. I didn't phone him to arrange that meeting with Gary at Brunton Park; there was no need as we were to meet the lad at United's first away game of the new season.

11

Home Park to Wembley

United's starting XI for their first game of the 2010-11 season featured six debutants, including forward Francois Zoko, already the next cult hero after pre-season friendlies. Keogh had moved to Championship Coventry. I saw Zoko in the carpark before the opener against Brentford and asked him, in my best pigeon-French: *"Vous etes dans le premier onze?"*

"Oui!" he replied, smiling.

Zoko brought smiles to most of the six thousand crowd during the game too. He was skilful, bemusing opponents and teammates alike. "We haven't a clue what he's going to do half the time," Greg admitted. Zoko had played at the top level in France, Belgium and Turkey.

Madine and Harte, with another successful penalty just before half-time, scored in the 2:0 win. At the break Bryan showed me the embryonic League table. United were top.

I whisked Diane away for a mid-week wedding anniversary break in Paris. On the train to the airport for the flight home we passed La Stade de France. Twenty-four hours later I'd be just as excited catching sight of Home Park, Plymouth.

It wasn't the brightest idea to schedule Carlisle's longest away game of the season on a Saturday in August, but we'd not done Plymouth before. Sam and I had an overnight stop in Gloucester (I headed off soon after we'd landed) before making an early start on Saturday.

It was just as well we did. Rob and Sue set off from Swindon, where they'd broken their journey, and only just made kick-off. Luckily we arrived at Home Park in good time, but only after taking five hours to drive 172 miles. The car park next to the ground was accessible to ordinary supporters; it was also free. I liked Plymouth immediately.

Home Park, as the name says, edged onto a park. I wish I'd brought either my running shoes and/or a plastic tub for blackberries; the park's paths and bushes beckoned. We walked back to the ground to wait for the coach. When it arrived chairman Andrew Jenkins gave us two complimentaries to add to the pair Paul Thirlwell had for us. He was confident United would win. When Gary Madine walked past, I seized my chance.

"Gary! Can we have a photo, please? I was your sponsor last season."

"Ah! The Harrogate Blues," Gary said, guiltily.

"I wrote you a letter at the start of the season," I told him. With the football lads making me his sponsor,

I'd invited Gary to reciprocate and be Honorary President of the team for the season.

"I never got it!" Gary replied quickly. Too quickly.

I felt like saying, "Gary, mate, I've taught lads like you for 25 years so I know you're fibbing." I didn't. Instead I punished him with details of my season up front, given that was Gary's position too. He couldn't wait to get away. He should've replied to the letter.

United took the lead midway through the second half, Harte heading in at the far post. It was nervy stuff from then on. Three minutes were added at the end, but the referee didn't blow the final whistle until the game entered the fourth. In the 18th second (yes, I was timing) Plymouth equalised. I'd been expecting it. I always do when United are a goal up away from home.

"They defended too deep," Sam sighed.

On the final whistle Greg called the players together, told them to get their heads up because they'd done really well, and sent them over to applaud the noisy Blues. It was a good piece of management. A week later United scored four goals in 22 blistering minutes against Milton Keynes. Zoko was unstoppable and Madine unplayable. United's passing game, centred around a diamond midfield, simply dazzled.

It was Harte's last game at Brunton Park. He signed for Reading, the fee reportedly £100,000. Like former teammate Michael Bridges, a spell at Brunton Park had kick-started his career. Reading won the Championship the following season and 35-year-old Harte played again in the Premier League.

With the money from his transfer, United could afford to pay the wages of another Leeds player to replace Harte: Slovakian Lubo Michalik, a giant of a defender who'd been a half-million pound signing from Bolton two years earlier.

United were also able to re-sign winger Ben Marshall for another loan spell from Stoke. Like Lubo, he would make his mark during the season. They both played in a 0:0 draw with Swindon, United's fifth League game unbeaten. Their next was already one we'd given the three-line whip to when the fixtures were published. Now it was even bigger: away to league leaders Sheffield Wednesday.

We picked Bryan up at Wetherby but had to turn back as he'd left his ticket in his car; we hoped that would be the only set-back. It looked that way at half-time. "Football doesn't get better than this!" I thought, for United led at Hillsborough, having played very well for 45-plus minutes. Over 2,000 Blues provided a vociferous soundtrack.

Towards the end of the half, United went ahead, the goal coming from an unlikely source, Craig Curran, one of those unfortunate strikers who finds that the harder he works, the less likely he is to score. His goal was one of just two in his first 26 appearances. United were attacking the far end, Hillsborough's mighty Kop, and as Curran shot from quite wide, we had no way of knowing from our angle whether it was on target or not.

There's a wonderful video clip of the goal (worth finding on Youtube if it's still there) filmed from a mobile in the away end. You can't see anything of the action, but that's not the point. It's worth watching because of the cheers; the *ole*'s which accompanied each accurate pass; the *U-NI-TED* when the move ended with a corner; the *"Go on then!"* from a lone voice as Curran shapes to shoot; and when he does, the second of silence as everyone takes an intake of breath. Then the roar when we know it's a goal and the film ends abruptly.

United started the second half as they'd finished (and started and middled) the first. So did we. Non-stop support. "If it goes pear-shaped now," I mused, "you can't take the last hour away from me."

All the old favourites were there, and the newer ones: *"We love you/And everywhere we'll follow/Because we support United/And that's the way we like it..."* and *"Zoko! Zoko! There's no limits!"*

I was still expecting Wednesday, like Plymouth, to equalise late on. I stopped looking at my watch. My heart was thumping, surfing the crest of wave after wave of Blue Army chants. It wasn't as stressful as Leeds away for my head was saying, "Sheffield won't score, they've created nothing and United are too good."

United played for one-nil win in the closing minutes. They ran the ball into corners, kept it there, kept calm, kept control. The final whistle was greeted in part with relief. The greater part however, was joyous celebration. United don't win at Sheffield Wednesday. They were a Big Club, and in the natural order of football things, they were far too big for League One. Afterwards Steph sent a text: "Paul told me the players were saying the fans were amazing and gave the players such a lift." Music, like the *ole*'s, to our ears.

United were kept off top spot because Peterborough had won their game by more goals. The unbeaten run stretched to seven with a home draw with Brighton, who'd end the season as champions. United's first defeat came at Bournemouth.

The Tuesday after, Gary Madine had quite a day. In the morning he pleaded guilty at Carlisle Crown Court to assault in The Beehive. He was remanded on bail and warned that he could face prison when sentenced a month later. In the evening he was up front for United at Hartlepool.

The away end was packed. A drunk lad fell into our row, knocking me sideways and nearly flattening the couple beside me. They moved seats and there was no more spillage, not least because the new Bloke Beside Me told the wobbling one, "I'll knock your fucking head off if you do that again!" Fans aren't always united.

Lubo scored his first Carlisle goal with a 35-yarder and United added three more. Their scorer? Gary Madine. Quite a day indeed for the lad. Madine was sentenced to do Community Service in the week before the Saints game in November, a cracking match and a corker of a result (United won 3:2), both because of what Southampton did to United at Wembley, and because theirs was the strongest squad in the Division; they would finish runners-up to Brighton.

United went fourth, but that was as good as their league position got. Before Bristol Rovers in January, we sat in The Sportsman overlooking the pitch as Sam read the team news off his phone. "He's gone!" said Sam. We knew who he meant. A few clicks later and we knew where. Gary Madine was a Sheffield Wednesday player.

My mate Otley Adam was at their game with Charlton, so I sent him a text. He replied a few minutes later: "It's true: 800k." Whether the fee was that high or not, Madine's goals would be missed; he'd scored 13. Come the end of the game however, the lads in front, in another variation on the 'Goal Machine' ditty, asked, "Gary Madine? Gary Madine? Who the fuck is Gary Madine?" because United won 4:0.

Three days later they scored four again, this time at home to Huddersfield in the Semi Final First Leg of the Johnstone's Paint Trophy. Victory over two legs would mean their sixth final in 17 seasons. The margin of success at Brunton Park more or less guaranteed an immediate return to Wembley. More or less…

'They haven't so much a foot in the final, but a couple of flip-flops, beach towel and we're pulling the sun lounger over,' I wrote confidently in the build up to the Second Leg. Come kick-off, I wasn't so sure.

I was as nervous this morning as I was for any Big Game. At the start of the season I wasn't that bothered about a return to Wembley in the JPT, but after the First Leg, if United are not there, it would be down to a monumental cock-up.

I calmed down in the pub. Sam had no worries. "We're four up for heaven's sake!" I had three pints ("one for each goal!") with Bryan, who'd picked me up. The pub was quiet, despite being one of the nearest watering holes to the ground. The number of home supporters was half that at the League game a week before, when Town had beaten United 2:0.

The gaps in the home sections were in stark contrast to the queues at the away end. There was a party atmosphere among the 1600 Blues. Several lads donned beachwear (in February) and we had to shuffle slowly through the crowds on the gangway to our seats. I vowed not to sing the word 'Wembley' in any of the refrains, but two syllables slipped out. A mistake.

Greg's team selection had attack in mind: Marshall, Zoko and Curran just behind Madine's replacement Rory Loy, a young lad from Rangers. "Best form of attack," Sam said. But for all the football United played, Greg might've stuck 10 centre-backs in the team; the game plan appeared simply to be 'boot the ball away from goal at every opportunity.'

Huddersfield scored, but on the plus side, 29 minutes had gone. On the law of averages (conceding a goal every 29 minutes) United would go through. United survived the half and started the second better. For a while I almost felt relaxed. Not for long. Alan Lee headed in from a corner. 4:2 on aggregate and 21 minutes left.

Collin tipped a header over, but from another corner Lee headed in again. "I've stopped watching Town corners," Sam messaged Rob, somewhere in the increasingly fearful away end.

"So have Carlisle's defence," was Rob's terse response.

Ten minutes to go plus time added. United were well and truly on the rack. Having spent the whole game booting the ball clear of their box, it was too late to try to play football. All they could do was hoof and hope.

Fortune smiled on United when Lee, on a hat-trick, headed wide from closer range than either of his goals. Five minutes were added. I'd made the mistake of looking at my watch at 43. It was a long, long two minutes, plus an extra five. The end, when it came, was greeted with relief. Last year after the Leeds semi-final, Steph's text simply read, 'And breathe.' This evening she sent another: 'Almost brought on labour!'

The mood wasn't as euphoric as it should've been; we'd been through the wringer and, as Sam said, relief couldn't hide the awfulness of the performance. Still, now I could say the W-word: "WEM-BER-LEY! WEM-BER-LEY!" Once again, Football Karma had kicked in. The memory of the pain of that first semi-final defeat to Huddersfield 17 years ago was just that. A memory. WEM-BER-LEY here we come again!

The rest of the league season was relatively stress-free, and, of course, we had another Wembley final.

Sam and friends went to Wembley in full Carlisle kit with frizzy wigs and full-sized masks. Sam was Lubo, Giles Taiwo, Mike Zoko and Leechy Kav. I should've worn a suit, stuffed a pillow up my shirt and gone as Greg. As for Ian, Hannah (who met us at the ground) and me, we wore the three Madine shirts. The lad had scored at Wembley after all.

We'd watched Arsenal v Blackburn on the Saturday and stayed in the capital overnight. It didn't take long to reach Wembley. It was only eight miles away and there was a lot less traffic than the previous visit. Brentford was a few miles to the west of Wembley. I couldn't imagine their fans coming by car and parting with a wad to park.

The official car park wanted £30, another forecourt £20 but one round the corner was a tenner. The Italian who took our money was an Inter Milan fan. "They lost last night!" he said. Not a good omen. Inter play in blue.

We'd arranged to meet other Blues at The Torch pub, just up the hill from Wembley Park station. It had a grassy bank for a beer garden and the banks were Blue. The full colour kit and masks didn't go unnoticed. Sam overheard someone comment, "With shinnies too!"

On Wembley Way they drew more admiring glances. Sam and his mates must've been the most photographed

Carlisle fans at Wembley, so much so that Sam bemoaned not being able to eat his hot dog for photographers wanting his picture. Ironic then, that the photo which appeared in the *News and Star* was of Sam eating it.

Friday's *Cumberland News* had a photo of the Harrogate Blues in full voice. We're standing whilst others sit. I photocopied and enlarged that one for The Wall of Honour of my classroom at school.

"Why don't you have them above the whiteboard?" a pupil once asked of the Carlisle pictures displayed above their work on the back wall.

"They're not for your benefit but mine," I explained. "They are there to remind me why I do the job."

"What's that, Sir?"

I fixed the oik with a steely stare. "To earn money to watch Carlisle United."

On Wembley Way we met Rob, then Hannah and at the tops of the steps, Deano!

"Tim Pocock!" he cried. "How are you doing, pal?"

I'd been recognised by Dean Walling! A good omen? Couldn't be anything else! He asked how Sam was and couldn't believe my little lad was the big Blue beside him. Mind you, it was an easy mistake to make; after all, Sam was dressed as an afro-haired Lubo.

Inside we were at ground level, closer to the action. Although I was disappointed at first that we seemed to be between the main groups of Blues, we actually got the best of both noisy blocks. We sang far more than last year. The *Cumberland News* photo proved it.

As the teams lined up for the National Anthem, the PA man declared: "The presentation party will be led by the chairman of Johnstone's Paint, who will present the trophy, Mr Stephen *Pocock*!" There! The ultimate omen! The trophy was as good as ours! All I had to do was get through the next couple of hours.

United had three corners at the far end in the first 10 minutes. None of them were that good, but Carlisle had the upper hand and nearly the opening goal when Zoko's header flashed past the far post. On looking up at the big screen, Zoko had gone even closer than it had first seemed, with Brentford's keeper just getting a touch to deflect the ball.

So, a fourth corner. James Berrett swung the ball out this time and Zoko met it with a meaty header. It would've gone wide had the ball not hit Murphy, who controlled it on his thigh, and quick as a flash, volleyed. His shot beat the keeper and the back of the net billowed. Murph sprinted back to half-way pursued by teammates and we were hugging each other in delight. Mike's chilli-burger was a victim of the celebration; it drowned in coke.

I knew it would be Murph (well, Murph, Michalik or Marshall) because the only other Blues to have scored in open play in five finals were also M's: Murray and Madine. I should've had a bet on him for first scorer. Sam did. It had to be Murph too, because the football gods had decreed as much a year earlier when, almost to the match minute, his handball had pulled the plug on any hopes of a win over Southampton. The football gods agreed he'd suffered enough.

Another M, Ben Marshall, didn't have such a good day. Brentford were a big team and just this side of brutal. They targeted United's two fleet-footers, Marshall and Zoko. On 19 minutes Marshall was hacked down by Adam Reed. We didn't have a clear view of the severity of the foul, but TV pictures showed it was bad. Reed was booked but might've walked. Marshall hobbled off before he was wheeled away on a stretcher.

United led and the clock was ticking. They were defending okay; Brentford weren't much of a threat; plus a Pocock was presenting the trophy. Then Brentford were down to 10 men. Diagouraga fouled Paddy Madden and Tom Taiwo in quick succession. I still didn't look at the time (he was actually dismissed after 86 minutes) and there was no noticeable movement of stewards to the perimeter to give a clue either. I couldn't however, ignore the PA declaring: "Five minutes of added time."

I stayed strong and didn't look at my watch. Like United I resisted the temptation to switch off concentration, not until Ian leaned over and said, "Only two to go now!" I could've swung for him. The next second the ball flew across the United goal. Ian had nearly jinxed United.

'Another attack and Berrett boots the ball into the wide open space of the Brentford half and suddenly arms are in the air, and I look at the referee and his whistle's in his mouth and his arm is pointing at the centre circle and YES! YES! YES! United have won at Wembley. Five simple words, but oh! How much happiness they brought!'

By the time Thirlwell had climbed the steps, disappeared from view (a ridiculous design flaw of the stadium) then reappeared, most Brentford fans had gone. There'd been two of them to every one of us, but now we had the stadium to ourselves.

This time, unlike 1997, I had a clear view of the presentation. As Jon Colman wrote in the *News and Star*, "Paul Thirlwell joins an exclusive list of two Carlisle captains to have lifted a trophy at Wembley." And I used to teach his wife!

On Monday the caretaker at school (another I'd converted to the cause) said he'd watched the game on Sky+ not knowing the score and found it so tense he had to pause the recording to find out the result before watching the rest.

"Treat every trip to Wembley as if it's your last," Sam said as we walked down Wembley way. Say what you like about the new Wembley, it's still an iconic place and winning there is special, particularly when, as happened at the old stadium as well as the new, United had lost there first. Defeat intensifies the pleasure of victory

Carlisle finished the season mid-table and started the next well enough, but a poor September saw their form dip; they also went out of both the League and JPT to lower division teams. Ten minutes from the end of the Stevenage home game, some lads in the Warwick held up a sheet with 'Abbott Out' painted on it. It wasn't a great piece of timing; United were on their way to a 1:0 win.

Sheffield Wednesday were one of the front runners and they came to Brunton Park on a Tuesday evening at the end of October. Their line-up included Gary Madine and Ben Marshall, United's best players of the previous seasons and both (in their own very different way) lived up to expectations. Marshall was the outstanding player on the park by a long way. Madine was, well, Madine.

Wednesday were a team in manager Megson's narrow-minded image. He was my Number One Football Public Enemy for mocking the JPT, withdrawing his keeper after a minute and two more players after 15 in their tie at Bradford. The rules insisted six players from the previous league game started, so as not to devalue the competition. Megson smirked on the touchline as he tossed the rule book to one side. Wednesday lost but the damage to the competition had been done. Who'd want to sponsor a competition when one of the biggest club's treated it with such distain?

Their style (and that's stretching the definition) suited their kit: grey. Rocket science it wasn't. Indeed it was barely even science. The plan? Kick the ball high and kick it long. Madine had done well off it; he was the Division's top scorer. But if Megson had any awareness of United's soft underbelly, he'd have made sure any game plan was based around Marshall's pace and poise. What United centre-backs Livesey and Lubo did best was win headers.

Marshall scored a stunning early goal, coming in off the touchline (not the best place to be in a Megson team) and putting the ball beyond Collin's outstretched right-hand. He didn't celebrate; the Warwick chorused: "One Ben Marshall..."

United stuck to their guns and tried to avoid being drawn into a long ball game, not that it mattered when they did because United's new signing Lee Miller was in his element. Sam turned to me and wondered if we'd ever seen a better target man. The Scottish international (three caps) had scored five goals in his first 10 United games after transferring from Middlesbrough.

United's passing game was built around him and they began to chip away at Sheffield. It was still 0:1 at half-time as the players went into the tunnel, where Megson picked an argument with Liam Noble, apparently for a tackle on Marshall. Greg wouldn't have needed to fire his team up. United had been playing well enough even before Megson intervened.

'United fans need to be careful what they wish for when they moan about Abbott,' I wrote the next day. *'At the very least, Abbott tries to get United to play the right way. This evening, in a 14-minute spell after the re-start, United passed Sheffield off the park and scored three very good goals.'*

Noble got the third and to celebrate he ran straight towards the United bench (so we thought) but actually came to a halt in front of Megson, and stood an inch his side of the touchline, arms out-raised. Up yours, Megson! The entertainment however, didn't end there. Enter The Goal Machine.

Only a few days prior to the game Gary had discovered Twitter. His initial attempts at friendly banter with Carlisle fans soon degenerated into ill-natured abuse, so there was already a caldron bubbling nicely before kick-off. That said, Gary was applauded as he came off after the warm-up and clapped the Carlisle fans back. He'd played at Brunton Park the previous season without incident and with mutual appreciation at the end. Not tonight.

United were 2:1 ahead when Madine was penalised, correctly, for handball. We jeered him for that, as you do, and Gary directed his own abuse at the ref (as he does) for which he was booked. United scored the third and Gary was even more unhappy.

Ten minutes from time he challenged for a loose ball. The odds on him getting the ball were 10-90. Indeed, when he went into the tackle the player and ball had long since gone. Nevertheless, his attempt to get the bouncing ball had him raising his foot SHOULDER-high. I kid you not. To no one's surprise, the ref showed him another yellow, then red. But Gary wasn't finished! He veered away on the short walk to the tunnel to go over to the ref to remonstrate again before storming off, pausing only by the tunnel to scream at us in the Paddock: "You're all fucking shit fans!"

Later, Tweeting again, he blamed the ref and United for winding him up: "useless fans! Needed the man in black 2 get u the win. Enjoy mid table peace out."

To which one CUFC messageboard Blue responded: 'Gary Madine wishing us peace is like the Dalai Lama declaring war.'

Victory was, I wrote, '*A triumph for the Good Guys of Football over the Bad.*' It was one of those games that kept on giving. Sam was still chuckling at the mention of Madine's name when I took him his cuppa the following morning. "He really is Five Star entertainment!" he laughed between slurps.

Preston away on Boxing Day was also a humdinger. It was set up to be with over 4,100 Blues in a crowd of 17,500. United conceded an equaliser in added time but that didn't hurt as much as it might've, because it had been a great day out. PNE deserved a point after the 3:3 draw as much as United.

Greg hit the spot with his reaction: "I was so proud to be able to stand on the touchline today for everything: for our fans, for the game of football, for the type of football, for the goals, for the excitement, for the aggro. It was just a phenomenal day, better than any turkey." Sadly Miller's fellow Scottish striker Rory Loy had his leg badly broken in a challenge. That was devastating for him and impacted on United's season. The lad had been playing very well.

Sam and I went corporate for Notts County away in March, the first and only time we've done that together.

Way back in my early days as a Blue, and long before club marketing was what it is now, I did watch a game from United's hospitality box. In the early 80s it was just that, one box at the back of the Main Stand.

I was friendly with a receptionist at Lancaster University's Student Union whose husband worked for Younger McEwan, United's first shirt sponsors. I worked in a bar where drinkers had a choice of three bitters. Unless they specified, I would pour them a pint of McEwan's to support those who supported United.

I must've told the receptionist that and she must've mentioned my product (and club) loyalty to her husband, who invited me to a game as his guest. The opposition? Leeds. In those day I was ambivalent about them. The rest of the drinkers in the box were, nominally at least, Leeds fans. I suspect the attraction of free beer turned the Lancastrians for the afternoon.

We were squeezed into the box and invited to open the cabinet at our knees and help ourselves to a four-pack each. It was an offer a cash-strapped student wasn't going to refuse. Come the final whistle, and having made sure I'd drained every last drop of free beer, I needed the loo. My host said he had to make a quick getaway as he was taking his wife, the receptionist, out for the evening.

"No worries," I thought. "I'll pee behind the Waterworks before jumping in his car. It will be dark and quiet enough." Only it wasn't. With Leeds the visitors the police were out in force and most of them, it seemed, were waiting behind the Waterworks. I had no option but to jump in the car and sit and wait. And fidget and wait. And wince and wait.

I can't remember anything of the game, not without reading my diary report, but I can still to this day picture the dark alley where I eventually relieved myself seconds after I'd been dropped off in Lancaster.

Fast forward to March 2012 and Leechy was a Notts County physio. He sweet-talked the restaurant manager into adding us to the hospitality guest list. She was worried that, as away fans, we might cause trouble. We were treated to a free buffet, made polite conversation with the couples who shared our table, and handed back the signed Notts County shirt we won in a hospice raffle when we returned for tea after the game.

We didn't want it, especially as County won the game 2:0. We didn't have the chance to thank Leechy in person as he was celebrating too long with manager Keith Curle and the County players. It was a big win for County who, along with Stevenage, were vying with United for the last play-off spot.

United recovered from that defeat and went on a season's best nine-game unbeaten run, including three goals in the last 13 minutes to defeat Bury and a 95th minute Lee Miller winner against Huddersfield. The last of the nine-games unbeaten was a goalless draw with Scunthorpe on Easter Monday, after which United slipped out of the play-off places.

It was ironic that on the day when the A1 was finally cleared of the 50mph limit which had been in place a season and a half, United's outside lane cruise to the play-offs hit traffic. What caused United to hit the brakes was an injury to Lee Miller in the Scunthorpe match. It looked innocuous, but after a turn in the box, Miller raised an arm to the bench. He limped off, hand pressed to his midriff. The groin strain would rule him out for the season.

'Miller's been the difference,' I wrote, 'not only for his goals, but also for making the 4-5-1 work.' In the three and a half games he'd missed earlier in the season after an unfair red card at Hartlepool, United dropped eight of 12 points. 'A return of one in three points between now and the end of the season won't see them sneak that into the play-offs,' I gloomily predicted. With five games to go and United only out of the play-off places on goal difference, they lost 0:1 at home to champions-elect Charlton. They didn't play badly but, without Miller, they couldn't score.

It was a tough run-in. Stevenage away were next. They were three points behind United with a game in hand and had a superior goal difference. It was also the furthest the Harrogate Blues had travelled for a mid-week game. "Stevenage! That's London!" Diane cried.

"North of London," I replied, swiftly changing the subject. Stevenage itself is a concrete jungle, according to second cousin and occasional Blue Matthew, but the ground was on the edge of town just a stone's throw from the A1 with a free car park the other side of the road and plenty of greenery behind that too.

One stand had an old-fashioned gable and clock in the centre; the ground had a non-league feel to it, which is meant as a compliment and wasn't surprising, since that was where they'd been two seasons before. Now they were within sight of Championship football. Their win was more convincing than the 1:0 scoreline suggested.

United's last home game was against Exeter. "I just want to see a Carlisle win!" I sighed before kick-off. Having watched the season slip away, I needed the Brunton Park chapter of the season to end with a memory to keep me happy over the summer. I also wanted United to win so we could go to Oldham still with something to play for, no matter how remote the possibility of reaching the play-offs.

United won easily, 4:1. Exeter were poor and defeat sent them down. It was routine stuff. Half-time wasn't. Earlier in the week Lee Miller's wife Donna, who had been ill for a while, died from a brain tumour. Miller came out onto the pitch with his sons for a kickaround. Everyone in the ground applauded. It was prolonged and heart felt. When it stopped the ground was silent, as if no one knew what to do or say.

The moment didn't last long. A blast from the tannoy shattered the silence and Donna's name was displayed on the screen. Football can be clumsy when it comes to acknowledging grief but the club and supporters did their best for Lee and his lads, who seemed to thoroughly enjoy their little game.

United started their last of the season at Oldham still in with a chance of promotion which, by any Blue's reckoning, was a cause for congratulation, if not celebration. I'd have settled for that at the start of the season. Admittedly United were the rank outsiders in a three-horse race for the last Play-Off spot, but there were over 1700 in the away end. A sudden cheer had us thinking that either Stevenage (home to Bury) or Notts County (home to Colchester) were behind. If both failed to win and United could beat Oldham, the Blues would sneak into sixth.

It was misinformation. County then Stevenage took the lead. At half-time a Blue told me United needed five goals to reach the Play-Offs: one at Stevenage, who were winning 1:0; three at County, 3:0 ahead; and one for United. That wasn't going to happen. United were staying down. The 1:2 defeat wasn't costly.

'It's been a good season, an eight out of 10,' I wrote to close the 2011-12 reports. 'Here's to promotion in 12 months' time!'

12

Kav and Keith

Much to Rob's chagrin (he refuses to accept them as a legitimate club), our first away game of the 2012-13 season was Milton Keynes. I'd broken my drive down with a Parkrun at Leicester. A Saturday on the road would now regularly feature an even earlier start than usual to take in a new Parkrun. Away days just got better, even if results didn't.

A run always puts me in a better mood, so I tolerated the conversation of a Milton Keynes programme seller as I waited with Sam for the Carlisle coach to arrive with two complimentaries from Paul. *(We wouldn't have gone, Rob, if we had to give Milton Keynes money, honest…)*

The programme seller was testing my post-run, pre-match feeling of bonhomie, and when he tried justifying left-back Lewington's sending off the week before for elbowing an opponent in the face, Sam turned his back on the programme-seller. He didn't suffer fools. I held my tongue. It wasn't easy but it would be a waste of words trying to reason with him. But things got worse.

"See that old boy," the programme seller enthused as an elderly gentleman was helped out of a plush chauffeur-driven motor. "He's 90 and has had two triple heart by-passes, but he still loves the game. He was one of the original directors who brought the club here from Wimbledon!"

My reply was swift and spontaneous: "He should have kept them there!" I walked away to stand with Sam and no, we didn't want a programme. United played poorly and lost 1:2. Thanks goodness for the free tickets and Parkrun.

Coventry three weeks later was a much better away day even before kick-off. We found a gem of a watering hole for a pre-match pint, the RAOB club on the other side of Tesco from the Ricoh Stadium. The bar was Cov through and through, as much museum as working men's club.

Leechy said the ground was the best in League One when he'd gone with Notts County. We reckoned he was right. If we were wavering in where we ranked the Ricoh, we were swung by their Man with the Microphone. "Now I want all three side of the ground to give Carlisle fans a big round of applause!" he urged. And they did! What's more, he later praised the Blue Army for not disrespecting the presentation of former players at half-time.

What a nice club! They let United win too. A Coventry lad, Greg's delight at the end was obvious. United climbed to tenth but that was as good as it got. By mid-November they had slipped to 15th and didn't get any higher, but nor did they fall below 19th. Despite it not being the most exciting season in terms of promotion (not good enough, obviously) or relegation (not bad enough, thankfully), that's not to say it wasn't enjoyable.

I was excited about the home game against Notts County in October because I was going to receive a United shirt pitch side. At a Tuesday night game the previous season, a photographer was snapping fans for *United Scene*, one of those glossy magazines the club from time to time produced. It was almost exclusively children being photographed, but as someone who's always enjoyed the limelight, I muscled in and had mine taken, adopting the goofy grin and thumbs up pose of uncool dads.

I forgot about the photo until we bought a copy of the magazine and there I was, complete with a 'Shirt Winner' star. The other winner was a cute little lad, as were most of those in the five-page spread. I felt rather guilty. I wasn't bothered at all about a signed shirt. They tend to look scruffy, plus you can barely make out whose are the signatures and there's always the suspicion that youth players were told to forge them because the pros couldn't be bothered.

Winning the shirt however, did mean I could walk down the tunnel and get on the pitch, always a thrill. The presentations were made before kick-off. The cute little lad was first; Joe Garner was the player chosen to hand the shirt over. After his photo was taken, I walked over to Joe.

"No problem," he said, shaking my hand and nipping down the tunnel. He had obviously assumed I was the lad's dad and why wouldn't he? What reasonable adult would gate-crash a children's competition like that?

The rest of the starting XI followed Joe down the tunnel, leaving my shirt, the club official, me and the subs on the pitch. "Pick one of them," the CUFC man said. I chose Alessio Bugno, an Italian left-back whose Carlisle career featured just four appearances over six months, on the grounds that Sam's girlfriend at the time thought he was the most handsome. He was also the son of a famous Italian cyclist, which attracted me more than his looks.

The presentation made and photo taken, I walked off, heading for the Paddock gate next to the tunnel. I looked up to see where Sam and Giles were, only to be met with abuse from a group of Blues I'd never met, let alone upset. "A bit harsh," I mused, even though it might've been justified had one been the dad of a lad who'd been denied his signed shirt.

I put my head down and was passed by County's Francois Zoko, on his way to the team talk. Zoko's decision to leave Carlisle for the bright lights of Nottingham had rankled with some United supporters. He was the target of the boos. Whilst I was relieved it wasn't me who'd incurred their wrath, I quite enjoyed the novelty of being on the receiving end of abuse from the Paddock.

If that was a momentary insight into what it's like to be a player, we experienced something similar at Bury the following Tuesday. The game was dreadful and wouldn't have merited a passing mention in these pages, but it did have quite a finale. With United's first on-target effort of the night, Joe Garner scored an added time equaliser. That in itself was joyous but, over the course of 40 plus seasons, not out of the ordinary.

Sam and I were heading for the exit (we never leave a game before the final whistle) and as we reached the bottom of the steps, Joe took the ball past a defender before his close-range finish. Bury's away end was one where the last few terrace steps are below pitch level. It had been built for standing and seats were clamped to those tiers to make the end all-seater. In delight Joe jumped off the pitch and, give or take a pinch of dramatic licence, into our arms.

The Sky TV footage, which I played over and over, showed Sam, with a massive smile, pulling Joe towards him, while I am just half a hug behind. We were soon jumped on by other fans plus Paul Thirlwell, who'd leapt off the pitch to join in. Sam had form for celebrating with players after he'd helped get James Berrett booked at Scunthorpe, dragging him almost into the seats, but this was the first time I'd celebrated a goal *with* a Carlisle player. Not just that, but we'd been the first two Blues, players or supporters, to go bonkers with the scorer.

The players were booked, of course. We should've been carded too. "That was stupid on my and Joe's part," Thirlwell admitted. "Sometimes you get a bit carried away and you just can't explain it. We were celebrating the goal and the fact it had come so late, but if we didn't have passion about what we were doing, there would be no point in playing." Or supporting either.

Into November and onto Griffin Park, Brentford. Arriving early, I strolled around the ground. One corner, where the away end and popular side joined, backed onto new apartments. Their carpark sloped up to the wall, which wasn't that high. If I stood on tiptoe, I could see into the ground, including both goals and nearly all the pitch. Throughout the game I kept peering over to see if anyone was watching for free. No one was. Surely the locals must've known about that spot.

Griffin Park's main entrance looked like it was trying desperately to muscle its way in between the terraced houses. This time the freebies wouldn't be from Paul Thirlwell, who needed them for his brother, but from Mike Edwards, thanks to the Leechy/Notts County connection.

I congratulated him on being the only Carlisle player to keep his shirt tucked into his shorts. He tried to wriggle out of that fashion *faux pas* by claiming the t-shirt beneath was too small, or some such excuse, but I told him to be proud of wearing his kit the way he did. It's how I insisted my school teams dressed, the staff one included.

We had seats for the upper tier of the away end; they were only £1 more expensive than standing. Ours were in the bottom row with almost a bird's eye view of the goal below. They also allowed us to peer down the tunnel to our right, where Peter Murphy and a Brentford striker continued their on-field push and shove spat.

We had beer in one of the four pubs on the ground's corners and a Bovril before kick-off. I couldn't have been in better mood. Not even a United defeat and Joe Garner failing to score a penalty affected it much.

In February we were on the road to tropical Portsmouth, for the sun was shining and it was almost warm. "My! You guys do some miles!" said Greg Abbott as he stepped off the coach. Paul saved us more money with a couple of complimentaries. It was a pity he hadn't one for the car park, as the driver had to pay £20 to leave his coach there, an indication of how desperate Portsmouth (more precisely its administrators) were for money.

The entrance to the covered away end was in the corner with a heavily stewarded approach, state of the art barcode turnstiles but crumbling steps to the back of the stand with grotty toilets half-way up. The team wasn't in great shape either. They finished bottom, with United seven places and 23 points better off, one coming from the draw at Fratton Park.

United's first away game of the 2013-14 season was at Valley Parade. Terrace chants reflected how it went. Before kick-off we were all, *"Amoo! He's magic! You know, David Amoo, he scores goals!"*

During the game Bradford's Kop home fans mocked us with, *"Nahki Wells, he knows that you're shit!"*

And at the end, *"Abbot Out!"*

United, three down in 30 minutes, lost 0:4. City's third goal was scored by United reject Wells. He came from Bermuda on trial, didn't impress and left. His 'Look at me!' celebration in front of the Blues in the double-decker did not endear him to us at all.

League One managers knew early in the season that all they had to do to beat Carlisle was play two up front, attack from the start and a goal would come sooner rather than later. United heads would drop, their team would get another and then pick United off at will. The sinking feeling at the end reminded me of Stockport, Ward's last game before he was sacked. Greg, stony-faced, had to withstand a barrage of "Abbott Out!" chants as he headed to the changing rooms. I couldn't see him lasting the month, the week even.

Greg however, was at the helm for the next game against his hometown club Coventry. United conceded two goals in the first five minutes and lost 0:4. "If this was Championship Manager, you'd be pressing 'exit' and 'delete'," said Sam at the end of United's third successive league defeat (and 'defeat' is putting it mildly.)

We couldn't see how anything other than 'exit delete' would follow for Greg. He cut a lonely figure. We sheltered in the Warwick before the final whistle; Greg stood on the edge of the pitch, getting a soaking in the downpour. The only things coming down harder than the rain were the boos and jeers from the terraces. It was hard not to feel sorry for him.

Greg's way of plugging the holes in the leaky defence was to send player after player down to the hold; the Vale game saw the 26th different face in a United line-up, and it was only the first Saturday in September.

Troy Archibald-Henville (a month's loan from Swindon) was making his home debut at centre-back against Port Vale. He looked the part and had some pedigree as a Spurs youngster. United didn't concede when drawing at Brentford and were seconds away from another clean sheet when Troy had United's best chance to win the game, stabbing the ball over the bar from right beneath it.

Had Troy's shot gone in, United would've have had their first win of the season, a three-game unbeaten run and they'd have lifted themselves out of the relegation places. Two minutes later Vale scored at the Waterworks. Greg described the goal as "cruel." He must've known what was coming. He was sacked on Monday.

His assistant Graham Kavanagh was the predictable, pragmatic choice to succeed him. He was the cheap option and the Board, sensibly in my opinion, didn't splash the cash because it had so few coppers to throw.

The new manager bounce after Kav's appointment in September 2013 sent United even higher than Ward's six seasons earlier. Under Kav, United won their first, second and third games. Poor Greg. The stat that he never managed United to three league wins in a row had been a millstone which weighed heavier by the two-wins-and-oops sequences throughout his five years in the hot seat. Now here was his successor, his assistant, for fox sake, completing a hat-trick of wins at the first attempt.

Exactly half-way through the season, United were 16th with 27 points. 'They're a mid-table team but there's no harm in that,' I wrote, 'not when they're on the up, which they seem to be under Kav. I like the way he's wanting central defenders to pass, and the way he'll surprise us with his line-ups.' A positive endorsement to slip into the file marked *Where ignorance is bliss, 'tis folly to be wise.*

United lost five of their first six league games at the start of 2014. 'If you want a reason why United lost,' I wrote after the fifth, 'and why they are now just a place and a point above the bottom four, try this: United fielded their 42nd and 43rd debutants of the season and it's still only mid-February. *(One was a young keeper from Sunderland, Jordan Pickford.)* That means United have had at least one new player every game.'

Little wonder then, that United's match day squad resembled something less than a solid, well-drilled unit, something we noticed from our seats in The Sportsman bar, the back window of which overlooked the Paddock.

We watched the players split into cliques for the warm-up: the Alpha Male In-Crowd together, the younger pros on their own, youth teamers Brough and Dempsey passing to each other and Drennan (another loanee) desperately looking for someone to play with. He could've played with Kav's son, who, once again, was given the freedom of Brunton Park as his own back yard. I'm sure he's a nice lad, but at how many other grounds do you see a child playing, other than the mascots? (United's are corralled into a space on half-way.) It doesn't look right. And what will the United players do when they see the boss's son out there? That's right, have a quick knockabout with him, just to keep in with dad.

Here are two simple things Kav should do to get players in the right frame of mind: (1) Cut out the cliques by getting all the players to do their warm-ups together, and (2) give young Kav the keys to the Neil Sports Centre and let him have a knock-around there.

United stopped the rot with a home win over Bradford City and followed that up with victory at Coventry's temporary home in Northampton. We were two of the 191 Blues inside the ground, one entire side of which was shut. When a ball in the warm-up was kicked over the perimeter fence, Sam nipped to fetch it and kick the ball back, whereupon a steward rushed over. For a moment Sam was in danger of being thrown out. The steward placed a temporary barrier across the walkway to keep the Harrogate Hoolies out.

The three points at Northampton/Coventry took United's tally to 36. We reckoned four wins from the remaining 15 games would see them safe. "They'll get those," I said. "In Kav we trust."

Things however, didn't quite work out as predicted. Four games and no win later, lowly Stevenage came to Brunton

Park. The game ended nil-nil. "I just don't think they've enough goals in them," Sam said afterwards.

Kavanagh's post-match comments spoke volumes. He blamed United's poor start to the season (under Abbott); he blamed the referee for not sending off a Stevenage defender; he had a pop at loanee Sam Byrne for not anticipating Tom Miller's header flashing to the far post, especially because United had practised set pieces all week. If ever he was trying to throw up a smokescreen for his and his team's failings, this was it. And like United's attempts to win a crucial relegation six-pointer, he hadn't done a good job of it.

United's 48th player of the season started two winless games later at Prenton Park. Ninety minutes had passed, a dreary ninety at that, when Brad Potts made his second, but only his second, threatening burst into the Tranmere half. Looking up, he spied his striker racing into the box. Potts hit a low, firm pass to his latest teammate. The ball came to Player 48 with back to goal; his swift turn gave him half a yard. He volleyed, the ball shot over the bar. Player 48, the Goal Machine that was Gary Madine, had nearly scored a storybook winner.

Given that Gary's last appearance in front of us was yelling, "You're fucking shit supporters!" as he stormed off after that red card, he'd received a somewhat surprising and appreciative, if not rapturous (there weren't enough of us for that) welcome at Prenton Park.

Released from prison after another fight in a bar and loaned by Sheffield Wednesday for what was left of the season, Gary said he'd sat in his cell looking forward to the moment when he could repay Carlisle. Today's game, and that 91st minute chance, was it. In fairness to him, Madine was the best player on the pitch by some distance, which doesn't say much for the rest in either team. Carlisle were fourth bottom, Tranmere a place above. It showed.

In the 38th minute of United's next game, against Swindon at Brunton Park, and following another Potts burst from half-way, Madine took a touch, feigned to take another, and keeping his finish low this time, poked the ball past the keeper. He celebrated with a run to Kav, kissing the badge. In prison he'd dreamt of doing just that, he said.

His was the game's only goal and it ended a run of eight without a win. I ended my report with: 'So, to Preston with hope in our hearts. I expect a five-goal hammering.'

I should've kept that flippant one liner off the keyboards. At Deepdale Madine scored again and Preston hit six. "Two-nil in your cup final!" crowed the Preston fans at 1400 of us in the away end. Then "Three... Four... Five... Six..." Carlisle were back in the drop zone with five games to go.

After defeat in the third of those at home to Oldham, Sam's reaction was damning: "The table doesn't lie. Well, wrong. It does. I can't believe there are two worse teams than Carlisle in this division." The Goal Machine agreed. "Fucking shambles!" we saw Madine say to assistant manager David Irons during a break in play.

United's season ended at champions Wolverhampton. They lost 0:3. In the 15 games since United beat Coventry, they'd won just once and scored only seven goals. Carlisle finished third bottom, five points adrift of safety. Relegation brought an end to eight seasons in League One.

The 2014-15 season didn't start any better (two points from 15) and coming out of the first Staff Meeting of term the following Monday morning, a colleague called across the yard, "How many was it on Saturday?" Answer: Five at Cambridge. At that very moment my phone buzzed, a text from Sam: *Kavanagh sacked.*

Paul Thirlwell and Tony Caig held the fort while United searched for a new manager. In the interim Bury came to Brunton Park, scored three and United went bottom of League Two. On the Friday before Mansfield away, Carlisle appointed Keith Curle.

Twenty minutes into the new regime there was no difference to what had gone before. "New manager, same shite," I sighed. Carlisle were a goal down and the longer the half dragged on, the worse United got. Curle had left team selection to Thirlwell and Caig, but he was pitch-side from the start. "He'll be checking his contract to see if the ink's dried," I said. By half-time United were three down and, for only the third time that I can recall, I lost it with the team I love. Here's how and why:

To the Cemetery End at Bury where United made my boy cry, to April 2001 when I let poor Matthew Pitts have it with both barrels (2000-01 was a long season and a shanked pass from the young full-back was one shank too many), add the moment the half-time whistle blew at Mansfield to the list of Times I Let United Have It.

"FUCKING SHITE!"

Gillespie was the nearest. I wanted him to hear just what I and every other Blue behind the goal thought of what had gone on that half and, indeed, for most of the previous 23 league games. One relegation, a second looming large (even this early) and a meagre one win.

"What really pisses me off is the lack of effort, the lack of bottle, the way they give up so quickly," said Sam. It must've upset Curle too and he'd only endured 45 minutes of it. I can't think of many times and places when I was so out of love with my team than in the away end at Mansfield at half-time. I couldn't see things getting any better. But twenty minutes into the second half, Sam turned to me, grinning: "One thing we now know about Keith Curle," he said, "is he delivers the best half-time team talks in football!"

United were transformed. Curle subbed off Potts and Sweeney, which was somewhat of a surprise as they hadn't been as bad as some, replacing them with Amoo and Mark Beck, neither of whom had been game-changers for a long while. He also set the formation to 4-2-4 and must've put the fear of unemployment into the rest of the line-up.

United were a different team. It wasn't rocket science. United's players simply worked harder, closed Mansfield down, came out on top in 50:50s. Beck won everything in the air and Amoo was as effective. He terrified Mansfield's flank. Defenders who were schoolyard bullies in the first half could only put the ball out of play in fear Amoo would get it and make them look stupid.

United scored when Billy Paynter's miss-hit volley bounced across the box to Amoo; he took a touch before turning it over the line. Dempsey added a second, a really good one, when he carried the ball across the edge of the box, evading challenges, before whipping a shot with his right into the far corner. It might've taken a deflection but United were making their own luck.

Troy won two headers from corners which, to his frustration (see, he cared), he put over, and the ball was in front of the goal below us all half. I was joined by Parkrun Blue Nick. "Whatever happens now, I'm happy!" he enthused. "There's hope!"

The atmosphere behind the goal was the best it had been for a long while at an away game. At the end, United were given a standing ovation, which was quite remarkable, given how bad, how very bad, they'd been in the first half. "It's still another defeat," said Sam, and it was a defeat that leaves United even further adrift (four points) at the bottom of League Two. But I didn't want to think of the bigger picture. I just wanted to enjoy the feel-good buzz that United gave me second half. Welcome to Keith Curl-isle United!

Over 800 Blues felt the same as I did, because that was the size of the Blue Army at Hartlepool the next game.

Hartlepool had generously (ha!) knocked a fiver off the £25 ticket if bought in advance.

It was cold but the away end afforded (pecuniary pun intended) some shelter. We sat further to the right than we normally did. Just below us was a boisterous, noisy group of lads, two of whom were arrested for pitch invasions after the first goal, but they added to the entertainment. When they lit a blue flare after the second and started bouncing it was, as Sam captioned the footage later, "Like the Sano Siro!"

If United were going to score, we suspected it would be from a set piece. Grainger had got a good long throw on him, and Beck won headers. Grainger launched it, Beck's near post flick headed the ball on and Steven Rigg got his foot to it before the keeper. Cue a charge to the far corner flag in front of a stand of elated Blues.

A second goal would settle it and a second goal is what we got. Grainger crossed to Potts, who volleyed the ball first time. It whipped low across the box and sub Stephen Elliott was on the end of it, sliding to divert the ball into the net. Elliott went bonkers too. United were well and truly on top as Hartlepool caved in and Beck converted Dempsey's cross for the third. It looked a simple connection but the video showed that Beck had dragged his left foot behind his right to flick the ball in. Showboating indeed!

United thoroughly deserved their win, just as we'd deserved the luxury of wondering, "How many more?" with 10 minutes remaining. United swapped places with

Pool and sent them bottom. They looked a broken team, as Carlisle had two weeks before. Some turnaround! Altogether now:

HE'S KEITH CURLE
HE'S TAKING US TO LEAGUE ONE!
AND THAT IS WHY WE LIKE HIM,
IN FACT WE FUCKING LOVE HIM!
WOAH-WOAH-WOAH!!!

We carried on WOAH-ing after Curle made it three league wins in three against Stevenage. There probably was more to the turnaround than this, but Curle had used a simple system and put players in their best position: round pegs for round holes. Victory took United out of the relegation zone; they were up to the dizzy heights of twentieth.

"I'd be surprised if they were to return there again under Curle," I wrote in the euphoric glow of the morning after the glorious afternoon before. United however, won just two of the next eight league games and were back in a relegation spot before Christmas. Curle started to tinker with the team, a managerial tick he couldn't curb throughout his four seasons at Brunton Park.

The last of that eight-game run was at Exeter. It was the longest there-and-back-in-a-day drive we'd done to watch United (Plymouth was further but we stopped overnight) and well worth the 598-mile round trip for the ground alone. In fact, given the result, a 0:2 defeat, worth it for the ground full stop.

No way today would St James have been built where it was, not far from the city centre, not far from pubs. We found a very good one thanks to Rob's mate Pete, a Devonian policeman and Carlisle fan. He didn't get to see United often, but he showed us a photo with Greg Abbott at Torquay. Although Pete was in uniform, he was snapped in his United scarf.

Exeter's home end was the biggest, in terms of capacity and probably height, of any standing terrace left in England. The away end behind the goal was flat and closed to us, so we stood in the corner. There was a snack bar and when Rob asked if his pasty had mushrooms (he doesn't like them), he was told, "If it has, bring it back and we'll give you one with a different filling!" Now that's customer service. Rob enjoyed his mushroom-free pasty so much he went back and bought another.

Exeter also seemed a club that cared for all its supporters. I counted six covered shelters built into the foot of the stand opposite, and another couple at the bottom of the home end which, presumably, were there for fans with mobility issues.

The best discovery however (and you wouldn't get this at its Newcastle namesake) was a half-open window in the wall of the stand between the steps to the loo and the top of our little section of terrace. I had a peep straight through it, down a corridor and right into the home team changing room, where City manager Paul Teasdale was giving his team talk.

He was pointing to a white board onto which he'd written (though I'm having to presume this because

I couldn't see what it said), "Attack this lot and they'll crumble if you score first." His team did as I supposed they were told. It took Exeter an hour but having scored, that was it. They added a second late on as Curle fiddled and tweaked to no avail. Billy Paynter ended the game as a winger. Rob described him as a male Kim Kardashian: "Both are high maintenance and serve no useful purpose."

Newport was another new ground for us. We met Rob at a nearby pub. It had no carpet but sporting mementos aplenty, signed shirts and photos on the walls. Perfect. The ground was another curiosity, but unlike Exeter's, the wrong side of quaint and picturesque. If you were a fan of modern identikit stadia, you'd say it was a mess. We're not, so we didn't.

We sat in a new stand which ran down one side. The gateman popped out of his booth and told us to sit higher up in case it rained. Opposite was an older stand with a paddock, where most of their fans gathered. It was similar to Brunton Park's East Stand, in that the far end overlooked temporary seating erected on what had been the in-goal area of the rugby pitch.

Courtney Meppen-Walter headed United in front but Danny Grainger conceded a soft penalty before Newport scored the winner with a miss-hit shot. We'd had a good day out though: a new ground, a Parkrun, a pint in a decent pub in friendly company and jam-free drives to and from another country. Once again, the game itself was just a part of the match day experience.

United's next away was Wimbledon. They owned the home of Kingstonian, who shared as tenants. Wimbledon FC were planning their move back to Wimbledon the borough, down the road from their old Plough Lane ground to a greyhound, stockcar and former speedway stadium. Rob, who likes his motor sports, sympathised with the motor sport enthusiasts. It was the last remaining venue in the London area.

We arrived in good time, had a walk round and wandered into the home end. The Wimbledon social club bar had its doors open as well so we popped in for a couple of pints of the aptly named Plough Lane Ale. The ground was a tidy one, covered on all sides, though ours only had a roof in the middle. We could've sat behind the goal. There weren't many   seats for the Blues, and there was no division between them and those for Wimbledon's fans, bar one steward. A refreshing change.

Wimbledon had only expected 100 or so Blues. Five times that number turned up so the terracing was quite crowded. We did well to get in before kick-off. Plenty of Blues were still outside at three. The first half wasn't a great spectacle, but United weren't losing at the break and had even come from behind, thanks to a header from Sean O'Hanlon (ex-Milton Keynes), who'd been serenaded by the home fans with: "You know what you are, you franchise bastard, you know what you are!"

At half-time Dougie from Temple Sowerby greeted me like a long-lost brother. "I'm a bit pissed," he explained, "I've been in the pub all day!" The Harrogate Blues weren't the only ones enjoying their away day. It got better too. The second half was an absolute cracker.

United were under the cosh. Their goal led a charmed life, but in fairness to United, they made their own luck with some heroic defending and Gillespie's goalkeeping. With the ball up the other end so much and not having a clear picture of how close the Dons were to scoring, things were even more stressful.

Wimbledon recorded 22 efforts on goal, seven on target, and 11 corners (to United's three), most of those in the second half. But in the midst of the second half pressure and doughty defending, United scored.

Right-back Matt Young, a Sheffield Wednesday loanee who'd underwhelmed on his debut a week earlier, now looked a decent player. Just up from us he crossed with his left foot. It was the ball of the game, swinging into the path of Steven Rigg, who directed his header low and wide of the keeper.

He ran in front of us and was engulfed in Blues who were quicker to react than me. I was behind a barrier but hey! Did I care? United were ahead, which made the next 35 minutes (plus time added on) even more stressful, for United had more to lose: three points, not one. Wimbledon came closer still. Dempsey acrobatically cleared off the line before Gillespie sprinted across his goal and flung himself to keep out a shot, with Grainger, on the deck himself, heading away for a corner.

The fourth official's board went up. Six minutes. SIX MINUTES! Wimbledon were going to score. My

Daventry Parkrun time en route had been 22.22. The game would end 2:2, I was sure. Sam was working out just how much time would be left, should (when) United concede until they would be safe with a point.

Wimbledon, desperate, pushed higher and higher. United cleared and suddenly Dempsey was away. He dithered and was tackled but he still had the ball. He cut back (waste time, waste time!), started again, and fired in a shot from the edge of the box. The keeper parried and Amoo, offside surely, slotted in the rebound. Except there was no flag! The goal stood!

He sauntered over to the mayhem and madness of our celebration. He was soon joined by teammates who jumped on him, pushing Amoo nearer the fence where Sam and Rob, having ducked under the barrier, joined in. Sam got a man hug from Mepham-Walter ("On a par with the Ian Harte hug after the Leeds semi-final!" he cried) and Rob slapped Amoo on the head.

Wimbledon's previous home game had been a FA Cup replay with Liverpool, who'd beaten them 2:1. United had gone a goal better and won 3:1. It was numerically true then: Carlisle were better than Liverpool. It felt that way.

When Shrewsbury visited early February, United were up to 18th, their highest position of the season. United played well and Charlie Wyke put United ahead with less than half an hour to go.

"I'll take a point," I said to Sam. The first of four minutes of added time had passed. This was an

insurance deal with the football gods. I was preparing myself for a Shrewsbury equaliser. Were United to finish with a point, it would have been a point more than we'd expected before kick-off. Shrewsbury were one of the best teams in the division (a win would take them top) and a point would keep United's run (three wins and a draw in the last five) going. As for a win, well...

But we were getting ahead of ourselves. Shrewsbury's keeper kicked the ball straight into touch as two minutes of the four passed. Young went to take the throw. Take your time, pick up a booking if needs be. Put the ball down the line, throw it to a team mate to boot towards us in the corner.

Instead, a short throw and Shrewsbury won possession. A powerful shot from outside the box. Dan Hanford pushes the ball into the air. He chases the rebound but it goes off for a corner. It's taken in front of the Shrewsbury fans. A Shrewsbury player attacks the ball. He's not picked up or challenged. Shrewsbury score.

Kick-off. Carlisle lose possession again, Shrewsbury attack down the left. The ball's crossed (it took, apparently, a deflection) and falls to the only Shrewsbury player in the box who smashes it past Hanford. We're stood with Bryan. He storms off. One last chance? Amoo has the ball in front of us but doesn't cross. He passes back to Young. His cross is headed clear and there's the whistle.

Brian later tells me he returned to the rugby club where bemused Blues, sorry, stunned Blues wander in. "I've never known it so quiet. It was like... it was like someone had died. A mate who wasn't at the game tried to wind me up. I just blanked him. We were all traumatised."

'It was the speed of what happened,' I wrote next morning, more cathartic process than match report, 'the shock, yes, shock, of being 70 seconds away from victory. Seventy seconds. Time enough for Shrewsbury to score one goal. But two? Two! I've not known a United game which turned so late on as this one. If it ever happens again. I don't want to be there.'

Curle felt the same. "The last time I felt like this was when I went into a restaurant to meet my partner and I saw her with another man. I was heartbroken. Cruel is an anagram of Curle," he muttered.

A mile from home Sam broke the silence. "One thing about tonight," he said, "the football gods owe us – and owe us big time. This has been banked."

We needed a game to put some distance between us and the Shrewsbury pain. We headed south to Luton. After Tuesday's trauma, it was back to normal with a run-of-the-mill defeat. The shame was that we had to be there to suffer it, for Luton was a town and ground that must've inspired the chant, "I want to go home! I want to go home! (Insert club name here) is a shithole, I want to go home!"

Sam said Luton reminded him of Johannesburg, South Africa; he and Leechy had been to the World Cup in the summer. It wasn't meant as a compliment. Around the ground the streets were tired and tatty with rubbish dumped on pavements; every other house was 'To Let.'

From the outside the ground was grubby too. It was squeezed onto an embankment and to get into the Oak Road away end (the oaks had long been felled), we had to enter through turnstiles beneath the first floor of terraced houses. The stairs to the stand are in the back yard; you can see through the frosted glass into someone's bathroom. In the next-door yard was a broken toilet dumped against the stand wall.

The away end was dark and dingy. The roof was too low, seats were bolted onto terracing with no leg room at all, and there were pillars and pylons everywhere. The only part of the ground with a clear view of the pitch was the ugly strip of private boxes which ran right down one side. The ground felt claustrophobic. To get a clear view of both goals we had to stand in the aisle at the back.

A line of stewards sat to our right and the home fans were a coin's throw away, but the stewards were more intimidating, if only because every time I glanced at them, they were staring back at me, especially after I'd instinctively sent a dismissed Luton defender on his way with the appropriate farewell gesture. I feared for a moment I was going to be thrown out. I could see the steward nearest me reporting to his mate what I'd done.

It was a long way from being a pleasant afternoon, and United's performance wasn't anything to lift the oppressive gloom. Carlisle remained rammed in the relegation cul-de-sac. At least they weren't the only tenants. Despite defeat, Carlisle were three points clear of the two eviction spots.

With eight games to play, United were four points above those relegation places. The first was at Oxford. As new out of town grounds go, it was a good one: three smart stands and a fence. Through a gap in the gate at the Fence End we could see most of the pitch; from the gap in a gate at the home end we could see *all* the pitch. Oxford was another ground where you could watch for free.

We spent a happy couple of hours in a diner the other side of the car park. We had coffee on arrival, stayed for lunch and a beer with Rob and Sue. Oxford Away was his 50th birthday present. Sue knew how to treat her man.

We sat high in the stand opposite the main one, not least to be sheltered from the wind and rain which blew in from the exposed Fence End. Below us in the corner was, of all things, a tank, part of an Army recruitment campaign. Carlisle scored with a fluke of a free kick that caught on the wind and bounced in off the bar before Oxford scored twice, Troy was sent-off and United lost.

Back at Brunton Park United scored a last kick equaliser against Portsmouth, but the over-riding emotion was still one of anxiety that they'd be relegated. Yes, Wyke's goal was very welcome, but I was finding it hard to believe they'd stay up. 'United are slipping and sliding on the thinnest of ice,' I wrote. But they hadn't crashed through it, yet.

We missed the Easter Monday game at Accrington. Sam had a stag weekend in Krakow, Hannah had the car and I decided not to spend time and money on a public transport trek to Accrington. It was a good decision. United lost 1:3 and Curle received nationwide media coverage for his post-match comment about players "lacking male genitalia". We knew that already.

He sounded like a manager about to be sacked, settling a few scores. We awaited an announcement. It didn't come. Curle remained in charge. The relationship between Curle and his eunuchs was, to say the least, strained.

But there were three worse teams than United and, crazy though it seemed, United were almost safe after a 1:0 home win against Dagenham, especially because those below United all lost again. In the last three rounds of fixtures, Cheltenham, Tranmere and Hartlepool had managed a meagre two points between them from a possible 27.

Curle didn't speak publicly afterwards but he'll have felt justified that his public humiliation of the squad had motivated them to victory. As the Blue Army's adaptation of a Peter Andre song went, he was a 'Mysterious Curle' indeed.

The first of United's remaining four games was at leaders Burton. Their new ground had been built opposite the old from the proceeds of a cup tie against Manchester United. Despite the terracing not being that steep, we had to climb stairs to enter the away end from the top, which I always prefer. I liked the price too, just £15; Luton was £20. There was an indoors bar area for away fans, which made a refreshing change from a cold concourse.

The game was one of the strangest I've seen for the second half was, and I don't exaggerate, 45 minutes plus eight in added time of attack v defence. United would boot the ball clear, either into touch or into the Burton half, where keeper Jon McLoughlin (who was at school with Sam) would sprint to retrieve it, pass to a defender, and another attack would begin.

At one point McLoughlin, a thoroughly nice lad by the way, came out of his box almost to the half-way line, with no Blue bothering to challenge. As he did so, United were getting into position to defend again; the formation was 5-5-0. It was the football equivalent of *Zulu*. A colleague sent me the BBC match stats. Burton had 30 efforts on goal and 15 corners; United three and two. It was as impressive a defensive display as I've seen.

United led after a 90-second opener. Some goal it was too. Derek Asamoah won a free-kick, which surprised us as much as the Burton defenders as it looked like he'd handballed, and Grainger smashed the ball over the wall into the top corner. Carlisle then retreated into their defensive shell, Burton went straight on the attack and the pattern of the game was set.

United weren't helped by playing 20 minutes of the half with only 10 men after O'Hanlon clashed heads with a Burton striker. It took the doctor 20 minutes to sort O'Hanlon out. No sooner had he returned then he went up for a header and the stiches split. O'Hanlon had to be subbed now, so United's trio of centre-backs was Grainger plus Middlesbrough loanee David Atkinson, in just his third league game, and Nathan Buddle, on as sub for only his second piece of first-team action.

Immense credit to that trio, and the other seven defenders, for withstanding the pressure from the league leaders for so long. "We've been hammered and lead 1:0!" I texted Bryan at the break.

The battering intensified second half. United continued to defend remarkably well; this from a team with the worst goals against record in the division. Gillespie couldn't have done more to keep a clean sheet, or to wind up the home fans with delaying tactics that stayed just this side of a booking. His best save was from a 95th minute penalty. There was no doubt it was a spot-kick. Jason Kennedy stuck out a tired foot and tripped his man.

"It wouldn't surprise me if he saved it," said Sam. "He's stopped everything else."

My thoughts were more pragmatic. The delay in taking the kick would reduce the amount of time Burton would have for a second. The ref had signalled seven minutes added time (there'd been six in the first half.) But Sam was right. Gillespie's full-length dive was a great save.

Sam jumped down a step or three to celebrate with Rob. I kept my feet on the ground of the back step. There were still a couple of minutes to go, plus added-added. I suppressed that rising scream of glee that was welling in my chest. The game wasn't over.

The seven minutes came and went. Burton abandoned their careful crafting of crosses and lobbed one last ball into the box. Gillespie had to punch this one. He did, but the ball didn't go far enough. The ball bounced off his hands to a Burton player and despite three defenders on the line, his shot beat the lot of them.

Burton's players and fans went ballistic, but the cheers and *U-NI-TED*s from the 404 Blues didn't stop. As soon as Carlisle kicked off the referee blew for time, and the cheers from the away end continued. The players came over, Curle waved them closer. This wasn't the first time he'd done that. I found myself down at the front, pumping my fist at Danny Grainger. "WELL DONE DANNY! WELL DONE MATE!" I yelled. He pumped his fist back.

I didn't feel as gutted as you might expect, not just because it was a point I never expected United to come away with before kick-off, but also because there was no way any Blue could say that Burton didn't deserve at least a draw. This was a ballsy performance without a doubt, not bad for a team that, just one away game ago, had been missing its male genitalia. The Burton bonus took United six points clear of the bottom two. If United's result against Plymouth was better than Cheltenham's or Tranmere's, they'd be safe.

And that's what happened. Both rivals lost while United won 2:0. Carlisle stayed up with two matches to spare after another really good performance. The celebrations in the second half, with all three sides singing, and that wonderful lifting-of-the-weight feeling in the car on the way home, would carry me though the summer.

The happy end to the season took the edge off my frustration, even anger at times, when I looked back. Curle hadn't won me over but there was no doubt United had done better with him than without. Against the four who finished below them, Carlisle had returned 17 points from 24. Statistical proof then, that United were too good to go down, even if it hadn't always seemed that way.

13

Anfield, Everton, Exeter

Curle had obviously told United to pass the ball more when the 2015-16 began. Or to put it another way: "ROLL THE BALL OUT! FUCKING ROLL THE BALL OUT!" when Gillespie had the temerity to kick it out of his hands. Luke told Sam that Curle wanted to play a "passing game", but we passed that off as loyal Luke toeing the party line. Whatever the tactics, results would determine whether the new season would be an improvement on what had gone before.

In the Premier League Claudio Ranieri had been nicknamed the Tinker Man for fiddling with the Chelsea line-up. That however, was fine-tuning a smooth-running machine. Curle, in contrast, took a sledgehammer to United each week. He smashed up the pieces, put them in a box, gave it a shake, and the first eleven bits that tumbled out were the team for the next game. United's season was in the hands of Tombola Man.

It was a slow start in the league but United beat QPR in the League Cup. The reward for defeating a team two tiers higher was a rich one: Liverpool away in the Third

Round. Before Anfield, we were off, once again, to the Victoria Ground, Hartlepool.

It felt strange being at a game without Sam, who was visiting his girlfriend (and future wife) Sarah's godparents down south; he managed to get to Woking's ground on a run. So I went with occasional Blue Ian. We stood on the back row almost above the corner flag. Below us were lads full of alcohol and bravado who spent most of the game goading the Pool posse to their right. It was a busy afternoon for police and stewards. Two fans were ejected, a policeman's helmet ended up on the pitch and at least one seat was broken.

A lot happened in the game as well (not that those below us would've noticed) and if you could pick a perfect scenario for an away day win, it would be coming from behind, twice, before scoring a late winner. That's what we got.

With 20 minutes to go, United trailed 1:2. New striker Jabo Ibehre had equalised in front of us before Paynter (it had to be him) restored Hartlepool's lead with a penalty. Five minutes later the ball was cleared from a Carlisle attack to another new Blue Bastien Hery, who slid the ball between defenders for Tom Miller to run onto. The right-back cut the ball onto his left and curled it into the top corner. Cue celebration, with Miller running across the Blues to our left and the boys below spilling onto the pitch.

United weren't finished. A Pool player clearly controlled the ball with his arm in the box as he ran it out from a corner, but the referee didn't spot the offence. It didn't matter, for Grainger tackled him and, rather than shoot or loft a cross in, he drove the ball into Jabo's feet. I didn't see the ball hit the net. I didn't need to, because Jabo was wheeling away with arm raised.

He celebrated in front of us. One Blue jumped onto the pitch and into Grainger's arms. Half the team followed. Troy took the opportunity to turn to sub Joe Thompson and tap his head: "Concentrate! Concentrate!" Joyce urged the same, before turning to the away end with a fist-clenched roar of triumph. Concentrate they did and United had their first league win of the season.

It wasn't the time to get carried away. Remember how happy we were leaving Victoria Park a year before, the blue smoke from the flare still in our eyes and with chants of, *"He's Taking Us To League One!"* ringing in our ears? And remember what happened next. But United did seem in a better place, with better players and a manager who had improved on what he'd done the previous season.

Hartlepool has been a relatively happy hunting ground in my time following United; Bootham Crescent the opposite. I'd only seen United win there once in the league, and that had been way back in 1986, so being two-up against 10 men with less than 20 minutes left meant I was looking forward to a rare success.

But as Ian said (after Hartlepool he didn't need to be invited twice), "There's a thin line between confidence and cockiness." Carlisle stepped right over it, slipped and were left with egg on their faces, banana peel stuck to their size 12s and squirming with embarrassment. Don't, repeat, don't start thinking you're a team good enough to run the game down. Don't trust yourselves to ease off and sit back. Don't trust a teammate (Angelo Balanta) not to stupidly tug a Yorkie's shirt in the box and gift a penalty.

York converted the spot-kick and had the momentum to go with their sense of injustice for the earlier red card. They equalised and nearly won, but for a Gillespie save. Curle, to his credit, brought the players over to the away terrace at the end to applaud - and apologise. I didn't clap back. I was too annoyed, too angry. They'd spoilt my day. I caught midfielder Gary Dicker's eye. I shook my head and he looked away.

I sounded off to Parkrun Blue Nick all the way down the alleys to the station. I was still huffing and puffing when we went our separate ways. He must've been pleased he wasn't travelling to Harrogate. I needed another game quickly to get that one out of my system. Liverpool would do nicely.

Funny game football. On Saturday I'd rarely felt angrier with United after they blew that two-goal lead at York. It felt like a heavy defeat.

This evening they lost but I left the ground prouder than ever to be a Cumbrian, for this was right up there in the top Carlisle games I've seen in my 38 years as a Blue. For United, this United especially, the work in progress that is Division Two's most porous defence, to go to Liverpool, prevent them scoring more than once in over 120 minutes, to take them to penalties, and all in front of one of the best away followings for noise as well as numbers was, well, the stuff that very happy memories are made of.

I didn't get home until one o'clock. The game didn't start till eight (United entered the Big League of kick-off times) and it wasn't over until 1030. I couldn't get to sleep though, and all next day at school I was still on a high. If I felt tired I didn't notice it; I was too busy luxuriating in the euphoria of Anfield.

Yes, United lost, but only on penalties and only because Liverpool's keeper saved three of the five (Gillespie saved two.) Sam was gutted. He was so sure United would win, especially when we realised Gillespie was heading our way for the shoot-out, giving United home advantage for the spot-kicks.

This wasn't a shoot-out anything as stressful as that at Wembley way back in 94, when I turned to Sam to focus on That Which Really Mattered had Stevie Hayward missed. Because score or not, win or lose, Anfield had been an epic, yes, epic performance, one that made all the prospecting at the likes of Newport, Luton, Burton worthwhile. This evening was a big nugget of football gold, pure gold.

Before kick-off we walked around the ground, past a fan park (a fan park at a United game!) and under the girders of the massive new tier of the main stand. Liverpool the club is awash with money. In the Arkle pub, which was buzzing with Blues (and Reds), Sam received the team news on his phone. For once, Liverpool's mattered as much as United's. They were fielding, in effect, a full-strength team. Manager Brendan Rogers was under fire and the team hadn't started the season well. The value of their starting line-up in transfer fees was a cool £131 million. United's hadn't cost a penny.

I bought a Liverpool fanzine, a link to better times, according to its writers, when the Kop was terracing and local lads could afford a ticket. The atmosphere was better then, Liverpool's football too. The writers were right. Bar a rousing 'You'll Never Walk Alone' at the start, I barely heard any noise from the Kop all night. There again, we Blues hardly stopped, nearly drowning out their anthem (which was led by the PA anyway) with chants of our own.

At the pub I met Lee, who'd flown over from Germany for the game. We had a couple of pints and headed for the Anfield Road End. The concourse was heaving; that first view of the ground as we headed to our seats had, as expected, the Wow Factor. Bootham Crescent it wasn't.

Curle had dropped his selection bombshell by dropping Jabo, the country's top scorer, to the bench. It didn't surprise us, (a) because that's what he did at QPR, and (b) dropping selection bombshells was Curle's modus operandi.

At least Hery was in the eleven, but Sweeney's presence suggested United would line up on the defensive again, possibly with the 'box' formation which Curle has tried to patent as his innovation. Joyce, Dicker and Sweeney would, presumably, not wander far from the back five, and Hery always puts in a defensive shift too.

Asamoah was the lone striker. He was up against a Liverpool back four comprising the England right-back Clyne, Liverpool's hard man Skrtel, multi-million pound Lovren from Southampton and multi-euro man Moreno from Athletico Madrid. If Asamoah managed to get caught off-side against that lot, it would be an achievement.

United defended the Anfield Road end first half. Nearly 6,000 Blues filled the lower tier. I was worried that we'd be amongst non-singers, but right behind us were some young lads who were quickly on their feet. Noise was never an issue. We made lots of it. True, there were silent types around us; a father and daughter in front of me stayed seated throughout, which suited me just fine. The seats weren't made for terracing, let alone long-limbed lads like Bryan, Sam and me, but that didn't matter. We had seats, here, at Anfield! COME ON YOU BLUES!

Liverpool had their first effort a few seconds after kick-off. Gillespie got behind it easily enough. It was the first of 48 shots and headers that Liverpool had during the 120 plus minutes but this was no Burton. There, Gillespie had to play one of the games of his life.

Most of Liverpool's attempts were from long range and off-target. Liverpool were really poor for a team boasting three current England internationals (Clyne, Lallana and Milner) and the Brazilian Coutinho, tipped to be one of the best in the world. But Liverpool were made to play like that by a United defensive display that was truly remarkable, not just denying a Premier League behemoth more than one goal, but because teams had found it so easy to score against Carlisle this season, and the two or three before then.

I can only think of a couple of occasions when Liverpool were able to work the ball behind United's back line. One was the goal, a bog-standard League Two affair: no one picked up Lallana's run on the left and his cross was headed in by Danny Ings. The other was when Gillespie came off his line smartly to save at the feet of Moreno, who'd broken through in front of the Kop, but that was well into extra time.

Gillespie indeed, didn't have to make any special saves. He kept goal well and bossed his box (he had to with Liverpool having so much possession), but for all their passing and poise, there was precious little penetration. Any attempts at intricacy or working the ball behind the defence were snubbed by United's defending. Credit the players for the way they pressed, pressured and didn't dive into challenges.

Early one we were 'ole'-ing United, the first sign that this wasn't going to be the rout we feared. On the way over I predicted a 0:5 defeat, which, I said, wouldn't be that bad; as for a 0:3 scoreline, well, I'd have grabbed that with both hands.

There were other signs too. Hery broke into their half, carried the ball on, shot. Okay, the ball went over the bar but it was a shot. Then Danny Grainger, benefitting from United's passing game, found space on the left, curled a deep cross towards the far post which wasn't (or so it seemed to us at the other end) too far off the Blue who came sliding in.

Credit Curle too. We've called him more often than not for tactics and team selection, but he got everything spot on tonight. The next time we criticise, we would do well to remember this. What other Carlisle boss has managed his team this well against this sort of opponents? United aren't a club with a giant-killing tradition. They've never defeated a team three levels above them. They never came closer than this evening.

At 0:1 my hope was that United might, just might, maintain that deficit until the break, when Jabo would come on and United would make a game of it at least. But things got better than that. Stand by for a Top Five All Time United Moment - Sam's words and I wouldn't disagree.

Bastian Hery, as he had a little earlier, broke down the middle. He likes to run with the ball and, as he's proved already this season, can play a penetrating forward pass. That's what he did, to Asamoah who'd found space between the back four (Liverpool's defending matched their finishing) to sneak through on the right.

Asamoah was in their box. Blinking heck! He was in their box and was going to shoot! Okay, the angle *wasn't great and, oops, he seems to have slipped just as he was going to get his shot away, but he has shot and, hang on, he's wheeling away and the ball, no, surely not... the ball's gone past the keeper and (memories of that momentary intake of breath from the massed ranks at Hillsborough when Curran scored at their Kop End) GOAL! GOAL! GOAL! CARLISLE HAVE **SCORED** AT ANFIELD! CARLSLE HAVE **DRAWN LEVEL AT ANFIELD!***

Football doesn't get better than this.

What's more, the score-line stayed at 1:1 until half-time and through all the second half too, despite Liverpool attacking the Kop where, over the years, visitors' resistance crumbles. Not United's. Not by a long way. Indeed, the longer the game wore on, the stronger they grew. Liverpool's shooting got worse. Only centre-back Lovren was capable of accuracy from distance. Gillespie had to make one of his better saves from Lovren's strike, and there was another when he dived to parry round a post but, really, there mustn't much else.

Jabo did come on, a straight swap for Asamoah. There was no need for Curle to change the system. It was working. United didn't get the ball up our end that often, though there was one corner when the ball just seemed to skim in front of Jabo's attempted header, drawing a huge 'OOOH!' from the Blues. And then the 90 plus minutes were up. United had drawn at Anfield in normal time. They'd got the better of Liverpool, and we in the Anfield Road End had been the better supporters.

United had worked their socks off, their shin pads too. Surely they'd tire now, surely their defensive line would dent. No. It didn't. Liverpool had that one half-chance denied by Gillespie's challenge; and Jabo had a chance late on, running onto a pass behind the defence and forcing a save from the keeper. If United conceded a late goal, so be it. They'd done enough in such a big game against such big opponents and oh! so much more than I'd ever expected from them. And if it went to penalties...

"They'll win!" said Sam. "I'm sure of it, they'll win." He was too. Nodding his head dismissively of my doubt, especially when we realised United had won the toss over which end the kicks should be taken.

Liverpool took the first, coolly dispatched by Milner. Let's face it, Liverpool's players should be better at hitting the target than United's. They're the master craftsmen after all. You get what you pay for and some of them (and this won't be an exaggeration I'm sure) would be earning 100 times more than some of United's spot-kickers.

Grainger was next. Bogdan went to his right and saved, 0:1. German international Emre Can's penalty was arrogant. He chipped it down the middle as Gillespie dived. Dicker's wasn't quite as cool, with the keeper sticking his hand back behind him, getting fingers to the kick, but Dicker scored.

United were one down with three to go. England winger Lallana was next. He aimed for Gillespie's right. Gillespie dived to his right. SAVE! We rounded on the

Liverpool fans to our left with a triumphant, "WHO ARE YOU? WHO ARE YOU?"

We'd gone too early. Luke's penalty seemed a good one but Bogdan saved. The Liverpool fans threw our taunt back. One later posted it was the lowest point of his Liverpool-supporting life, having to jeer a team three levels below for not scoring in a shoot-out.

But hold on... Coutinho's kick was the weakest of the 10. Gillespie saved it by sticking out a foot and hand behind him. And Coutinho's supposed to be the next big thing? If Alex McQueen scored now, scores would be level. Score he did, and how, with just about the best penalty anyone could take. He curled the ball high into the top left corner, the ball hitting the side netting just inside the post. No keeper could've saved that.

"Are you available to stick some stamps on envelopes?" Sam tweeted McQueen after the game. He read that and liked it, retweeting Sam's message.

So, 2:2 with one kick each to go. Ings drove his kick down the middle. 2:3. Bastian Hery had to score to keep Carlisle in the tie. He didn't. The little Frenchman's kick was too close to Bogdan who, in fairness, was the only Liverpool player to come out of the game with any credit. He might've let Asamoah's shot sneak between him and the near post for United's goal, but three penalty saves from five is impressive stuff.

Sam was gutted all the way home. Imagine if United had won, just imagine... Yes, but had we dared imagine *they'd come so far, that they'd be so close to actually beating Liverpool? I hadn't, not in my wildest, glass seven-eighths full dreams.*

It felt like a win - and it feels so good to be a United fan.

Four days after United held Liverpool, a team 65 places higher in the league ladder, they lost at home to Newport, a team 14 places below, gifting them their first win of the season. They also lost to Morecambe at Brunton Park and were heading for another defeat at home to bottom club Yeovil, conceding twice in the first seven minutes.

Yeovil's opener came from a corner after centre-back Kevin Raynes, not for the first time, slipped. "I played 700 games and I can't remember slipping once," Curle grumbled afterwards. Raynes redeemed himself by scoring twice as United recovered to win 3:2.

'Being a Carlisle fan has never felt so good,' I wrote afterwards. *'Selective memory, perhaps, but given the past few years, you'll forgive the hyperbole. Carlisle are playing better football and they're in the top ten. Indeed, I'll be surprised if they slip into the bottom half at any stage. The only blot on the horizon is the threat that Curle might leave (he admitted on Radio Cumbria that he still hasn't signed a contract.) Who, a few months back, would have thought I'd be thinking that?'*

Heading into December, United were still enjoying a decent season. They won again, home to Crawley at the end of November. It would be United's last game at Brunton Park for two months.

At Welling on the first Sunday in December 2016, Charlie Wyke hit a hat-trick in a 5:0 Second Round FA Cup victory. Back in Carlisle, Brunton Park and much of the area around the ground was underwater. For the second time in 10 years, the rivers burst their banks in the wake of Storm Desmond. The levels were so high water poured over defences built after the 2005 floods.

When the club coach arrived back from Welling, players found their cars submerged. The water was, once again, at crossbar height. The players, led by Danny Grainger, helped clear 15 homes in Warwick Road. The next day those residents queued to help clear Brunton Park. Many houses remained empty for months.

Pupils and colleagues at my school, few of whom did not know I was a Carlisle supporter, saw the pictures and asked what they could do. The school is called St Aidan's, the same name as the church not far from Brunton Park. We launched an appeal and sent money to the church.

Just as they did a decade earlier, United had to play their scheduled home games away from Brunton Park. The first ground to host them was Deepdale. United beat Notts County 3:0. The crowd, all things considered, was an impressive 3,300. It was a significant fixture for us. Afterwards Sam popped the question to Sarah and they were engaged. I missed the game as I was watching Hannah in a pantomime in Ludlow. It was her first professional role following her graduation from performing arts college.

Sam and Sarah flew to New York for New Year. Back home (in the broadest sense) United's next stop was Blackburn. The attendance was 4,400, including 800 Plymouth fans, who celebrated a first half goal from a deflected shot. It was a close encounter before Plymouth added another at the death.

The third leg of their winter road trip was Blackpool for a Sunday kick-off against Yeovil in the FA Cup. Grainger's freekick opened the scoring. Former Blue Francois Zoko headed the equaliser and, in fairness, didn't overdo his celebrations. United weren't behind for long. Alex Gillead whipped in a free-kick and Mark Ellis dived to head home.

Yeovil hadn't been much of a threat so their added time equaliser surprised us all and meant a midweek replay deep in south Somerset, where Gillespie saved Zoko's penalty during the game and another in the shoot-out. That was followed by Ellis's tie-winning kick. United would celebrate being in the Fourth Round for the first time in two decades with a sell-out against Everton.

Brunton Park re-opened seven weeks after the floods. The devastation around Brunton Park was painfully clear. Skips lined the road and the houses were empty. A sodden wreath, washed off the war memorial, lay in Botcherby Community Centre gardens. Club offices were container cabins. The rugby clubhouse was a wreck. With only bottled beers in Brunton Park's bars, we wandered around the ground instead, buying a Bovril from the stall outside Claire's Bakery, another business hit by the floods. United drew the game with

York 1:1 in front of 7,500, many lured by the prospect of queue-jumping for the cup tie if they had a ticket for the league game.

The build-up to Everton felt surreal. United, the lowest surviving team, playing a Sunday game with an early kick-off live on television. The tie was the subject of much media attention, the focus on the club's recovery after the flood. Everton had to make do with temporary changing rooms and while Warwick Road was busy, its houses were empty.

It was strange having a pint before mid-day in the Fanzone outside the main stand. "I'm not sure I like all this," I admitted. I can get pretty selfish when it comes to *my* support of *my* team.

"If it was like this every week, I'd stop coming," Rob replied.

Queuing to get into the Paddock was another out of the ordinary experience. I feared we'd be squeezed out of our regular spot and have to rub shoulders with soccer tourists. We couldn't stand where we usually do, but we did find space just behind the dug-out. Luke, suspended and in any case injured, was leaning on the roof the other side of the wall, so we had a chat with him. I wanted to turn round and declare: "See, we're real fans, we know the players!"

It was a tight squeeze further along. Grant missed 20 minutes of the second half trying to get in and out of the loo. It was, after all, the biggest crowd since the

1989 Liverpool tie and the largest Sam had been in at Brunton Park. The official attendance was 17,101. I didn't fancy Carlisle's chances. I couldn't see recent history repeating itself. To hold Liverpool to a draw over two hours at Anfield seemed even more remarkable four months on.

Any hopes of a cup shock were dented after 94 seconds and dashed in 13 minutes, when Everton scored a first then second goal. Their players were head and shoulders above United's and Ross Barkley was head and shoulders above his own teammates. Given how good Barkley was and Everton's two early goals, for United to concede only one more in the next 80 minutes, and that a big deflection, was a decent effort.

Getting out of the ground took an age, and once out we had the weird experience of walking down the centre of Warwick Road, which the police had closed and used as a coach park. We'd been able to park in our usual spot, but match traffic meant we were half-an-hour leaving Carlisle. Later in the season we met Everton fans at Beaconsfield Services. We were on our way to Crawley, they were heading to the FA Cup semi-final at Wembley. "It should've been us," I told them.

At Crawley we were searched by two big, burly security guards who looked like they were hitmen for an East European mob. The game wasn't exactly high risk; there were less than 2,000 spectators. It wasn't a thriller either. The home keeper was even booked for time wasting at nil-nil but 14 minutes from time Charlie Wyke won it with a header in front of the away end.

There were no hold-ups on the roads back north. We arrived in Leeds just as Robbie Savage gave us a shout-out on *606*: "Thanks to Sam for driving the Harrogate Blues to Crawley where we watched next season's League Two champions cruise to a 1:0 victory!"

"This season had saved the best until last," I wrote to sign off the report. But I was wrong. I'd gone a game too early with that accolade.

I was in party mood for United's final game at Notts County. We were joined by Sam, fiancé Sarah (who had yet to see United lose in six games) and her bridesmaid-to-be Abi who, on the basis of what followed, should really come to another game with us at some point.

Nottingham was as warm as Mallorca had been the previous weekend for my staff team's annual European challenge. I sheltered in the shadows of The Navigation pub's beer garden and, with a nod to the continent, had a San Miguel, then a bottle in the concourse at County, which was bouncing with boisterous, boozy Blues.

Caught up in the excitement below, I stayed to finish my beer before climbing the steps to find the game had already kicked off. I've never intentionally missed the start of a game, or left one prematurely, so that discovery came as quite a shock.

Luke had saved us another £48 with two tickets. We'd seen former Blue Mike Edwards earlier, who'd sorted out a pair for us at Brentford. "Will you celebrate if you score?" I asked him.

"I always celebrate goals," he replied. "I don't get that many."

Out of earshot, I told Sam, "If he starts, United win." As it was, Edwards played only the first half alongside partner Hollis, though 'partner' was stretching it a bit; they might've been a divorced couple for the amount of time they spent together.

Edwards was yanked with County three down and Carlisle scored two more in the second half. They finished 10th, a considerable improvement on 2014-15. A 5:0 win away from home was some debut for bridesmaid Abi. Our bold claim on national radio after Crawley didn't seem outlandish at all.

Curle's signings for the 2016-17 season were decent. Nicky Adams was the pick. He'd had most assists in League Two the previous season for champions Northampton. Reggie Lambe, another winger, had impressed when Mansfield played at Brunton Park, as had Jamie Devitt in Morecambe's win. Curle had complained more than once that United didn't have enough pace. Backed by the Board, he'd gone out and done something about it.

At the very least, I thought, it wasn't a relegation squad. I was right. By the time United beat Stevenage in October, they'd broken the club record for their longest unbeaten run (14 games) to the start of any league campaign. They lost just one league game in the first half of the season, were second in the table at the start of January and seven points clear of a play-off spot.

Nothing encapsulated the joyous first half of the season more than a moment shortly before half-time in a comfortable win over Crawley, when Luke scored a screamer. The way he was jumped upon by teammates said everything about his popularity. He was a player who put 'defence' into defensive midfielder; a shot almost merited a mention in match reports. When Luke pinged one in from 30 plus yards, we couldn't help believing that yes, this *was* Carlisle's season.

The run eventually ended at Newport but United were still second in the table with 31 points. "Just 19 from safety," Sam was quick to point out, but a week later the unbeaten home run was disappearing too. With 88 minutes gone, they were 1:2 down to Exeter. Too many players were off the boil. I feared the season might unravel. Curle went for broke; United played with just two at the back as defeat beckoned. Fortune favoured the brave. In the 90th minute Shaun Miller equalised then Charlie Wyke won the game in added time.

"SHREWSBURY!" yelled Sam as we jumped and hugged. "SHREWSBURY! REMEMBER SHREWSBURY!" For this was a jumping, hugging finale, a jumping, hugging celebration that had been two seasons in the waiting. For even as, traumatised, we'd shuffled out of Brunton Park on that gut-wrenching, faith-flipping, torrid Tuesday night when United conceded two goals in added time to lose a game they'd done so well to come so close to winning – even then we

*knew that one day we'd cash that chip in. This was it.
This was "SHREWSBURY!"*

It was the best kind of win: against the clock, against
the odds, against the laws of natural justice. Of course
I felt something for the Exeter fans. I acknowledged as
much in the last paragraph of my match report: *'Their
time will come (please God, not at their place on the last
day of the season with United needing a point to go up),
but we've been there before. To feel This Good you
have to first feel That Bad.'*

A week later and it was better still against Mansfield.
"United are so good this season they don't even lose a
pitch inspection!" Sam said. Bryan had warned that the
ground in and around Carlisle was frozen solid, and it
wasn't until nearly 1230, with Sam and I parked up
near the Boroughbridge A1 junction, that he read via
Twitter the pitch had been given the all-clear.

There was nothing stopping United's surge to promotion
either, because United won 5:2, Charlie Wyke scoring a
hat-trick and we in the Paddock did our bit too. Curle
praised us for distracting Mansfield manager Steve
Evans during a first half throughout which Boston's
manager moaned at the fourth official, moaned to his
assistants, moaned to the Paddock. He was, as Curle
said, nicely distracted from what his team were
doing. Come the second half, Evans, like his team, was
burnt out.

While United were scooping seven points from nine,
leaders Plymouth were beaten for the third time in a

week, so come five o'clock, United were (excuse me while I CAP lock) TOP OF THE LEAGUE!

At Notts County on New Year's Eve, Carlisle won again. All three United goals came from headers: Wyke from Adams' tenth minute corner; Jabo bulleted his in from an Adam's cross; Kennedy's looped over the keeper after he'd flicked on Tom Miller's throw. We serenaded the marksmen: *"They're magic, you know, Kennedy, Wyke and Jabo!"*

United's results had been, yes, magic: 23 league games, one defeat. 2017 was going to be a good one. Sam and Sarah were getting married; Diane and I were moving house; I would go part-time and Carlisle would win promotion. Only the year didn't start well for United. Carlisle lost at home to Grimsby, again at Colchester then drew three in a row. In each of them, United ended the game playing against 10 men. They still couldn't keep a clean sheet; the sequence extended to 16 games. The bigger problem was they weren't scoring enough. Three of a paltry five in January were Wyke's.

It wasn't then, a great time to lose your top scorer. Wyke was sold to League One Bradford City for £250,000. To replace him, Curle signed Jamie Proctor on loan from Bolton. His debut was eventful. Proctor header the winner at Orient, United's first victory in six games, then picked up two yellows in eight minutes.

Curle increased his squad with other signings: John O'Sullivan, a right-winger from Blackburn; George Waring, a loanee striker from Stoke; and James Bailey, a trialist who'd been playing in Canada and India. I pick my verb carefully: 'increased' not 'strengthened'. Gary Liddle, a defender from Chesterfield, was a better signing. He replaced injured Danny Grainger, whose absence had coincided with United's loss of form.

The season was taking a turn for the worse. United were beaten in six of seven games from the end of February into March, failing to score in any of them. Unsurprisingly, United dropped out of the top three then the play-off places.

I won't dwell on the details, but here's a sentence from the Crewe defeat: *'After a bright but brittle start, United conceded and imploded, just as they used to do two, three seasons ago. I felt as wretched watching it happen as an alcoholic would feel waking up the morning after breaking a spell of abstinence, or a recovering gambler clutching a betting slip.'*

Curle's response was to do a Kav: throw new signings at the problem. Players were brought in on short-term contracts, including some who'd trialled and failed in pre-season. Curle couldn't help himself. He was a Tombola Manager after all. The excellent early season run meant even he had no need to tinker, fiddle or tweak the team. Now however, the balls were flying out of the drum so furiously that he was picking starting XIs off the floor.

United ended the sorry sequence with victory at Yeovil and on Good Friday we travelled to Hartlepool with five games of the season remaining. The Saturday before, Sam and Sarah were married but United couldn't give the Happy Couple the present of a non-defeat on their wedding day, blowing a lead in the last five minutes at home to Notts County.

At their reception Sam labelled the 11 tables after his favourite Carlisle players, many of whom had responded to requests to sign cards. I can't blame Michael Bridges or Pascal Chimbonda for not replying. One was in Australia, the other in France, and it was difficult to track them down. I'd asked the club to help but they were bound by data protection laws.

I knew what Sam's best team was because he had it published in an opposition fan feature in the previous season's Dagenham programmes. It read: Jimmy Glass; Paul Raven, Richard Keogh, Dean Walling, Tom Cowan; Chris Billy, Paul Thirlwell, Peter Murphy; David Reeves, Michael Bridges, Matt Jansen, with subs Kieran Westwood, Stephan Pounewatchy, Luke Joyce, Chris Lumsdon and Joe Garner.

It was a pity United couldn't have fielded that team for the five games remaining, the first three of which (starting at Hartlepool) were drawn. United's form was shocking, as was, thankfully, that of those around them. A 2:1 win over Newport, only their second victory in 13, moved Carlisle back into the play-off spots. Victory at Exeter on the last day of the season would guarantee them a place. Exeter were anchored in fifth; they wouldn't go up or down whatever the result, and if United did win, it would be Carlisle v Exeter in the play-offs.

Bryan went to the game with the West Cumbrian branch and said it was one of his best away days. At half-time United trailed 1:2 and were down in tenth, then a second Grainger penalty and a Proctor header meant Carlisle had done it. Celebrating a place in the play-offs, Bryan reported, helped the ale taste that bit sweeter.

Eight days later Exeter were at Brunton Park for the First Leg of the Semi-Final, which had a refreshingly reckless sense of abandon about it. At 1:3 down, Curle made two all-or-nothing substitutions; for the last half hour, United had three strikers and three wingers on the pitch. Paul Tisdale, Exeter's manager, didn't think twice. Off came his left-back, on went a centre-forward. United would be gung-ho in attack and exposed in defence.

They'd played well and despite the two-goal deficit, it was a much less painful watch than it had been of late. Both teams ripped up any *'it's-only-half-time-in-the-tie'* script and went for the win (or comeback) with gusto. The game had already done the occasion justice. It didn't seem to make much difference that it was live on Sky. All available home seats were filled. Curle said of the support afterwards, "I know you're out there now!" There were nearly 10,000 inside Brunton Park.

Exeter took the lead before an Adams cross was turned in by a City defender to level, but goals either side of the break had United 1:3 down. That's when Curle made those adjustments. He rattled around in his toolbox and threw a couple of spanners into City's works. Five minutes after the third of his substitutions, John

O'Sullivan's touchline cross veered closer to goal than he and the keeper expected, the ball spooning into the top corner.

Game on! The scores were level a minute later: Adams whipped the ball in and Shaun Miller connected with a meaty header. Brunton Park was rocking. Exeter nearly succeeded in putting the tie beyond reach again, with two efforts disallowed for off-side, both close calls. They hit the post in the last attack of added time and Gillespie made three very good saves.

Although City did have the better chances to score the winner, United hadn't blown up in front of a big home crowd. Indeed, having turned 1:3 into 3:3, it felt more like a win. Momentum was with United. *'And,'* I added, *'will be with them all the way to St James Park on Thursday.'*

Tisdale said the right things in his interview, but his voice couldn't hide a tone of resignation. At 3:1 the tie should've been done and dusted. It wasn't. Sam's Barnsley mate Jonny, who'd watched the game on Sky, put it like this: 'With that post, that linesman and Adams, Carlisle could win on Thursday, even if Waring starts.'

I expected United to go through to the Play Off Final, mainly because it had been a bizarre season when the unexpected had become the norm, even if Second Leg home advantage suggested Exeter should win. Back in November when United's late, late two-goal salvo saw off Exeter in the league at Brunton Park, I ended my match report with a nod of respect to Exeter's travelling support: *'Their time will come, but please God, not at their place on the last day of the season with United needing a point to go up.'*

The Good Lord has answered many prayers in my lifetime, but when it comes to football, he is the all-seeing VAR. He has blessed us with the game and there is no favouritism. Either that or he mis-heard my prayer. The *'not'* didn't register.

So to Exeter, or in our case, Burley Park, Leeds. It being a school night (and St James Park rather a long way from North Yorkshire) we decided against Being There. Instead it was to Sam's. The report/cathartic release below was typed the next morning:

The Football Gods closed the Jimmy Glass account last night. With (effectively) the last kick of the game, Jack Stacey (ex-Blue too) hit an unstoppable shot. The ball swerved away from Gillespie, taking with it all hopes and fears of Wembley.

Had the game finished 15 minutes earlier, defeat would've been easier to take. United were 0:2 down and second best all game. Not that they'd played badly, but Exeter had again created more chances. When Ollie Watkins scored with a strike almost as good as Stacey's, it was, so we thought, game over.

But, for the seventh time, no less, in four games against Exeter, United came back. Curle's substitutes did it again. Kennedy was first to a loose ball on their goal line after a right old scramble and United pulled a goal back. In the ninetieth minute, Adams sent over the sort of quality cross he's delivered, on and off but mostly on, all season, and Sullivan, steaming in off the right wing, directed his headed downwards, and a bounce later, goal, game and glory on!

Extra time beckoned against a team who must've felt they were jinxed no matter how often they scored against United. Then Stacey scored. Game, glory, season over. Heavy sigh time. Fair play to Exeter and Jack Stacey. They deserved it over the two games and, I suppose, the season too. They finished a place higher than United, albeit only on goal difference. You have to take the rough with the smooth. That's life. That's football.

14

Sheridan, Pressley, Beech

United's biggest league attendance of 2017-18 came at the opening league game against Swindon, with 5,500 Blues in a crowd of just over 6,000. That in itself is a plot spoiler for how the season panned out. United lost 1:2. Three defeats on the road and two tame draws at home further diluted pre-season optimism. The sequence started at Lincoln, which delighted Sam's in-laws. Sarah's family were Lincoln fans. Our fear was any grandchild might grow up to be an Imp.

Curle picked a team without two of his best players, Joyce and Adams, and Carlisle lost 1:4. The least written about the game, the better, except to share Bryan's post-match reaction. You can fill in the gaps yourself: '*CURLE IS A CLASS ONE* ******* **** *What the* **** *is he playing at? There was so much pride and hope after Sunderland* (a narrow League Cup defeat the Tuesday before) *so why did he have to change it? Answers please on the back of the fag packet where he does his team selections.*'

In Curle's defence, the defence did improve thanks to Clint Hill, a former Premier League player with over

600 games under his belt. The usual back four were Gary Liddle, Hill, Tom Parkes and Danny Grainger, all above the League Two average. With Mike Jones and Joyce chugging away in front of them, United conceded 14 fewer goals and finished with a better goal difference than the previous season.

The problem was United didn't score enough. Half-way into the season, their form was the epitome of ordinary: eight wins, seven draws, eight defeats. My highlight was the opposite. It was so close to being something extra special: I nearly (oh so nearly!) contributed to a United goal.

The moment of near glory happened in the home game against Port Vale, a forgettable 1:2 defeat. The ball flew off the pitch, as balls are wont to do in forgettable home defeats. Bryan turned his back, it bounced off him and I took the catch, immediately throwing the ball to Tom Miller, accurately, might I modestly add. United's full-back took his throw just as quickly and United kept the ball for half-a-dozen passes as the attack swept to the left.

"If they score now, I'm claiming an assist!" I enthused, already seeing myself in a highlights reel. But it wasn't to be. Tom Parkes, overlapping on the far side from us, ran into an offside position and my moment of glory was gone

We continued, as ever, to enjoy away day Saturdays. The New Lawns, Forest Green's new home, was the first League ground I'd approached down a single-track country lane. It was a Clint Hill clearance away from their former ground and had the friendliest stewards I've encountered on Blue Army Manoeuvres; they virtually valet parked the car for us right behind one of the ends, the frame of which had come from the old ground. Their colleagues on the door of the home bar weren't so keen to let us in, which meant we had to deny our allegiance to the Blues. "We're neutrals doing the 92," we lied, shamefully.

United beat Forest Green 1:0. The second half of the season was marginally better but United only finished 10th. Lincoln made it to the play-offs where they lost, like United a year earlier, to Exeter in the semi-finals. We took some comfort in that, but when the only thing you take away at the end of a season is a modicum of satisfaction at a rival's misfortune, it's a sign that 2017-18 wasn't much of a season at all.

United started 2018-19 with a new manager. Curle had left at the end of his contract, an unusually smooth parting of the ways. His four seasons in charge saw United's league position improve for three then stall. We needed a change, someone to liven things up. Enter John Sheridan, who did just that.

One of his signings was Anthony Gerrard from Oldham. His contract had been cancelled after a fall-out with the owners. I suspect Gerrard was the type who spoke his mind and didn't suffer fools. Sheridan was the same. Every response to a post-match question started with a sigh. "You saw the game, you know what happened, why ask me?" was Sheridan's default tone. Curle, by contrast, would take a deep breath and launch into a 10-minute monologue.

But if Sheridan could manage, I wouldn't mind a jot if he were the most miserable man in football. Three league wins in a row at the end of August made me a quick convert. "Are you still a Sheridan fan?" Sam asked as he met me the other side of the turnstile at Mansfield. He'd driven down separately in case he had to dash back to Pontefract. Sarah was expecting any day.

Sheridan, he explained, had changed his three-in-a-row winning team and formation. "In Sheridan I trust," I replied, but there were uneasy echoes of Curle.

I suppressed those concerns and enjoyed the warmth of a sunny Saturday afternoon, or tried to, because I wasn't in the best of moods, having had to park a long way from the ground. I'd also had to queue an age while the lady in the kiosk had torn tickets perforation by perforation, probably because they were so valuable. I had to pay £24 for mine.

I was in a worse mood come five o'clock. Sheridan had done a Curle. He'd overcomplicated, changing a simple, effective winning formula. United were all over the place. The players were as confused by a five-man defence as we were and lost 0:1.

My next game wasn't until four weeks later. A lot happened in the meantime. We'd been on holiday (in term time!) to Corfu to see Hannah, who was working out there; I was retired and a grandfather, for Sidney Arthur Pocock debuted on Saturday 8th September. Carlisle celebrated his appearance with a win at Cambridge, by coincidence the nearest league club to the place of my birth, Ely. The family was now four generations Blue.

My first game as a grandad was a home defeat to Stevenage. The season was panning out more of the same: win one, lose one, win again, lose again. Inconsistent and decidedly average. 'I can't see anything other than mid-table mediocrity from here on,' I wrote. Sheridan, I sensed, felt the same. After the Stevenage game he praised defender Gary Liddle for being, "*(SIGH)* a seven and a half every week. And you wonder *(SIGH)* why he's played 600 plus games," Sheridan added, the inference being, "so why can't the other buggers be the same?"

Sheridan brought in a second loan signing from his former club Fleetwood, midfielder Jack Sowerby, to join striker Ashley Nadesan. They improved the team. Sheridan also gave youth a chance, with winger Liam McCarron, only 17, lively in cameos off the bench.

United found consistency of sorts: they won away (three on the trot after Mansfield) and lost at home without scoring. Morecambe was the fourth in this sorry sequence, after which fans were quick to message Radio Cumbria criticising a lack of effort. Lumsdon defended the players, to an extent, by pointing out that it wasn't that United's players didn't try, but they showed no confidence or belief. They would much rather pass the ball backwards or sideways than take a risk and lose it.

This was evident right from kick-off. Sheridan yelled at Rotherham loanee Jerry Yates, "THAT'S TWICE!" after he turned and passed back instead of taking on Morecambe's right-back. Sheridan's blast did the trick (Yates didn't try it again) but it couldn't mask a weak spot in United's psyche.

Afterwards Sheridan revealed, and quite a revelation it was, that with Gerrard absent there were no leaders and, worse than that, no talkers or organisers. That used to drive me potty when I played for our staff team. "You might not be as quick, fit or talented as your opponents," I told them (I definitely wasn't), "but you can still talk to teammates to help and encourage them."

We were a group of mates playing friendlies on a Friday after a week at work, so the last thing anyone needed was more grief, but in the case of professionals, who should be able to take it, players ought to give each other a good rollocking if required. Lumsdon said he used to do that and didn't care who he upset on the pitch.

Sheridan's comments ("after Gerrard, Regan Slater's the only one who does that") didn't say much about the attitude of the senior pros. I suspected they were just too soft, too nice. Slater, a young lad on loan from Sheffield, was putting them to shame.

Morecambe wasn't an easy watch. It did feel right however, to be at Brunton Park for the minute's applause before kick-off, and another at 42 minutes, for Tony Hopper, who'd died (aged 42) earlier that week of motor neurone disease. Hopper it was who warmed up with Sam when he was mascot and, by all accounts, a more likeable and popular footballer you'd struggle to meet. More's the pity then, that United couldn't put on a performance to lighten the gloom, albeit for a couple of hours, around the club and for those who knew and loved Tony Hopper.

Yeovil was the fifth successive home game United lost without scoring. Unsurprisingly it was a club record. The game followed a dismally familiar pattern. United looked good at the start, had a couple of half-decent chances but when they didn't score, players retreated into their ever-decreasing comfort zone: "Give the ball to someone else and get out of here!" Fan reaction was more "give and go", as in "give Brunton Park a miss and go somewhere else". The attendance was below 4,000.

Carlisle's last goal at home had been on 25th August, two weeks before Sidney was born. On the Saturday of the Newport fixture in November he was eight weeks old. United, as was their wont, started well. Devitt had one shot (wide) and Yates another, close in, saved by the keeper.

"Here we go again!" you sensed from the groans, not that there were many to moan; the attendance was down to 3,400 Blues. Then, oh joy oh rapture oh blessed relief! Eight minutes into the game and after eight hours plus since United scored at home, a goal!

Nadesan played in Sowerby, who crossed low and Devitt slid in, diverting the ball into the corner of the Waterworks goal.

"I'll go now," I said, making my way up the steps. I was pleased I stayed when three minutes later, Devitt was back celebrating in front of us again. Instead of crossing, he whipped the ball in waist high to the near post. The keeper had left a gap, defenders weren't expecting him to shoot, and before the goalie could get his hands to the ball, it had crossed the line.

"I don't know what all the fuss was about!" Sam joked. It was his first United game as a dad. Two up, 11 minutes gone, Dev on a hat-trick and United comfortable until Newport pulled one back and equalised with four minutes to go. Then Danny Grainer scored with that rocket from outside the box that opened these memoirs, and all was well with the football world.

Confidence restored, United won at Crewe in the FA Cup and thumped Swindon at the County Ground 4:0, before inconsistency kicked in once more. Come mid-December, United were 13th and out of the cup. The season was turning out to be every bit as dull as 2017-18.

Not for the first time, United proved me wrong, this time gloriously so. They beat Colchester at Brunton Park and won at Crawley, which meant a bigger crowd on Boxing Day for the Oldham game, nearly 5,500. Sheridan had managed the visitors in three separate spells and had played well over 100 times for them.

With Gerrard having left Boundary Park under something of a cloud, it had the makings of a tasty afternoon and a close encounter.

It wasn't. United won 6:0. Sheridan's reaction was as remarkable as the result.

"A fantastic performance, John!" the post-match interview began.

"*(Sigh)* I wouldn't say it was a fantastic performance, clinical yes, but I was unhappy at two-nil. We shouldn't have been two-nil up..." Sheridan was more than unhappy. He was angry. I later watched the interview. It was anything but the usual post-match banalities. It had me fearing for the interviewer and backing away from the screen.

"I am a demanding manager. If you don't accept the way I am, I won't be here. If people don't like it, I will leave. I am getting sick and tired of it."

Carlisle beat Macclesfield 2:1 three days later. On New Year's Day they won at Morecambe. Five wins out of five. Mansfield, who'd not lost for 17 league games, were next. United won a cracking game 3:2, their sixth victory in a row, but Sheridan missed it. On the eve of the game he quit.

Sheridan had been offered the Chesterfield job. They were a division below but Chesterfield was closer to his Sheffield home and, I assume, his new contract was as good if not better than the one he had at Brunton Park.

We didn't need to hear the whispers of changing room unrest to work out that Sheridan was not a happy gaffer, despite United's five-out-of-five form. The Oldham reaction made that clear, especially with rumours of a big bust-up at half-time between Sheridan and some of United's senior players.

Given Sheridan's prickly personality and, fair play to him, demanding standards, it wasn't surprising perhaps that relations would be strained. What was unusual was that things came to a head during United's best spell of his short time in charge. The team's success might even have been in spite of Sheridan rather than because of him, not so much a case of us against them, more us against him.

Sheridan's premature departure and the manner of it should not detract from the improvement he'd overseen. United were in a play-off position and the signings he'd made were making a big difference. The problem however, was that Yates, Sowerby and Nadesan were doing *too* well. Their parent clubs, Rotherham and Fleetwood, wanted them back.

Yates was first to go, recalled before the Mansfield game. Nadesan was next and at the end of January, Sowerby had gone too. The trio had shown up the strengths and weakness of taking players on loan. If they do well, it's the parent club who, in the long term, benefit while clubs like Carlisle are left in the lurch. But loans are the easier, cheaper and safer option than offering a player a permanent contract. Catch 22 indeed.

Carlisle's winning run ended in defeat at Northampton and before the next home game, United had a new manager: Steven Pressley. He'd had some success at Coventry, despite their financial and ground problems. He'd not done so well at Fleetwood, his only other English club, and his most recent post had been in Cyprus.

First impressions of him were favourable. "I've seen Pressley smile more in a minute than Sheridan in five months," I zapped Sam from the Paddock in his first game. Devitt scored and made the other for Hope in a 2:0 win over Cheltenham. A week later they won at Port Vale.

Seven wins from eight games meant United were fourth by the end of January. Even without that trio of quality loanees, I was optimistic. "The play-off push is still on!" I said after a home draw with Exeter. Pressley's first three games had brought seven points from nine.

Exeter saw the home debut of Callum O'Hare, borrowed from Aston Villa where Pressley's son was a trainee. O'Hare, only 18, came with glowing testimonies from Villa fans. They weren't wrong. He was that bit better than any of the trio United had lost. The problem was that O'Hare couldn't plug the gaps on his own.

The league table following victory over Swindon early in March was the last time United would fill a play-off spot. They lost at home to Notts County, drew at Forest Green and at home to Cambridge. "This team isn't as good as the one earlier in the season," Chris Lumsdon sighed, Sheridan-like, on Radio Cumbria.

Sam made the point that Pressley's January signings weren't sensible. He had brought in a central defender and a couple of midfielders who weren't really needed, whereas a centre-forward was. There again, Pressley was unfortunate to see loanee Mark Cullen, a striker from Blackpool, crocked.

We were writing off United's chances but on Good Friday, against smug leaders Lincoln, who hadn't lost in 19 league games, Mike Jones scored the only goal and with the indifferent form of other clubs chasing the last play-off place, United found themselves on the front row of the grid en route to Grimsby.

We were confident enough for Sam to check the play-off dates as we drove east. Grimsby were safe from relegation but on a very poor run of form. Plus I'd just run the Ackworth Half Marathon and seen Sidney (we even parked in Sidney Street, Cleethorpes!) The sun was shining and the roads, despite this being Bank Holiday, were clear, unlike our route into the ground because we went in the wrong entrance. In fairness this was more easily done at Grimsby than elsewhere and we found ourselves in amongst the locals in their antique home stand. No worries, we'd just ask to go through the gate and join the Blues in the corner section of the away end.

But it wasn't that simple. We explained what we'd done to a steward. He called over his supervisor. He radioed his line manager and asked us to wait five minutes. The Fire Marshall came over too. We waited until, at last, a radio message came through that we could go through the gate.

A little later a quartet of injured or dropped players came to take their seats in the away section and simply stepped over the low wall. The stewards' walky-talkies nearly went into meltdown and the Fire Marshall was reaching for his bucket. Come the final whistle we could've done with its contents poured on us, for we were fuming. O'Hare was the only player on the pitch worth paying the £14 to watch (reduced from £21, thanks Grimsby.) For United's play-off aspirations, the 0:1 defeat was a Season Over result.

The recurring theme throughout my 2018-19 match reports was: *United just aren't good enough.* Nothing supported that better than those two Easter results. United could follow up beating the leaders on Friday with losing to a team that hadn't won in 10. To make matters worse, other teams' results actually went Carlisle's way. Had United won they'd have been two wins away from a guaranteed place in the play-offs.

United beat Crawley easily to end the season at Brunton Park; they were four goals up in half an hour but, mirroring the season, tailed off. Final score 4:2. They drew 0:0 in their last game of the season at Yeovil, already relegated. Colchester scored three first half goals at champions Lincoln, which made the outcome at Yeovil irrelevant. Infuriatingly (Fire Marshall at the ready, please) had Carlisle won at Grimsby, they'd have been in the play-offs.

That said, it wasn't a bad season overall. I saw some cracking games in the 22 I'd got to (the lowest total for many a season, mainly because Sam was otherwise engaged), even if I'd suffered some very poor performances. For the third season running, it was a mid-table finish. The club announced that Pressley's contract had been extended to the end of next. 'I'm not hanging out the bunting,' I wrote.

For the first time in 10 years, United won their opening game, 2:1 against Crawley. Ten of the 14 players used to start 2019-20 were debutants. "Maybe this season will be different after all," I mused.

"Only another 47 points to safety," added Sam.

Harry McKirdy headed the first. "He's the sort of player who's going to be very irritating when things aren't going well," observed Sam. I found him pretty irritating on a day when they were. McKirdy spent much of the half in front of us asking for bottles of water, to the point where Pressley shoo-ed him away from the touchline.

"He takes a bit of managing," Pressley admitted, "but he's a good kid underneath that," which is the sort of euphemism that I used countless times in school reports: *'He/she is a lively character and has the potential to do well but is a pain in the backside.'* I never did add the last bit, tempted as I often was.

A photo appeared on the United website of fans in the Paddock and I am positively beaming as I applaud Stefan Scougall's Crawley winner. If I was happy then, I should've been snapped at Barnsley on the Tuesday.

Barnsley were two divisions above United and hadn't lost at home in 28 league and cup games dating back 17 months, so what unfolded was as unexpected as it was exceptional, both in terms of the result and performance. "Dull game!" I remarked happily midway through the second half, because United were already three goals up. We gave every Blue an eight in our ratings bar McKirdy, a nine. He was almost unplayable.

Pressley was beaming at the end. He left the pitch (the tunnel was in the corner below us) with arm raised. Sam brought us down to earth somewhat as we left the ground: "Let's hope this isn't when the season peaked!"

"It won't be!" I replied confidently.

The Barnsley wonder show seemed a long time ago four days later. United lost 0:2 to Mansfield and were poor in defeat by the same scoreline at Cheltenham. During the warm-up at Whaddon Road Adam Collin half-volleyed a ball into the burger bar. Somehow it bounced off the back of it and flew straight out, leaving chips and greasy burgers intact.

Nephew Tom (Gloucester Blue) and I were then joined at the back of the stand by United's non-travelling reserve Aaron Hayden, a thoroughly nice bloke, who initiated conversation and revealed what a United corner routine was going to be just before his colleagues cocked it up.

United won four and lost six after Cheltenham; went out of the League Cup at Rochdale; then went through to the FA Cup Second Round after beating Dulwich Hamlet 4:1, a game screened live on BBC2. Next game saw them exit the Football League Trophy after losing at Morecambe, which mattered not to me. I had long since ceased to care about the competition formerly known and loved as the Autowindscreen and JPT; the Football League spoiled it by inviting Premier and Championship clubs to enter Under 21 teams.

Carlisle however, had never lost at Morecambe in a competitive match. The significance of that defeat was considerable. The following morning Pressley was sacked. Results under his charge, both in the second half of the previous season (when, in his defence, he lost his best players in January) and the first part of 2019/20, suggested a sacking could happen, but Carlisle didn't tend to sack managers mid-contract because they couldn't afford to. Pressley's record wasn't even that bad: 18 points from the season's 18 league games. Of course it should have been better, but it could have been far worse. I wasn't however, sorry to see him go. The rest of the season would've been uninspiring stuff.

Gavin Skelton took charge for the defeat at Port Vale and a draw at home to Cambridge. For a while Michael Bridges was odds-on favourite to be appointed, presumably on the basis that he did the Golden Gamble draw at half-time of the Macclesfield game, but at the end of November United announced the name of the new manager: Chris Beech.

"Chris who?" was the common reaction to the appointment. Who, sorry, Beech was Rochdale's assistant manager. "The cheap option then," was the next response. I didn't fancy his chances. The squad had too many players from the bargain bucket, either passed their sell-by date or unlikely to reach one; Beech himself wasn't from the luxury goods aisle. We weren't over enthusiastic at the announcement. But a little more than a year later, the appointment looked inspired.

Beech's first game was a draw in the FA Cup at Forest Green; United also drew his first league fixture at Morecambe. His home debut was a victory in the Forest Green replay, followed by a goalless draw in the league at home to Grimsby, watched by fewer than 3,500 Blues. They would win only one of the next eight, even if that run included a worthy draw at Championship Cardiff in the FA Cup and a narrow defeat (3:4) in the replay.

United's sole win from those eight was at Walsall. The Bescott Away Day started well for us. We had a good chat with *News and Star* man Jon Colman (I congratulated him on the Matt Jansen autobiography, a quality read) before heading into the Park Inn next door. I had a couple of pints as well as burger and chips while we waited for Rob. I was expecting nothing from Carlisle but I was enjoying the Away Day.

It got better when, for the first time ever as a travelling Blue, I claimed a concessionary entry fee. I'd already handed over £22 before Sam pointed out that Over 60s had a cheaper rate. I asked the turnstile operator if that was the case and could I get a refund? I could: £4!

Although we sang, "We love you Carlisle, we do!" it had been hard to love Carlisle in 2019, but they took the lead, conceded an equaliser which wasn't anyone's fault, and just as I was preparing for a stressful last 15 minutes while Walsall pounded the home end goal, the hosts had a player sent off. That meant the ball was down our end more than up theirs. Three minutes into the five of added time, McKirdy scored in front of us. The perfect away day ending.

Chris Beech joined in the "We love you Carlisle, we do!" celebrations. The players came over and I found myself stood next to former favourite Francoise Zoko, who'd come down to watch with his lad. He knew sub Olufela Olomola. United were a happy band of winning wanderers, bar one, hero of the half hour Harry McKirdy. He it was who got the Walsall player sent off after he'd been hauled back when clear. McKirdy had also set up United's first goal.

McKirdy's part in that hadn't stopped one belligerent Blue abusing him. McKirdy heard and made it clear he'd heard. He was more concerned with mouthing off to his fake fan than watching the ball for the next minute or two, and his first reaction after heading the winner was to pick out his man. McKirdy headed straight for the changing room at the final whistle before being brought back by team mates. "The new Madine?" Sam wondered.

After a draw with leaders Swindon three games later, the improvement under Beech was measurable. It was the fifth unbeaten league game in a row. Beech also proved himself a better man manager than Pressley in the case of Aaron Hayden. We weren't the only Blues wondering why Pressley wouldn't give him a chance. It wasn't as if Carlisle's defence had been watertight. Pressley had hardly used him at all; Beech put him into the team straight away.

Hayden repaid his manager's faith. Against Swindon he was, I enthused, 'the new Deano, a colossus at the back.' Hayden scored United's equaliser, a far post header at the Warwick from a corner, which had been won after just as sweet a ball from Callum Guy, one of four new signings. Beech, it seemed, could recognise talent.

There was a positive feeling about Carlisle again. United were a long way from the finished, promotion-chasing article, but for the first time in a long while (certainly since Barnsley in August) I felt buoyant about the Blues. Starting with a draw at Oldham, United only lost two of 11 games, though they still found victories hard to come by. Their League Two status was, even in mid-February, assured. 'Fast forward to August as this season is over,' I wrote.

If I knew then what I know now, I'd would have chosen my words more carefully.

My route to Brunton Park for the Newport game on the second Tuesday in March was longer than usual. My day had started at five when I was pinning a ewe down in the lambing shed on my sister's farm in Wiltshire. I then drove to Gloucester to call in on my parents before heading north. I wondered, more than once, why I was bothering. The season was over, United were safe. My loyalty was rewarded with an easy win after two early goals and Newport had a man sent off on half-time.

Sam and I were planning a trip to Grimsby on the Saturday but the day before, football leagues halted their programme of games in response to the spread of the corona virus, initially, it was said, until April.

The 2020-21 season, the 14th since a Carlisle promotion (and ninth since they'd won the JPT) was not a good one for any football fan. I don't want to waste words writing about what happened. This book, after all, started life as an escape and celebration. And we could still celebrate, for United went top at the start of 2021 after another win at Walsall. Except, of course, we had to celebrate alone, in Lockdown isolation.

I was luckier than most, certainly than Sam, because I did get to the four home games in December when fans were allowed into Brunton Park, albeit with a 2,000 limit. I missed the Southend game in September, a post-Covid trial run so to speak, of just 1,000. The decision to let fans in came late in the day and I'd already arranged to meet Sunderland Steve, my Best Man whom I'd not seen for over 20 years, at a Northallerton Town game.

Sam couldn't have made it either at such short notice (parental responsibilities) and besides, I reasoned, we'd be there for the next one. But the Monday after the Southend game, Boris Johnson declared that stadia would be closed again until March at the earliest.

I could still, for a time, receive a regular football fix at Northern and North-East Counties League grounds. It wasn't the same as watching United, no football is, but it was live football. I couldn't however, bring myself to watch the live streams of United's home games. It was too painful. It was only when we were stopped from going to non-league and I had no other option on a Saturday afternoon or Tuesday evening than to sit in front of the laptop, that I started to watch.

I wasn't looking forward to that first game against Newport in November. I couldn't ignore the empty Paddock and the ache that *"I should be there – yes, THERE in my spot!"* but United played so well I stopped hurting.

I could also feel good about Carlisle United the club. They were one of the first to have things in place for crowds to return; they also dealt with issuing season ticket fairly, keeping fans informed, trying to allocate the same seats and terrace spaces when we were allowed back. Friends who were Bradford and Leeds fans were far less complimentary about their efforts, not that any club had it easy with the government's eleventh hour decision making.

I emailed Chief Executive Nigel Clibbens thanking the club, along with my preferred option regarding a season ticket refund. I chose the option which allowed United to keep my money and I would make do with live streams of home games. 'Keeping my season ticket payment seems a small price to pay for the part United has played in my life,' I wrote, 'even though I might not get to many of the games.'

I was touched when Clibbens replied immediately. 'The generosity of support is humbling,' he wrote. Hardly any supporter asked for their money back.

At least (and at last) I had those four games in December, the first on the Wednesday evening when national restrictions were eased. The kick-off was put back 24 hours to allow fans to attend. After it, I could write a match report again.

My pleasure in this evening can best be measured in Sam's pain. "I wish I could've been there," he said when I phoned him as I walked back to the car. He'd been following the action on I-follow. "I didn't really enjoy watching."

Covid restrictions (don't get me started) mean that Pontefract is in Tier 3 so he couldn't come. Ripon and Carlisle are Tier 2, so I could. He might've struggled to make the earlier than usual seven o'clock kick-off but he'd have been there, because Being There was what mattered. Indeed, I'd go further and say it was all that mattered. After nearly nine months, I was back at Brunton Park.

I'm still not allowed to watch non-league but I can watch Kirklington, the team from the next village. There's neither logic nor fairness (see, I've got myself started!) and it wouldn't surprise me one iota if we were stopped again from attending games at Brunton Park before the end of the season, despite pre-match chat that Covid vaccinations will begin this month.

This evening however, I Was There. I arrived early, walking around the ground, savouring the anticipation. There's nothing quite like the sight of the ground lit up at night. The moon was bright and clear, looking in from above the East Stand/Waterworks corner. Not for the first time during the evening, I felt a thrill, and at regular intervals during the game I'd think, "I'm here! I'm here at Brunton Park watching Carlisle again!" And my stomach would spin with delight.

I'd been to the Ticket Office to pick up my season ticket. The one sent out yesterday had me in the newly-numbered Section 14 of the Paddock when I'd asked for Section 13. I emailed this morning as soon as I realised the mistake. Lucy from the Ticket Office phoned back at once. Later I asked after her in person so I could thank her when she handed over my replacement for Section 13.

I bought a coffee from Claire's then met Rob and his mate Mark, one of the lucky few non-season ticket holders who was able to get a ticket. We went in at the top end of the Paddock together. Our tickets were scanned by the turnstile operator, so I didn't have to use the Covid App as I had been doing at non-league grounds.

We had to walk to Section 13, now identified with a number painted on the ground, by going to the foot of the

Paddock steps rather than walking along in front of the hospitality boxes. We also had to wear face coverings as we did so but not once we were in position or outside the ground. Those were the only changes to our usual routine.

We had space around us; Blues were scattered either side, down to the corner as well. There wasn't anyone at the bottom of the steps because the club had had to erect a temporary covered bench on the other side of the perimeter wall so subs could be socially distanced, despite the fact they train together all week.

We were joined by Bryan and Parky. I'd not seen them, or Rob for that matter, for nine months. I sensed that every Blue was going to be that bit louder and more supportive. We clapped the players off longer than usual after the warm-up. Their efforts so far this season (United were eighth) merited that anyway, but we clapped mainly because we were simply happy To Be There, to be back.

United made the evening happier still by winning. I wouldn't have minded, I really wouldn't, had they lost. In some ways it would have been reassuring that things really were returning to normal. United usually lose more than they win, though not this season at Brunton Park. The 2:1 victory was their sixth in seven games. Lewis Alessandra curled a beauty into the top corner of the Waterworks goal and, second half, Rhys Bennett dived to head in Guy's free-kick.

After Alessandra's goal the Blues in front made a big show of fist and elbow-pumping (handshakes and high *fives are 'non rigueur', hugs a definite no) before the East Stand and Paddock broke into chants of U-NI-TED! Boy, was that sweet music to the ears. Come the end of the game the Blues in front were shaking hands and slapping shoulders. For a few minutes it was like Covid never happened.*

We had to leave through the exit at the top end of the Paddock (face coverings back on) rather than being able to walk along the back of the Paddock to the Warwick Road exit. That meant I could stay and cheer the team off before walking down Warwick Road with Rob and being able to give Sam a call. I wished again he could've Been There.

Face coverings had to be worn all the time for the other three games. It was annoying but the majority of Blues, Sam included, didn't have the luxury of that irritation. Indeed, it was still painful, he said, watching on i-follow. I saw United beat Stevenage and Mansfield before Bolton on Boxing Day. In normal times, there might well have been 10,000 at Brunton Park.

On Christmas Day the club announced that Chris Beech's contract had been extended another 12 months. It was the least he deserved. United were 40-1 to be champions at the start of the season. Before the Bolton game on Boxing Day those odds were down to 4-1.

Six minutes in and there was one of those great moments, a goal every bit as explosively intense as the Danny Grainger winner that opened this book and to the one which will soon close it. United were already one up when Alessandra scored and I was screaming with joy on the Paddock (Section 13) steps. If I could have articulated that feeling, it would have been something like this:

FUCK COVID FUCK BORIS FUCK TIERS AND DRIVEN BY FUCKING SCIENCE! MY TEAM HAS JUST GONE TWO UP AND THEY ARE GOING TOP OF THE FUCKING LEAGUE!

As it happened, it didn't happen, well, not for longer than forty in-play minutes. That early lead, increased to three half an hour later, didn't last. Bolton pulled a goal back before half-time from their one and only on-target effort (it had echoes of that late Leeds goal at Elland Road in the Play-Off Semi Final) and United conceded twice in the last 10 minutes. A combination of defending into a storm and a referee every bit as weak as the gale was strong meant United were denied their table-topping triumph.

But what a moment the celebration of that second goal was, another to savour (it had been nine long months since I'd shared anything like it) and to reinforce again the reason I love football – and more specifically, why I love Carlisle United.

It hurt, of course, to see United's two-goal lead disappear. I sent Sam a text to say I was gutted, but it didn't feel as bad as that. It was hard to fault United, either collectively or individually. Maybe they could've 'game managed' better in the closing stages, but I hate that (it was one of Curle's favourite phrases.) Beech and his players wanted to attack.

A few fans sent texts to Radio Cumbria saying United had to sign a centre-forward who could finish off more than three of the 18 chances created, but two of United's front trio scored again, so I didn't see that as an issue, not when Hayden or top-scorer John Mellish were also chipping in. Mellish hit the post with the last kick of the game.

No, any frustration came with the fear that I wouldn't get to see United again for another month at least, so I hung onto that sixth minute moment: *FUCK COVID MY TEAM ARE FUCKING TWO UP!* United's next game, their first of 2021, saw them win at Walsall and they did go top of the table, but it was a bitter-sweet moment, for with another Lockdown declared, we weren't there.

95

Jimmy

There is only one place these Memoirs can end. After over 40 years' worth of reminiscing, two years of writing and editing (halving an original word count of 194,000), we're approaching the final whistle. What comes next however, isn't a footnote, because what happened on 8th May 1999 was the single most defining moment of my life as a Carlisle United supporter. If I could go back and re-live just one game, one moment, the 95th minute of Carlisle v Plymouth would be it. On my shelves it has a scrapbook all of its own.

To recap where United were at the end of the 1998-99 season won't take long. In two words: rock bottom. They'd been relegated from League One the previous season and were three points off the foot of League Two with three games to go. Below them Scarborough had two games in hand. Relegation loomed large.

Carlisle were given special permission to make an emergency loan signing of a goalkeeper, Jimmy Glass from Bournemouth. Richard Knight had been recalled by Derby and reserve Paul Heritage was out with a back injury. Despite United's precarious position, Glass claimed he didn't feel any pressure. "I didn't put the club in this position but I will do my best to get them out of it," he told *The News and Star* before the Darlington game.

We missed it because of Diane's birthday; I treated her to Blackburn v Liverpool in the Premier League. Diane had said she'd like to see Liverpool play (she was a St Helens lass after all) and with Matt Jansen at Blackburn, I surprised her on the morning of the match with tickets for the sell-out Premier League game. Matt signed a card for her too.

Liverpool won 3:1. At the end the players applauded the travelling Kop but not, I noted, 'with the passion or appreciation that Damon Searle and mates had clapped a few hundred Blues at Rotherham.'

We knew from the half-time scoreboard that United were a goal down to Darlo. We had to wait over an hour in the carpark before we heard the final score. The battery was flat and it was only thanks to a Blackburn fan that the car started and the radio came on. "Carlisle 3, Darlington 3," the second run through of the results declared on Sports Report. And a few seconds later: "Scarborough 1, Cardiff 2." It was their fifth defeat in a row. United had come from behind twice to level and the point took them four clear of Scarborough, who lost for the fifth successive game.

If United won at Hartlepool and Scarborough lost at Halifax (quite likely as Halifax were in a play-off position), United would be safe. Hartlepool were no great shakes. They were down the bottom too, needing a point to stay up. They wouldn't even require that if Carlisle won and Scarborough didn't. Only one team would be relegated from the Football League. 'We could be celebrating with the Monkey Hangers at the end,' I wrote in my preview.

Post-match I praised the Blue Army: 'The best vocal support since Wembley! Almost constant chanting. All the seats behind the goal were taken, plus part of their Main Stand, with more Blues standing behind our seats and in the gangways.'

A minority jeered "Judas!" towards Hartlepool's Peter Beardsley, 38 now and playing his penultimate league game nearly 20 years after the first. We didn't join in. Beardsley laughed it off anyway whenever he came over to take a corner. Come the end the "One Peter Beardsley!" chants from the away end were much louder than "Judas!" He acknowledged our support with a thumbs up.

The only time we were quiet (impressively so) was during the minute's silence for England's World Cup winning manager Sir Alf Ramsey. The players' efforts were great too, but their performance, like the game, was 'pretty dreadful.'

Glass touched over a full-blood Beardsley free-kick and from the corner Richie Prokas cleared off the line. Glass had to save another shot spectacularly but there wasn't much going on in either box. Young Richard Tracey ('frailer than most of my Sixth Form players') had United's best chance but the ball ballooned over the bar. We bumped into Tracey at a service station on the way home. By coincidence, he now teaches in Featherstone. Sam can almost see the tops of the school building from his house in Pontefract.

At half-time rumours had Scarborough level, then behind, then level again. No matter how important this game was, Scarborough's result mattered more. The PA didn't give the score, a deliberate decision I'm sure. The noise didn't abate but throughout the racket, quality football slept. We still gave United a standing ovation, even as news filtered through that Scarborough had won at Halifax.

"They've been crap but they still get that," said Gerald (the Rochdale Superman). "Just think what it would be like if they were any good."

'The present Carlisle United,' I wrote later, 'have just one more tomorrow and, I predict, just seven days left in the league.'

That probability increased after Scarborough's game in hand on the Wednesday. They beat Plymouth 3:0 and went a point above United. On Saturday they were home to Peterborough. Their goal difference was better too so United would have to win and hope/pray that Scarborough didn't if they were to stay in the Football League.

'WE COULD BE JUST 24 HOURS FROM FOOTBALL OBLIVION!' screamed *The Cumberland News* headline. The photo from the files to illustrate the point showed 'FACES OF DESPAIR' from the front row of the Warwick. One fan had his face in his hand, behind which a grimace was visible. That's me. Sam has his hands clenched tightly together. There are seven of us in the photo, a range of ages and gender. None of us were smiling. Faces of despair indeed.

The newspaper's point was well made but a classic case of journalistic licence. The photograph had actually been taken two seasons earlier when United were stumbling over the promotion line. We were smiling not long afterwards.

The day before Plymouth a tense atmosphere was made worse when details of the newly filed club accounts were published. Another *Cumberland News* headline declared: 'Bottom-of-the-league Carlisle made more money than *(Premier League)* Leeds.'

The club's profit was £1.4 million. It had received £2.12 million in transfer fees (Jansen, Delap and others) but paid out just £100,000. The amount owed by CUFC Holdings, a company which controlled 93% of United shares, fell from £1.55 million to little more than £100,000. Normally those figures might have been well received (they seemed to show a club in sound financial state), but on the eve of the club losing its league status, they were, as Andy Baker of *The Cumberland Sausage* fanzine said, "The final straw for Michael Knighton's relationship with the fans."

Knighton claimed his wife was too frightened to shop in Carlisle and his son had been bullied out of his private school. He also asked for police protection at the game. His request was refused. "He expects a rough ride from angry fans," the newspaper said, the understatement of the season.

In Harrogate on the Saturday morning, I'd gone in goal during Sam's boys club training session, 'pulling off some smart saves too,' I wrote, 'though I did let a few soft ones in.' An omen? Sam and I drove straight from the playing field to pick up Plymouth fan John.

"I've been on the internet and Plymouth fans reckoned the players didn't try at Scarborough, so some are saying the least they can do is play with a similar lack of effort today," John said. When he wasn't watching Plymouth, John was a high-ranking police officer and pantomime dame. I wrote the scripts for Sam and Hannah's primary school PTA and John was the star of the show. He liked the theatrical.

I wore Deano's "prized possession", the shirt from the championship season he'd sent me. It was the first time I'd put it on. I'd been saving it for special occasions - or emergencies. Beneath that (I didn't want to get Deano's shirt sweaty) I wore a Wembley 95 t-shirt.

I had the usual excited rush as we headed north. I fancied Peterborough, who were still in with an outside chance of a play-off spot, to at least not lose to Scarborough. So far as United's result was concerned, a draw or defeat were one and the same thing. On second thoughts, no, I sighed, expelling that air of optimism, I couldn't see a United victory. A record of two wins in 19 was the cold flannel of reason.

Warwick Road was busier than usual. At 7,500 the crowd would be double the season's average. The Riverside car park was well over half full. The attendant reminded us to pick up our special free parking voucher for a game next season. "Who says we're coming?" I retorted. But I knew we would.

John met a couple of Argyle friends so Sam and I went into the East Stand to save seats for them (John said he was swapping allegiance for the day) plus my brother Guy. We chose to sit a dozen rows back, right on half-way to have some shelter from the showers. It was 2.15 and Jimmy Glass was already warming up.

He'd been first out at Hartlepool. "Do you want his autograph?" I'd asked Sam. He wasn't bothered, he was growing out of that. "I'll get it then," I said, going down to the perimeter wall of the away end. I wished him luck. "You could be our hero today!" I told him.

A week later every Carlisle player who emerged from the tunnel to warm-up was cheered, and I led the East Stand ovation when they jogged across together. I nearly always joined in the chants but rarely started them. The boys at the back of the East Stand were singing but the Blues nearer the front needed geeing up.

The game wasn't, of course, one that I would enjoy, but I did feel waves of masochistic pleasure early on (later there was only pain) and eight minutes in there was a rush of real excitement across the East Stand. John had a radio with him and was listening through an earpiece. Peterborough had scored! I was out of my seat.

"They need two," I thought. "Scarborough need two! And they're not good enough to get two!" The noise increased. The roar wobbled the floodlight pylons. A minute later Tracey flicked on a header from the left and the ball bounced off the bar via the tips of the keeper's fingers. From corners and crosses United looked dangerous. Not so from free-kicks. Graham Anthony and Damon Searle wasted three from good positions. The whole ground was singing, often in unison. "How often does happen in a season, never mind a game?" I wondered.

Jimmy Glass leapt smartly to his right to push out a shot, but he had few saves to make. I'm not saying that Plymouth were going to *let* Carlisle win, but they weren't up for it like United. Plymouth's players were better but they had nothing to play for. It was plain they weren't going to behave like the mourner at a wake who turns up in fancy dress to party.

From another centre Scott Dobie beat his man to the ball, headed goalward and despite getting a hand to it, Plymouth goalie James Dungey couldn't prevent it crossing the line. We were out of our seats but instinctively I looked to the referee because I sensed Dobie had fouled his man. The ref wasn't running back to the centre circle. I was right. The goal wouldn't count.

I hadn't checked the name of the referee before kick-off. Just as well. It was Frazer Stretton, the 'Sheriff of Nottingham' who had form for gross acts of injustice against United in seasons gone by. He owed us, but allowing Dobie's header wasn't one of the repayments.

Brightwell, from another corner (United had seven but it seemed more) had a header cleared off the line, frustrating again, but at least United were creating chances. That was an improvement on Rotherham and Hartlepool.

With half-time approaching and my confidence, though brittle, still in one piece, Tony Hopper dived into a tackle (it was no foul) with Plymouth's Paul Gibbs. It was on the far side but we heard the CRACK straight away. When Gibbs didn't get up and lay there twitching instead, we knew he'd broken something. The lengthy delay before he was stretchered off meant United's game would finish later than Scarborough's.

Then we heard Scarborough had equalised.

At half-time I went to the loo. I passed Alan, a Yorkshire Blue and regular at the branch meetings. We looked at each other, shook hands, said nothing. It was back to square one. United had only half the time to save themselves and rely on Peterborough not conceding again. "Scarborough have just missed an open goal!" John reported as we waited for the second half to start. The next 45 minutes were not going to be easy.

United went on the attack. They'd taken their time to get going in the first half but edged possession and made chances. Brightwell won a header which hit Ian Stevens at close range, and the ball was going in until Dungey dived to his right and turned it away. Dungey only played a handful of professional games, 27 in total. This would be his last. A goal was coming; I could sense it.

It did. United full-back Rob Bowman lost possession and Plymouth broke. Lee Phillips cut infield and set himself up. No one closed him down. He shot, placing the ball to the right of Jimmy Glass inside the post. Carlisle were a goal down. They had 42 minutes to score twice and hope that Scarborough didn't manage the one.

Tracey was substituted, burnt out after less than an hour. "But how can you expect a lad that young and inexperienced to cope with this," I said, "let alone lead the line?"

Tracey's replacement was Paul Bagshaw, just as young, equally inexperienced, but you wouldn't have thought so from the excitement of the man behind the PA: "LET'S HEAR IT FOR PAUL BAGSHAW! COME ON LADS! GET BEHIND THEM!"

From the stands and terracing, the "KNIGHTON OUT!" and "FAT GREEDY BASTARD!" abuse increased. We were still giving it "U-NI-TED!" and "WE LOVE YOU CARLISLE!" but with each failed attack, anger grew.

Stevens broke free in the box, squared the ball, no one was there. Seale was fouled in the far corner, there was a scramble for the ball and Anthony steamed in, sparking off a ruck among the players. If the man behind the PA was losing it, so too were the players. United needed a goal before things got really desperate.

Another promising position is wasted; the ball's cleared to Brightwell, 25 yards out. He lopes towards it and thumps the ball in his stride. It doesn't rise much beyond waist high. The goalie dives to his left but OH GLORY BE! He's missed it! YES! IT'S IN!

The first three rows of seats are taped off, another example of the foolish man building his house upon the sand, because the lads to the right of us are through the tapes and on the pitch. The players don't celebrate, Brightwell legs it back into his own half and we jeer those still cavorting on the pitch. They're not there long. There's still half an hour left.

Centre-back Stuart Whitehead, who took a clean sweep of Player of the Season awards before kick-off, slipped on half-way. A Plymouth player raced through, one-on-one with Jimmy Glass, but Whitehead recovered and whipped the ball off the forward's toes. Panic over. For the moment.

The ball breaks loose in Plymouth's box. Stevens is onto it but the keeper's onto it first. Then a better chance for Stevens; United sub Peter Clark ("PEE-TERRRR CLARRRK! COME ON CARLISLE!") threads the ball straight down the middle into the forward's path, but his first touch is tacky and he's forced wide. Tony Hopper knackers himself in another tackle and limps off, replaced by David Bass ("DA-VVVVID BASS! LET'S GET BEHIND THEM! COME ON UNITED!") *the slowest player in a Carlisle shirt this season. Hopper and Prokas have given their all.*

Graham Anthony was a more creative player than Hopper and Prokas, albeit only occasionally, not that we had seen much creativity in the game, but Anthony had a great chance to open up Plymouth.

He's given half the pitch to run at the stretched defence; his man's backing off him; Anthony has a teammate to his right, another to his left. All he has to do is give the ball to one of them. Instead he checks back, once, then twice, and lays the ball off 20 yards behind him.

Prokas had let rip from outside the box early on (a Prokas shot wasn't something you saw every game) then he tried a delicate chip (ditto) which dinked over Dungey and, like his attempted screamer, also cleared the bar.

And time's running out. Time's running out. Carlisle push further and further forward. Plymouth break, it's one against one again, but Jimmy Glass is focussed and saves at the forward's feet.

The board goes up: four minutes added time.

"THERE'S FOUR MINUTES LEFT! IT'S FINISHED 1:1 AT SCARBOROUGH! COME ON! WE NEED YOU NOW! U-NI-TED! U-NI-TED!"

Scott Dobie drives from the edge of the box with his right. His shot slams into the side-netting. There's a

*nanosecond scream from the Paddock who think, from
their angle, he's scored.*

*There's only seconds left. United win a corner. And
Jimmy Glass is coming out of his area…*

*I clutch our Carlisle flag like a comfort blanket. Any
second now and I'll be sobbing into it. Sam said the tears
were already in his eyes. In just a few seconds United
would enter the Conference, the lobster pot league: easy
to get in, difficult to get out. I'd seen it coming since
transfer deadline day. Four minutes and more into added
time in the last game of this rotten season, we were
taking our last gasps of Football League air.*

David Brightwell said later he'd turned to the referee
before the corner. "How long have we got left?"
he asked.

"This is your last chance," came the reply.

As Anthony raced over to take the corner, Jimmy Glass
edged out of his area. There was no one between it and
the Plymouth penalty area, into and around which the
other 21 players packed. He started his run, then almost
stopped, stuttered, started again. He said afterwards he
was looking for a wave from Nigel Pearson. I like to
believe it was our roar which carried him forward.

*And we continue to roar as Anthony takes the kick with
his right foot from the right-hand corner of the
Waterworks. The ball drifts away from the keeper's
reach. Scott Dobie rises to head, connects firmly, and*

for a split second I think it's good enough for a goal, strong but straight at the keeper, and he throws his hands up to block.

(Thank goodness he wasn't quick enough to tip the ball over, or worse still, catch it! I've shuddered as I typed that, for what if the ball hadn't rebounded off his gloves, what if the ball hadn't dropped onto the six-yard line, what if -)

Jimmy's jersey is red. It blazes like a beacon in that box. He sprints into the area, checks as Dobie jumps, heads, Dungay saves and the ball drops. Jimmy sees it, seizes on it, right-foot forward, right-foot first, a half-volley, keeping the ball low, hitting it firmly. Six yards out and there's no defender in the way or on the line. There's no rebound off a stray boot. There's nothing to stop the shot.

There's – it's –

The ball is in the back of the net and I can see Jimmy Glass and his red jersey wheeling away to the left and I can see Jimmy jumped on by his teammates and 10, 20, 40 fans and I can see people rushing onto the pitch from all four corners and I can hear the noise and I can't move and I can't speak, not for a second, not a thing.

I'm numb with delight.

WHOOSH! Now I'm hugging the bloke beside me, now I'm turning and hugging Sam, now I'm crying or maybe I'm not or maybe I'm trying to mouth AMAZING

AMAZING and I don't believe it and hundreds of people are on the pitch and the PA man is screaming "GET OFF GET OFF GET OFF THE PITCH!"

And they do, just about, for the game must restart, the referee mustn't take the players off, mustn't even be given a chance to consider abandoning the match. The game must go on but – a second's shudder again – not too long, not long at all please, not long enough for Plymouth to go up the far end and –

"Who scored?" someone shouts.

"The keeper!" I reply. "The keeper!"

And the ref's blown. Plymouth have kicked off. And he's blown again. It's over and he's leading the cavalry charge. Half the crowd follows, Sam and I are there too.

And United, my United, our United have done it. Carlisle United, who've been doomed all week, who were down, dead and buried two minutes ago... CARLISLE ARE STAYING UP!

Forest Green Rovers, derby days with Barrow, Diane buying Premier League season tickets at Bradford because "surely you won't be supporting them in the Conference?" – all that rubbish now binned along with the doubt and despair.

THE BLUES ARE STAYING UP!

Twenty-three years on and I can still replay the goal as I saw it, not the film that I've seen a hundred times since. I can still see too, an image of the two men who sat behind me. They weren't celebrating. Quite the opposite, they were po-faced. I can pick out their carrier bags from that image, for they were programme collectors, spectres at the feast, only there to pick up the last Football League programme of Carlisle United.

On the pitch I skip ridiculously to the thousands thronging in front of the Main Stand. I hug a beery, shaven-headed Blue as we sing, dance, chant and boogie to the Great Escape. "Steve McQueen had nothing on this!" I shout.

We cheer every Blue who bursts into the Directors' Box. John Halpin's the first, punching the air in irrepressible, joyous disbelief. Richard Prokas and Tony Hopper can't keep still. It matters to them that bit more to them. All the players emerge, stripping off and throwing whatever they have to us Blues beneath. They're all there, bar the man we want the most.

"JIMMY GLASS! JIMMY GLASS!" we yell.

Dramatically, theatrically, Jimmy Glass appears, still in his red jersey (though that soon went) and arms open wide with an almost casual, Last-Minute-Goals-By-Keepers-Are-Run-Of-The-Mill smile. He leaves the laughing, the shouting, the dancing to us.

Someone taps me on the shoulder. It's Bryan who's come over the Paddock wall. We look at each other, hug, laugh and keep saying over and over: "Unbelievable! Can't believe it! Unbelievable!" His brother-in-law Matt, a professional volleyball player in

Europe, was with him. He'd never known anything like it in all his years as a sportsman.

Nigel Pearson took the microphone and said the usual stuff: players gave their all, let's sort things out in the summer, thank my coaching staff, frustrating season… Knighton (to no one's surprise) hadn't appeared in the directors' box.

Finally Pearson thanked us; we should've been first, well, second behind Jimmy, then departed to more cheers. Sam and I wandered off to where The Goal went in. A couple of stewards stood between the posts. "I feared they were going to pull the nets down," my brother Guy said about the goal celebrations.

A boys club had their photo taken in front of the goal. I knelt with The Blue Beside Me on the spot where Jimmy had slid in. "Forget Lourdes!" I told him. "This is where they'll be bringing the sick for miracle cures!" Then Sam and I crossed the goal-line in the same place that the ball had done. We kissed the net.

We walked past the Plymouth fans, standing bemused and, I'm sure, envious of our celebrations. They were Loyal Supporters, the 800-mile round trip proved it. They would know exactly how we were feeling. Some had given us "Going down!" grief earlier and had cheered the half-time score from Scarborough, but now they were our mates.

I took my Wembley t-shirt off and gave it to one of them. Sam gave another his scarf. "He asked if I wanted his flag but I said no," Sam said. Good for him. Let the lad keep his flag. We had something better. We still had our league status.

Walking down Warwick Road four Plymouth fans behind us broke into an "AR-GY-LE!" chant. We joined in. It was the least we could do. They'd been up for the week and were stopping in Scarborough. They were off to their clubhouse that evening. "I was on my phone to a Scarborough fan on the pitch when your keeper scored," one said. "He wasn't a happy man."

At the Riverside we said goodbye to the *Ar-gy-le* and turned on the car radio. Jimmy Glass was interviewed: "I just came up here to do a job... I'm back at Swindon... I'm just pleased I could help..."

Knighton, on a long time later once the ground had emptied, maintained he wouldn't have gone had United been relegated. Given the anti-Knighton anger he might not have been around at all had Jimmy not scored. As Graham Anthony was racing over to take the corner, City centre pubs were closing their doors and police reinforcements were heading down Warwick Road.

A few seconds later and pubs doors were thrown open, the police were turning on the heels and heading home. Knighton could milk the moment for all it was worth: "I believe in Methuselah! I believe in Frankenstein! I believe in alien beings! I believe in God! But most of all, I believe in on-loan keepers who score goals in the 91st minute!"

Knighton had got it wrong again. It was the 95th.

"Even you wouldn't have dared write something like that in your panto," John said to me.

We phoned Diane to tell her the score. She didn't know what had happened. Soon after we told her, she tried phoning Bryan for a full report (we were otherwise engaged in celebration) and misdialled, but the person who answered had been at the game too and was full of it, so gave her a report anyway!

That was the case across the airwaves too. Every call on Radio 5's *606* phone-in was about Carlisle. A fair amount of talk centred on the post-deadline day signing of Jimmy Glass. The opinion was that Knighton had conned the league in claiming he couldn't afford to buy a replacement keeper after selling Caig.

"So now the rest of football knows how it feels to be shafted by Knighton," I said.

For a Plymouth fan, even one who'd wanted United to win, John was elated. He'd seen football history. It was 25 years since Carlisle topped the old Division One, which had been the one thing you were guaranteed football fans would mention in conversation if I said I was a Blue. That wouldn't be the case anymore. It would be Jimmy's Goal instead and the question would be, "Were you there?" and I'd be able to reply, "What do you think?"

The 115-mile drive home had never seemed so quick. There was only one way to celebrate; I went round to the off-licence for a bottle of champagne. When I walked in the owners started clapping. And that was the start of another thing: everyone wanted to hear what it was like Being There. In school on the Monday morning it was almost as if I *was* Jimmy Glass. The Deputy Head (a Liverpool fan) gave me a Guest of Honour spot in his assembly.

"I'll give you two minutes," he said.

"I'll take four and a half," I replied. "Then pause for the invasion."

A few months later Sam and I met and thanked Jimmy Glass in person. We were down in Gloucester for a half-term holiday and drove to Swindon to watch him play against Port Vale. We took our Jimmy Glass scrapbook and, as the players warmed up, called one of the Swindon players over. He was Alan Reeves, brother of United's former striker and captain David.

He reached for Sam's programme ready to sign, only to be told, "Thanks, but no thanks. Please would you ask Jimmy Glass to come over when he has a minute?"

He did and Jimmy signed the scrapbook. He also said he'd reply to a letter I'd sent him a few days earlier inviting him to sponsor a Harrogate Hornets game. We were raising funds for a new kit and I wrote to a few former Blues asking if they'd like to make a donation. Matt Jansen and Deano were two; Graham Taylor, the Watford and ex-England manager was another, what with the Hornets link. I didn't specify an amount and everyone I contacted sent something, which was really good of them.

A few days later I received Jimmy's reply. He enclosed a £30 cheque.

'I was pleased to see you at the game the other night and hope you enjoyed seeing me play,' he wrote, 'even if it was in a different colour shirt than last time. I'm glad I could help Carlisle last season and would have signed had Knighton separated with a little more of his precious money, but maybe getting a chance for Swindon has turned out a better option for me. I would be glad to help your football team so please find enclosed a cheque. I hope it helps them to enjoy their football, as I am enjoying mine more since I scored that goal.'

They say you shouldn't meet your heroes in case they don't live up to your expectations. In Jimmy's case I'm pleased we did, because he surpassed them.

What happened next for Jimmy is well known to Blues. Unfortunately things at Swindon didn't work out and he didn't have long left as a professional footballer. Roger Lytollis, another of the fanzine generation, wrote Jimmy's biography, *One Hit Wonder*, which is highly recommended. His story does have a happy ending; at the time of typing, he is back in football working for Bournemouth FC.

A little while ago the country celebrated the 75th Anniversary of VE Day on 8th May 2020. The day before Rob messaged me. "I'm often critical of this government," he wrote, "but credit where it's due; they've finally given us a public holiday on St Jimmy's Day."

Added Time

The final whistle is about to blow on these memoirs. During the time it's taken to write this labour of love, Jon Colman of *The News and Star* published his excellent *Bolts from the Blues*, 40 chapters long and each one about an iconic United goal. It does what I hope this book will have done: bring a big smile to the faces of Carlisle fans, reminding them how good it is to support United.

It feels that way again now. My book goes to print with Paul Simpson back as manager and every Blue so much happier, this one with an extra reason to cheer as second grandson Bertie was born on 14th March 2022, the Monday after Simmo's fourth win in his first four games.

Jon's book celebrates what it means to be a Blue. At the end of it, the score is 40:0 to United! I've had to mention a few goals against in these pages, but I hope they haven't diluted the pleasure. They haven't for me and I look forward to the Saturday afternoons when Sidney and Bertie become the fourth generation of our family to watch, support and follow Carlisle United.

I've never played at Brunton Park, let alone scored a goal. My experiences have almost always been the other side of the perimeter wall, bar the occasional end-of-season celebration. Well, almost all…

The Carlisle Half Marathon, first staged in 2018, is based at Brunton Park. The race starts at the back of the East Stand and the course takes runners through the city, out to Crosby, then back through Rickerby Park to the ground. Competitors enter Brunton Park via the Paddock gates and the finish line is by the entrance to the players' tunnel. It is a well designed course whether or not you happen to be a United supporter, but those last 50 metres are extra special if you're a Blue.

I couldn't wait for that finish. I am a mid-table runner and by the time I rounded the home turn before the gates, through which Sam and I usually run out of at the end of the game for a quick getaway to the car, plenty of faster competitors had finished.

Many waited in the Paddock along with family members and friends of other competitors still out on the course. After 13.1 miles, runners are spread out, so it can be a little dull just waiting for folk to finish. I'm always grateful to spectators, especially those who encourage you. If I have enough puff, I try to thank them. Giving folk a thumbs up, smile or gasping a word of gratitude invariably makes those watching give a runner a bigger cheer; I know that from having taking part in and marshalled many races over the years.

I knew then, what to do when I rounded the last corner and ran into Brunton Park. My arms went above my head in triumph; I clapped the crowd; I jumped up, punching the air, though not too high as the legs had done 13 miles. Those spectators watching, the crowd in the Paddock, responded, giving me loud cheers and cries of encouragement as I dashed, well, ran as quickly as possible after those 13 miles, in front of them towards the finish, towards the Home Team bench.

And just for a moment, a few precious seconds, I knew how it felt to score for United.

Lightning Source UK Ltd.
Milton Keynes UK
UKHW010702220722
406233UK00002B/529